Profit from Strategic Marketing

Profit from Strategic Marketing

How to succeed in Business Markets

ALAN WOLFE

Director of Marketing Services
Primary Contact Limited

FINANCIAL TIMES

PITMAN PUBLISHING

Pitman Publishing
128 Long Acre, London WC2E 9AN

A division of Longman Group UK Limited

First published in 1993

© Primary Contact Ltd 1993

A CIP catalogue record for this book can be obtained from
the British Library.

ISBN 0 273 60161 X

Phototypeset in Linotron Times Roman
by Northern Phototypsetting Co. Ltd., Bolton
Printed and bound in Great Britain
by Biddles Ltd., Guildford

The
publisher's
policy is to use
paper manufactured
from sustainable forests

CONTENTS

FOREWORD

In 1985, I was invited to become Chairman of the business advertising agency Primary Contact after 15 years as a Board Director with Ogilvy & Mather. I had reached the age where a man's thoughts turn increasingly to reducing his golf handicap; and I fondly imagined that business advertising would prove to be less frantic than fast-moving consumer goods. Unfortunately, the agency misread my intentions and set off on a course of spectacular growth.

This had serious implications for staff training. We had recruited a large number of bright young people to service our accounts. Next, we needed a quick and effective way to help them share the experience and knowledge of our senior staff.

I persuaded them to express their expertise in a permanent form – and so the Primary Contact Viewpoints were born.

Our earliest Viewpoints dealt with such topics as 'How to evaluate advertising', 'Setting a budget' and 'Creativity – what works?'. As expected, they made a significant contribution to the education of our own people, and the continuing improvement of our work

Then the requests began to come in from our clients. Could we please supply so many copies of a particular Viewpoint? And what other titles were available? Perhaps this should not have surprised us. Business and financial advertising has never enjoyed the academic prestige of its consumer sister. As a result, published and authoritative information is hard to come by.

In subsequent Viewpoints, we formally recognised this need, and so emerged a series of papers that were specifically geared to the needs of our existing and prospective clients. Fourteen different Viewpoints were produced in the series – most went to at least one reprint to satisfy demand. In all, over 50 000 have been sent out to interested parties.

Most of the credit for this success must be attributed to Alan Wolfe, who was the editor of all, and the main contributor to most of them.

I can think of no one more suitable for this assignment than Alan. We first met at Ogilvy & Mather, where his incisive systematical thinking, constructive criticism and pragmatism helped to produce the very best in strategic planning. He has been my friend, conscience and personal 'guru' for many years.

This book forms the background to our 'Viewpoints'. It is devoted to explaining the role of marketing in the successful running of a profitable company and sets out the principles and benefits of good marketing practice.

I would like to acknowledge the considerable help my colleagues at Primary Contact gave in sharing their experience. They have been great partners.

I dedicate this book to the founder of the Ogilvy Group, David Ogilvy, who expressed precisely the spirit in which it is intended:

'Advertising could achieve better results if more people who create it would take the trouble to learn which techniques are most likely to work.'

Harvard Business Review, July/August 1982

John Armitage
Chairman
Primary Contact Ltd

AUTHOR'S PREFACE

WHO THIS BOOK IS FOR

This book is about the parameters of making a success in business. It uses as its focus commercial firms (i.e., those in the profit-making sector of the economy), based in Europe and which sell goods and services to *other businesses* as opposed to individual consumers or domestic households. It is aimed at those who are responsible for making a success of this kind: top management who need an overview of current thinking; the management of the marketing function who will already be applying the principles discussed but may value a second opinion; and those who have risen to a high level in other specialisations (perhaps production, sales or finance) but who suddenly find themselves responsible for, or inter-acting with, marketing.

This is not to say that managers in consumer goods and services, or those working in the public sector and in other non-profit-making operations, should not be allowed to open its covers, only that their special needs have not been catered for. Indeed business-to-business (or 'industrial' as it was once called) has learned a great deal from the pioneers of consumer marketing, and it may be that the time has come for expertise to become a two-way flow. Certainly cross-comparisons are instructive to both sides.

Nor is this a 'how to do it' manual for business students and their teachers: there are several excellent student texts available on the elements of marketing practice. While it is not totally free from check-lists, the book is there to help the reader think, not to tell him or her what to do next.

The readers are assumed to have already substantial first-hand business experience and indeed access to subordinates or outside agencies who can execute specific tasks. The chapters that follow concentrate on ways of helping to make sure their orders and the strategy on which they are based are workable and likely to achieve their intentions. They build up to a philosophy of doing business – one based on the marketing approach (or 'the customer is king') which has by now been adopted by many of the more successful parts of the business community.

Theodore Levitt, the great guru of consumer marketing since his seminal paper *Marketing Myopia* (Harvard Business Review, September–October 1975), wrote more recently: 'A strategy that doesn't speak explicitly about customers and the competitive environment will surely fail to generate and sustain a proper level of customer and competitive consciousness in your company, especially in the important nooks and crannies where the real work gets done.' (*Thinking about management*, The Free Press 1991). That quotation could be taken as the text for this book.

WHAT THIS BOOK IS ABOUT

For those who want to read the book at a single sitting, it condenses topics into short chapters, to help senior managers who do not have the time or inclination to wade through prolixity. There is supposed to be a consistent thread of development linking each chapter to the next, building up to positioning marketing as a central function of a successful business.

However, each chapter can be read in isolation, in that it opens with a statement of its coverage, and what the reader is expected either to know or to be willing to take on trust from previous chapters, and ends with a recapitulation of its key points. Each chapter is intended to challenge its readers to review their established ways and to analyse their company's (and their own) motives for doing things. Where the current approach holds water under such scrutiny, well and good; but often rules which were sensibly developed under one set of circumstances become jerk-reflex habits which persist into different and less suitable ones. They may even get handed down to others (who are not even aware of their origins) as 'corporate policy'. It is hoped that a reader will keep the book to hand at his or her work-place and when wrestling with a problem or working on a strategic plan might sometimes be tempted to dip in to the most appropriate chapter it may stimulate a new idea or at least a better justification for one under attack.

The approach is meant to be practical and professional, based on the collective, lengthy and wide-ranging experience of the writer and many colleagues and business friends. I hope I have never been too proud to accept (indeed eager to steal) good ideas and advice which have come my way, and I have read at least some of the works of, I believe, all the most respected management and marketing pundits from James Burnham (*The Managerial Revolution*) to Sir John Harvey-Jones (*Making it Happen*).

I make no apology for using first-hand illustrations to confirm or illuminate general principles. I am most sure about my facts when I was actually there. Many published cases are distorted to make a good story or miss essential facts because they are second-hand. I started to earn my living in 1955 at almost the very beginning of the development of modern marketing. I have since then observed or assisted in many disasters, and have been part of teams set up to pioneer several new developments, both of which contributed more to my learning than the many happy times when I was just helping a long-established success on its way.

Because I reached Department Head level in my twenties, when possibly qualified but certainly under-experienced, I had to view events from a managerial perspective for most of my working life; by the good fortune of working mainly in advisory roles in service industries, I gained experience of a wide range of client industries and organisational structures; by working for and on behalf of multinational companies as well as local British ones I was able to observe the range, market conditions and methods of doing business in different countries. I was forced to recognise that there is more than one way of making a success in business.

Politicians with unpopular policies try to get themselves off the hook by disclaimers: 'There Is No Alternative'. Many businesspeople search for magicians with 'Golden Rules' which will run their businesses without the responsibility of thinking the decisions out. I plead guilty to having written many lists of Golden Rules in business documents aimed at potential clients in search of a guru. However, I agree with my long-time boss David Ogilvy, himself a great writer of 'How To Do It' manuals, who constantly quotes: 'Rules are for the guidance of wise men and the obedience of fools'. The truth is that the use of a little imagination and creativity will show that there is almost always a series of alternative approaches to a problem, all with both advantages and disadvantages. These have to be evaluated overtly and balanced to make a workable choice.

It struck me quite early in my work experience that despite the high rewards of success and frequency of failure, business management as a whole did not seem to try to learn systematically from experience or to cross-fertilise ideas from one industry to another, or even from product to product within a firm. This is partly because those who climb straight career ladders rarely see a problem twice from the same perspective, leaving any issues they fail to resolve to their successors; and having to approach from scratch any crisis bequeathed by their superior.

More often than not companies prefer to believe they face unique circumstances rather than their individual variant of a problem or opportunity shared with many others. As the eponymous Colonel Batchelor told me after enduring my rather callow presentation on the marketing implications of trends in household eating habits of the 1960s: 'Young man, what you say may be all very well for people who make baked beans and products like that. But I make canned peas and they are quite different!'.

I strongly believe that many of the problems which a business may have to face are neither totally new nor totally unforeseeable. This book will have justified its price if it helps a reader avoid or at least anticipate only one such serious problem; or if too late for that, if it draws attention to an approach which has worked in parallel circumstances in the past.

The book will seem in places to be controversial. This is deliberate, and my colleagues may well say I have always preferred to challenge rather than to soothe. Circumstances change and the fashions of one period can be downright dangerous to a business in the next. Facts are facts and I have tried to be accurate with them, but I do not expect any reader to take unchallenged the deductions I have made from those facts. I take personal responsibility for my views, and Primary Contact in particular should not be expected to agree with every word as printed.

PERSONAL ACKNOWLEDGEMENTS

I have to admit that writing a whole book, even on a deeply-felt subject, has not been easy. I am totally grateful to my wife Nancy for showing tolerance and encouragement throughout the process. I want to thank my colleagues at Primary Contact, John Armitage and David Neaves, for creating this opportunity and for giving fearless second opinions on content.

There are many people from whom I have learned my trade over the last 35 years, too many to acknowledge individually. But I would like to remember here Ray Willsmer, in turn my client, colleague, boss and guru. He was a polymath: a highly successful marketing director, a founder of the Marketing Society, author of *Directing the Marketing Effort*, professional footballer, Olympic cyclist and a jazz guitarist who won a golden disc for one of his compositions. Ray encouraged me back in the 1960s to emerge from what was then the ivory tower of market research, to think my knowledge and experiences through from a managerial perspective and then to learn how to persuade other people to act upon the conclusions. His accidental death was a great personal loss and I believe also to the marketing business. This book would have been greatly improved by his insight.

Alan Wolfe,
Firle, East Sussex,
December, 1992

1 THE NATURE OF PROFIT

WHAT DO WE MEAN BY PROFIT?

As explained in the Preface, this book is about marketing and is aimed at those working in the so-called 'profit-making sector' of the economy. In the Western capitalist world at least, the generation of profits is widely believed to be the locomotive of economic progress. It is beyond the scope of this book to examine this tenet, and it accepts it as part of the climate under which writer and readers have to do their jobs. It takes as read that if marketing is to be of use to business, it must help in the generation of profits. Expenditure on marketing activity has to be looked on as a luxury, indulgence or waste unless it generates sufficient income to justify itself in the short- or long-term.

But profit is a technical term whose meaning differs between academic economists, professional accountants, business managers and lay people. Therefore as essential groundwork to dealing with the subject of marketing, we must be quite clear what we mean by profit, how it arises and why it is so important. Chapter 1 explores the meaning of profit and its role in the commercial world.

The general public appears to consider profit to be the gap between the selling price of a product and the apparent cost of its raw materials, and usually excessive at that. 'Twenty pounds for that deck-chair? Why, it is only a few bits of wood and a strip of canvas!' Somebody wrote to the UK Advertising Standards Authority that when their TV would not work they called out a repairman, and made a complaint that he charged £33.90 (42 ECU) to put a new fuse in the plug (reported 16/12/92). It is perhaps worrying that people who might know better, such as the media, civil services, consumer protection agencies and even the European Commission, often give the impression that they are unaware of such basic accounting concepts as cost of goods, fixed and variable overheads, economies of scale, let alone the economics of supply and demand.

But are we businesspeople all so financially erudite? When part of the Faculty at the College of Marketing run by the Chartered Institute of Marketing, I regularly addressed seminars for Product Managers; men and women, most of them young, each responsible for a brand or portfolio of brands and working for a large variety of industrial and consumer companies. To stimulate dialogue, I would often start by showing the Institute's definition of marketing (below) and asking 'what is the most important word in this definition?'; or 'what in one word is marketing about?':

> *The management process responsible for identifying, anticipating and satisfying customer requirements profitably.*
> (Chartered Institute of Marketing)

Usually I had a wide scatter of replies, but in most cases one came loudest and clearest: 'profit'. What might be a better answer is discussed in Chapter 4, but to help reveal why this one was not what I wanted, I then asked these managers to quote the profit targets for their own products, gross or net, in absolute or percentage terms.

It was always surprising how few of them knew. If profits are so important to their companies, why was it that those most responsible for generating them had not had the corporate needs drummed into them month-by-month by their bosses? And those that did know used a wide variety of measures: gross margin on sales, net margin before tax, a flat figure per case or tonne sold, percentage return on capital employed and so on. Even when we had sorted out some common denominator the apparent requirements of different firms might vary as much as five times from highest to lowest. We then had to debate: how come Company A expected to fall apart if it failed to achieve 25 per cent when Company B was content with 5 per cent?

This book is not intended to decry the profit motive in any way, if only to avoid most of its readers putting it down before the end of Chapter 1! Clearly making a profit is vital to every commercial business because if it makes continued losses on the costs of its operation it will eventually go bankrupt or be closed down. But the parameters of profit are not fixed by God or the laws of economics or even the stock markets of the world. Lester Thurow, Dean of MIT's Sloan School of Management, in his analysis of the relative economic strengths of USA, Japan and Europe entitled *Head To Head*, argues that one of the great strengths of Japanese industry is a willingness to accept low returns on investment (relative to world standards) in order to buy domination of their markets in the long term, while the USA has been hampered by a system which insists on maximisation of short-term profits in bad years as in good.

The amount of profit necessary for a specific product of a firm in a particular year depends on many factors, some of them under the control of product management, many of them not. For example:

- expectations for the industry ('the custom of the trade')
- general economic conditions
- future prospects for the firm
- the intensity of use of capital by the firm
- its method of financing long-term and working capital
- the product's market share
- the position of the product in its life cycle.

In practice, even if corporate long-term plans set targets for future profits at a constant percentage, the achieved net profits in the past will always have varied greatly by year and by product. Somehow the company managed to survive nevertheless.

During a period of (say) five years, there are likely to have been booms and slumps, competitive price wars, windfall gains or losses from stocks of raw materials, customers may have changed their technologies and so lost interest in a previously vital ingredient, management may have launched new products which inevitably took time to break even, or have retained products which regularly made substantial losses which had to be paid ('milked') from other more successful lines.

Some of the problems could have been foreseen, even prevented. For example, loyalty to loss-making lines might be through pig-headedness ('investments in management ego' as Ray Willsmer called them in *Directing the Marketing Effort*) or through over-optimism about their future.

But in other cases running a deliberate but limited loss might be a wise decision for the good of the company as a whole or as an investment for the future. Maintaining *The Times* newspaper as 'a paper of record' for 21 years was one of the conditions upon which the Canadian Lord Thomson of Fleet was permitted to take over this very British institution; nor did it make a profit for many years before or after. But the ability to use every day the printing machinery and staff which his *Sunday Times* could use only on Saturday nights did a great deal for the profitability of the latter!

On what basis should profit be calculated? To take an extreme example from the sector supplying services to business, according to the UK Institute of Practitioners in Advertising, the average advertising agency made net profits before tax of 1.2 per cent on its billing in 1991. Most of that agency's clientele would quite probably claim that their agency was over-compensated, yet consider such a level of profitability in their own company a disaster. If the agency was earning the traditional 15 per cent commission on the newspaper space, TV time and ancillary production services it bought for its clients and which make up its 'billing', it would be earning 8 per cent on actual income (which equates more closely with general industrial profits). And because typical advertising agencies have very little fixed capital, choosing to rent rather than own property and equipment wherever possible because of the short-term nature of contracts with clients, its Return On Assets might well be a ludicrously high 80 per cent even in that year of recession! Which is the truest (or most useful) measure of profitability?

COSTS OF CAPITAL AND ADDED VALUES

The classic approach of accountancy defines profit as the surplus thrown up by deducting from total income all directly attributable costs. This is supposed to be used partly to finance growth or build reserves for the future, and partly to distribute as dividends to shareholders and others who provide the fixed and working capital of the company. Is money retained in a business for the financing of growth or provision for crises a profit in the normal sense of the word? Companies who plough back part of regular income to create future wealth and employment are sometimes pilloried by political lobbies and the media for making 'excess' profits. They then have to spend some of these reserves in corporate image campaigns to explain themselves!

Defining profits as a 'residual' between income and costs implies that it is reasonable to expect profits to vary from year to year. Yet few businesses (and certainly not their backers) are willing to accept wide and unexpected variations in the rewards they pay to those who provide their capital. In the writer's experience most businesses treat a budgeted profit (i.e., the promises made to the backers before the start of a financial year) as a fixed cost, namely the reward for capital; just as salaries of permanent staff are usually treated as fixed costs as the reward for labour. What is called by economists 'Pure Profit' means any excess of income above what is needed to pay for materials, labour and capital costs of producing output. The implications on business strategy of not separating profit from pure profit are discussed in Chapter 2.

Economic theory approaches the operations of business more in terms of 'adding values'. In other words money is spent on inputs (raw materials, labour, machinery, transport, advertising, etc.) which are transformed into an output which is worth more. Added Value, equal to output minus input, is not part of the language of accountancy, but a concept which has considerable value to governments who are increasingly using it as a lucrative and efficient basis for levying taxes (VAT/TVA) on commercial operations. It will be discussed later as a sensible concept for developing profitable marketing strategies.

REWARDS AND RISKS

On whatever basis it is calculated, commercial profit occurs as a result of taking a risk. I was brought up very close to Epsom Downs, and from quite an early age would sneak off to attend race meetings. I quickly learned that there was no such thing as a 'racing certainty'. There were no odds at all on offer on a one-horse race, and that unless one had some very special source of information, the odds quoted by the bookmakers on each race could be taken as closely related to the relative chances of each runner winning. Outsiders promised attractive returns, but so few of them won that I quickly learned to 'invest' my half-crown pocket-money on favourites which paid only a small profit on the stake, but at least provided it reasonably often! On joining the work-force, it did not take long to discover that the same principle applied in the commercial world where rewards are also earned only by taking risks.

RISK MANAGEMENT

Planning a business is in effect the successful management of risk. Money has to be laid out *in advance* – on machinery, raw materials, staff, and so on – in the expectation that income will be generated later. These expectations form a continuum from high-risk–low-risk, and the operations themselves can be assessed as high reward (or 'profitable') or low reward ('unprofitable'). All enterprises (individual products, operations, divisions, whole companies) can therefore be located against these two criteria on the matrix shown in Figure 1.1.

In the top left-hand quadrant fall enterprises which offer high rewards at low risks. These are as rare as they are desirable. They happen occasionally; but can be maintained only by statutory monopolies or by firms with unbreakable patents. For example, everyone always knew that a pocket-sized powerful calculator that cost under £5 (7 ECU) would sell in millions to business-people alone. One day in the 1970s it became technologically possible and the office slide-rule was suddenly a museum-piece. But as soon as the first supplier started to make sure-fire profits, others hurried to share the opportunity. It has been suggested that these days patents get broken or

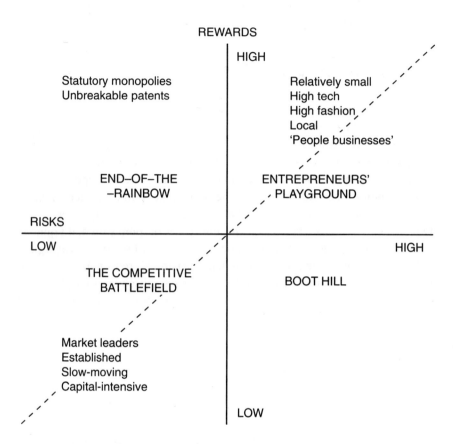

Fig. 1.1 Risk analysis

leap-frogged in a matter of months. For the originator, the risks remain low sure enough, but the rewards fall quickly to drop the pioneer product into the lower left-hand quadrant.

At the opposite quadrant are enterprises which offer low rewards at high risks. These rewards may not necessarily be negative nor the risks infinite, but such enterprises are highly vulnerable to economic down-turns, competitive activity and disasters generally. Wise managements shed them before they bankrupt the company. (When confronted with this diagram at a seminar, one Brand Manager said, 'you seem to have described my product portfolio!').

Consequently, just about all businesses operate somewhere along the dotted line connecting high-reward–high-risk with low-reward–low-risk. To develop a viable business strategy, it is essential that not only top management but also all concerned should be aware in which quadrant their operations lie. This knowledge can with benefit affect every aspect of business strategy and co-ordinate tactical decision-taking. The degree of acceptable risk must relate to the potential or 'upside rewards' of success and the penalties or 'downside risks' of failure.

At the top right of the matrix are to be found small companies with little to lose and everything to gain, and those operating in markets which involve high technology such as robotics or new computer chips or else those with a high element of fashion. These are best suited to develop business strategies which accept high risks; provided of course the rewards of success are also high. For example, hundreds of new pop records are released each month, but only 40 reach The Charts where the big money is made. One chart-topper will pay for the development costs of many failures, and underwrite the future profitability of new numbers from its lucky performers.

It is necessary for such businesses to be geared up to provide high-flexibility, low-fixed capital, short decision times and the ability to change direction fast. Many of this group describe themselves as 'people businesses'. This is where an entrepreneurial style of management is most likely to pay off, and indeed is how some highly-regarded tycoons get headlines in the business media when their enterprises hit the jackpot in the market place. For example, computer software where even school-children have made themselves fortunes from programmes written in a bedroom or garden shed. The many others who failed, of course, remain in obscurity.

In the low-risk–low-reward quadrant are found established businesses, particularly the leaders in their markets or those with capital-intensive processes. Suppose a company holds 25 per cent of its market. It would be unusual (not to say foolhardy) for such a company to set itself a short-term target of 50 per cent, 40 per cent or even 30 per cent share. Most would be content with a modest increase to 26 per cent next year, or, if circumstances were uncertain, would prepare themselves to maintain the status quo.

Such operations have little to gain by the extra 'upside payoff' from any inevitably small marginal success, but a great deal to lose in 'downside risk' of lost customer loyalty if they read their market only slightly wrong. Such companies tend to prefer defensive business strategies which minimise their risks. They will tolerate the resulting low profit levels providing they are relatively sure of achieving them.

This means that the high-risk strategies and entrepreneurial management styles which can bring a small new business fast growth and early success are totally inappropriate for a market leader. Indeed, long-established and highly-respected firms have been destroyed by new 'whiz-kid' managers replacing 'fuddy-duddy traditionalists' and initiating fast-growth strategies which the business was not set up to implement and their customers did not appreciate.

The most successful entrepreneurs are those who were able to recognise the need for a change in style when success had been established. Good examples are Paul Getty who not only made a fortune from scratch in the oil business but hung on to it, John Bairstow who built a single hotel into the Queen's Moat House Group, one of the largest hotel operations in the world, Sam Walton whose Wal-Mart overtook all his rivals in the discount-store business in the USA and Enrico Berlusconi the mega-multi-media magnate.

Others have shown themselves psychologically incapable of modifying their offensive approach or of handing control over to someone with the organisational skills needed to defend an established business against competition which has become direct and aggressive. This is why we frequently find the winners of the various 'Business Success of the Year Awards' facing deep trouble shortly afterwards (one at least created much embarrassment by going into liquidation between the announcement of the award and the ceremony itself!).

This problem of changing business philosophy to match market circumstances is not confined to small entrepreneurs. My first employer in the 1950s was Rowntree of York. For decades their market position had been a low second to their fellow Quakers, Cadbury, who had made themselves the generic name for chocolate in Britain. Putting the Cadbury name on a new line guaranteed it widespread trial, and a high content of Cadbury's Dairy Milk Chocolate gained it consumer acceptance even among those who did not buy regularly. Rowntree did not then enjoy such universal acclaim, and had worked out in the 1930s a counter-strategy of product differentiation exemplified by Aero: 'the milk chocolate that's *different*'. All their lines had strong branding but with the Rowntree parenthood played down, one not always recognised even by loyal buyers of Kit Kat, Black Magic and the rest. Marketing in the 1950s was aimed with success at out-flanking Cadbury by capturing those consumers least attracted to each line in the Cadbury range.

But 20 years on, Cadburys were bought out, fell on hard times and temporarily lost their firm touch in the market. In particular they had responded to rising ingredient costs by maintaining the price of their most popular size by progressively reducing its weight. Rowntree then launched the chunky Yorkie Bar which delivered the physical sensations desired by 'chocoholics' and which Cadbury's Dairy Milk no longer provided.

Rowntree found themselves almost overnight reversed into brand leadership and having to defend the high ground of their market. They realised this
demanded a radical change in strategy, but after so many years as number
two, management had for a while a great deal of difficulty in thinking like
market leaders.

DEVELOPING A BUSINESS STRATEGY

It is not the role of the marketing department to develop the corporate
business strategy, but marketing as guardian of the customers and the sales
income (see Chapter 4) is usually given a large role in its implementation.

It is therefore vital that marketing management make sure that any profit
targets (however defined) which they are set are realistic and commensurate
with the risks involved. And, since nothing in the real world is certain, they
must also ensure that the corporate business strategy admits to and evaluates
the possibility of setbacks and short-falls and where necessary includes
contingency plans to survive them.

Sales and profit growth are in practice unlikely to be constant from year to
year, and as discussed in Chapter 2, it is better if good and bad years are
anticipated. Certainly a company which reneges on promises of good profits
in boom years may have trouble in rolling its working capital forward when
there will be plenty of more lucrative borrowers available. But in recessions
when everyone is squeezed, where will the financiers move their money?
Better the devil they know!

A company which always delivers a planned return seen to be realistic in
the current circumstances is a better credit risk than one which switchbacks
from year to year from a growth to a recovery stock.

To recapitulate: 'profit' is an essential component of the capitalist system,
but it has no absolute value because the system has survived and grown
through a wide range of market conditions, and delivers a wide range of
rates of return. How much profit a particular operation must make to ensure
its survival or should attempt in order to provide for growth varies considerably between different types of organisation (even in the same market)
and from year to year.

Profit can be defined in many ways, and the percentage profit likely to be
achieved by any product in any particular year depends on a wide variety of
circumstances, some dependent on the actions of management, many
entirely beyond their control. Risk management is the basic component of
business strategy, because profit is normally unobtainable without facing

some degree of risk. For success, the risks willingly undertaken must be commensurate with the rewards likely to be obtained and with the consequences of failure.

2 THE RELATIONSHIP OF PROFITS TO MARKETING

THE CORPORATE CATACLYSM – SALES-UNDER-BUDGET

The detailed discussion of the nature of profit in Chapter 1 is there because of the close relationship between profit and marketing; perhaps one even more intimate than that with other parts of an organisation such as production, distribution and administration. Marketing ('spendthrifts') and Accountancy ('killers of initiative') have long been boardroom opponents, frequently because of lack of understanding of each other's functions and terminology. One of my most helpful colleagues was both a Chartered Accountant and a former Brand Manager from Beechams, and one of the most useful training courses I ever attended was entitled *Finance for Non-financial Managers*.

Chapter 2 illustrates this difficult relationship by means of a case history which is based on real life, but which has been simplified and slightly fictionalised to protect both the innocent and the guilty. It will show how narrow the gap can be between success and failure and it will also provide pointers to developing a business strategy which minimises the risks of the latter.

Consider XYZ Widgets plc (or s.a. or gmbh), a medium-sized company with a good financial track record since its inception in 1984. XYZ manufactures a single product which it sells to widget-using businesses across Europe. XYZ works on a calendar financial year and therefore round about September 1993 had to set its *budget* for 1994.

Suppose budgeted *sales revenue*, for ease of calculation in the example, is 100 million ECU (or millions of £, FF or DM, whichever currency the reader finds most familiar). Further, it budgeted *fixed costs* at 50 million (being expenditures which do not vary with sales or within the financial year, such as rent of premises, insurance, depreciation of assets, salaries and pension-fund contributions of full-time employees), *variable costs* at 40 million (those costs which vary more or less in line with sales volume such as ingredients, power, transportation, wages of staff paid by the hour). This leaves *'profits'* for 1994 of 10 million. The terms in italics are not precisely what accountants would mean by them and have been greatly simplified to avoid this chapter becoming a book on its own. The figures are shown graphically in the left-hand column of Figure 2.1.

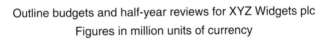

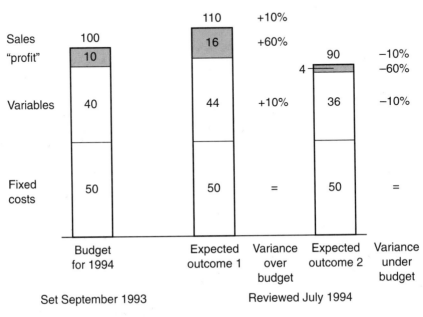

Fig. 2.1 The 'Sales-Under-Budget' Syndrome

Most companies keep regular track of costs and sales, and managers of XYZ receive monthly summaries of income and costs from their accounting department, with projections for the whole year based on year-to-date against budget. At the beginning of the year such comparisons are not particularly meaningful, as most of the year's work is still to come, and small variations from month to month cannot be given much weight, particularly if they are mutually compensating.

However, by the end of June each year, the outcome should begin to clarify. Income will be a half-year's actual sales, plus perhaps forward contracts and commitments, and the sales force's first-hand views of the customers' buying needs. Similarly many cost estimates will be firm, for example: rents and taxes will have been demanded, stocks, rates of use and prices of new materials will be known, and wage rates for the year already negotiated.

On the other hand, enough time is still ahead and enough of the budget uncommitted at least to be able to fine-tune the plan if necessary. For XYZ as for many companies the Half-Year is the key time for budgetary review. So some time towards the end of July 1994, the Board will be discussing their plans for the second half with their CEO.

Suppose, in the first instance, that for XYZ 1994 looks like being on track or a little better, as summarised in the centre column of Figure 2.1. At the half-year, sales for the full year are expected to be just a little better than budget, say 10 per cent up. Fixed costs (as they should be) are on budget, and variables will probably be up 10 per cent in line with the extra sales.

In these circumstances how will XYZ react? The leverage of marginal income on the relatively high fixed costs makes an enormous increase in apparent profitability. Perhaps this will not be fully achieved, because factory staff may have to be paid overtime to produce the extra product, raw materials above contract may have to be bought at higher spot-market rates and if the transport service is working near capacity unexpected deliveries may be expensive to arrange. The consequences and costs of such matters must be debated. But though there may be unexpected problems, there is now unexpected money in the budget to help solve them. The July Board meeting will probably be a happy one.

But just suppose January–June 1994 is only a passable period, with sales coming in regularly but not quite up to best expectations, and looking likely to end up by end-December 10 per cent below budget. Cost control remains good, with fixed costs still where they were fixed and variables running 10 per cent down against the lower sales. The position is then as the right hand column of Figure 2.1. Under the leverage of fixed to variable costs even a relatively small drop in likely income puts profit disproportionately below target.

How will the Board meeting go now? The company will still end the year in profit, not loss, and in any case how could sales and costs have been forecast more accurately a whole year ahead? Should XYZ not accept the rough with the smooth and hope for better luck in 1995?

Perhaps with a self-funded partnership the protagonists might just agree to tighten their belts a little and carry on with the plan. But in just about every company the writer has ever had dealings with, and certainly in those which funded their capital from outside, such figures would ring every warning bell in the building. As the Financial Director will remind the Board, XYZ has promised its backers (Merchant Bank, Debenture Holder,

Shareholders, Corporate Headquarters, or whoever) 10 million in returns. If XYZ does not deliver that sum, or something close to it, it will not be able to borrow enough money next year to support current levels of operations, let alone fund the exciting expansion programme everyone has been discussing. What do the Board propose to do, and quickly, to bring the situation back into line with Budget? As discussed in Chapter 1, budgeted profit has to be treated as a fixed cost, and cannot be avoided any more easily than taxes or fuel bills.

THE CLASSIC RESPONSE

So what typically will be proposed? Since the cost figures are exactly as expected, those responsible for them will point out that their housekeeping has been good, and the failure (if there is one) is in sales. Unless the cause is obvious, such as the bankruptcy or defection of a major customer, no doubt an investigation will be started to determine why sales are lower than expected, and whether this will be a temporary or permanent problem. But such market research takes time, and action must be started at once if results are to show before the end of the year.

Immediate Action (as the army calls it) is usually to crack the whip over the sales-force, and to give them some extra help in the form of price-incentives: such as extra discounts for quantities or new orders, or selectively to key customers. But will tinkering with the price solve the problem? Sales may respond in the short run, but if customers are merely stocking up ahead or intermediaries are refilling their pipeline without stimulating increases in final use, year-end volume sales may be no higher, and revenue even lower than now expected. Yet even if genuine new sales are made, unless the percentage volume increase is greater than the price cut, revenue will be down, not up (a problem further discussed in Chapter 12). Worse, temporary price-cuts have a habit of becoming permanent. Worse still, to get the 10 per cent drop during the first half back to budget, sales income has to be raised not by 10 per cent but by 22 per cent throughout the second half. Is this a realistic expectation in any market, however generous the incentives?

At best, Immediate Action 1 on price might be expected to increase sales a little, but not to solve the problem on its own. Where next? Immediate Action 2 must therefore be on *costs*. Fixed costs, by definition, are not available to provide savings within the financial year, although if the research suggests that demand is down for good, now might be the time to put one of the warehouses up for sale, to postpone the plan for a new delivery fleet and to call for voluntary redundancies to reduce fixed costs in future years.

Cost-cutting has to be done on the *variable costs*, and the axe seems invariably to fall first on *marketing*. This is not because anyone thinks marketing activity is not useful or effective (if so, no money would have been allocated to it in the first place!). It is partly because the effects on sales of such activity as advertising, market research and public relations are strategic rather than immediate; and, even more important in a cash crisis, can all be cut at short notice with only minimal cancellation charges. Any money saved drops immediately to the bottom line. Along with the marketing budget the first cost cuts are made (with effect from September 1st?) in other activities with the same characteristics, such as Travel & Entertainment, management training, and Research & Development. Such costs which are not directly product related and easily cancellable, usually go in the balance sheet under a generic heading of *Expenses*. Unfortunately, such cuts may contribute only marginally to the profit problem because by September no more than one third of the annual expenses budget will still be uncommitted, and in any case expenditure on such activities in most business-to-business companies is only a small percentage of total costs.

At this point the logical reader may wonder why instead of cancelling everything the marketing department did not go out to the customers with a crash programme to build sales. But imagine the reaction of their Financial Director, sitting in his office and gloomily extrapolating his spreadsheet to find out how long before he has to telephone the Receiver, if the Product Manager rushed in and asked: 'My sales are still down and my costs are up; please will you authorise me to spend an extra million on advertising to put things right?'.

So after cutting the product's price, its marketing budget and the expenses, and still not hitting the target, what is there left? This is where matters become really serious. Management have to accept cuts where they will show most clearly, namely in the largest cost items.

The most obvious will probably be on product specification. Can we replace real fruit juice with artificial flavour? Steel screws instead of brass? Reduce the gauge of polythene wrapping? Cancel the guaranteed next-day delivery? Scrap the night-shift on the 24-hour customer help-line, or start charging for the calls? Any of these may save significant sums this year, but all will reduce the quality and customer appeal of the product. It may become harder to sell in the first place and repeat sales could eventually be lost.

Similarly, money can be saved by reducing maintenance and postponing re-equipment scheduled for the current year. But neglected plant produces at lower quality and un-serviced delivery vehicles break down (thereby increasing costs or further reducing customer satisfaction).

The logical reader will also wonder about shedding staff. In the bad old days this would no doubt have been first on the list at many companies. Certainly XYZ should have cancelled overtime and temporary work early, in line with low sales as part of normal good housekeeping, and embargoed replacement of natural wastage. They might postpone salary increases and make cuts in staff benefits such as free meals.

But nowadays, full-time staff have to be treated as part of the fixed costs, partly because of potential Trades Union trouble, partly because of the high costs of legal redundancies, and partly because a company with the reputation of protecting its short-term cash-flow at the expense of its employees finds itself with morale and recruitment problems even in good years. This is not to say that XYZ might not shed a few salaries; particularly those it has already been looking for an excuse to fire and those who can cause least redundancy costs and problems, namely short-service junior managers.

THE CONSEQUENCES OF COST-SAVING

So where does all this leave XYZ? Perhaps following the tough decisions, hard work on the details, and a bit of luck in the marketplace, by the year's end the declared profit will be enough to satisfy the backers and ensure that a plan for 1995 will be reviewed sympathetically.

But can XYZ take advantage of any upturn in the widget market in 1995? It has left itself with a degraded product, a soft price list, reduced awareness or weakened image with the customers, no new replacement products in the pipeline, a short-staffed and badly-equipped plant, a de-motivated and underpaid management team, short of market data and technical training to guide them, with the best replacements for any vacancies already snapped up by the competition.

Probably all these future problems were envisaged, but management knew they had no choice. Such a situation has the characteristics of true tragedy. It is said that, once the action starts, *Romeo and Juliet* can end only one way. War-games players have failed to find any way of changing the outcome of many of the great battles of history. Once XYZ is irretrievably below its sales target it must do what it knows to be wrong in the long run to ensure it survives in the short run, because at that point it is the only action available. As the countryman is supposed to have said to the lost motorist: 'if I was going there, I wouldn't start from here'.

I go through this loop in boardrooms at the beginning of every recession and meet it at second-hand with many client companies. In dozens of seminars I have asked managers of all levels and from several countries what they would do in such a situation. They offer similar decisions and acknowledge the same drawbacks, and the more senior of them give case histories of having done it (or having it done to them!) for real.

But is there anything else XYZ could have done when sales were falling? Hold hard: who said sales were falling? Just suppose (since this is a fictionalised case) sales income in the previous year (1993) had been 80 million ECU. At the time the hard decisions were taken sales were expected to be *12.5 per cent up* year on year. Financial Consultants point out that companies do not go bankrupt because of low *profits*, only through shortage of *cash*. There are many examples of companies trading on through a whole series of unprofitable years, and going under only when they finally ran out of money and an exasperated creditor took them to Court.

XYZ and many other commercial companies run into trouble not because of low sales but because of unrealistic expectations. The 'sales-under-budget' syndrome strikes a company which expects an increase of 20 per cent and gets only 10 per cent just as hard as it does at one which expects zero growth and gets minus 10 per cent. Many companies face this problem if they refuse to retrench early in a recession, but a few even manage to go through it all on their own during a boom!

With hindsight, it is easy to blame XYZ's management for foolhardiness. But imagine how such an over-optimistic budget might have been arrived at. A small and relatively new but successful company would be used to achieving quite large annual growth rates as in Figure 2.2.

A target of 25 per cent up on 1993 could seem an exciting possibility. As a success-minded company, they may well at budget time (September 1993) still have been expecting to sell a bit more than 80 in 1993, which would have made the 100 seem even more likely as well as satisfyingly appropriate for their 10th anniversary next year. The company Cassandra muttering about exponentially diminishing growth curves, hardening competitive trading conditions and possible down-swings in the business cycle would easily have been talked over in a wave of corporate enthusiasm ('we'll sell the tonne when we're ten years on!').

Yet if XYZ had set a sales budget for 1994 of 90 and geared up to make a profit of 9 on it (say by borrowing less through restraining fixed costs to 45), they would have hit all the figures, had yet another record-breaking year and

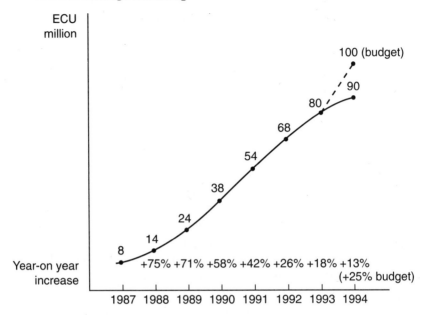

Fig. 2.2 XYZ Widgets plc: long-term sales

be in a good position to try (cautiously) for the magic 100 in 1995. As it stands, they will be lucky not to be taken over. It is hard not to be sympathetic. In mid-1993 when they laid their plans, the trend since 1989 must have looked close to a straight line, and the emergence of the inevitable S-curve might have been difficult to spot even if they had employed an econometrician. Disaster seems an extreme penalty for trying to do only modestly better than a straight-line projection, even in a business with such high fixed overheads.

To recapitulate: a company which sets itself realistic goals and consistently achieves them is a happy and successful one and popular with the financial community. A difficult year which has been anticipated in the corporate plan may not be pleasant, but it will be survived. Unjustified optimism in setting sales targets leads to shortfalls in expected profits. Financial prudence demands draconian action first by discounting the price, next by cutting the most easily cancellable marketing activities and finally by reducing product quality and service.

In even minor cases this action will weaken relations with the customers, in severe ones it can destroy the product. The 'sales-under-budget' syndrome almost inevitably leads to a policy of 'eating the seed corn' through the inexorable pressure to maintain short-term profits even at the expense of long-term growth. Marketing is always the first activity to suffer: it is therefore essential that marketing should for its own and the company's protection pressurise financial management to base their calculations on market-based reality, and to plan for the long-term as well as the next financial year. Pessimists are not popular in boardrooms, but the job they save may be their own!

3 PLANNING FOR UNCERTAINTY

THE HAZARDS OF JARGON

When dealing with the future, Chapter 2 deliberately used such words as budget, target, forecast, projection and estimate as if they were synonyms, as indeed they are often used in real life. Yet in a business context, each represents a concept which has a specific and different meaning. Any casual use which causes confusion between them can lead to dire consequences, as they did in the case of XYZ Widgets. Chapter 3 will explore the meanings of these concepts and their implications on profit and business strategy.

To be realistic, many businesses have developed their own internal terminology, but this is acceptable only so long as it is used correctly and all concerned understand it. Jargon is a convenient shorthand, which should be confined to consenting experts in private. Whatever they are called in different firms, there are three key concepts whose different meanings must be distinguished so that all decision-takers are clear what is being talked about. These are: budget, target and forecast.

The most easy to define is budget because it is a basic tool of accountancy. *Budgets* are about *money*: costs, revenues and profits. A business budget is a *plan* to allocate financial resources under various headings (plant, raw materials, staff, transport, advertising, etc.) in order to generate income from sales.

The essential nature of a budget is that most costs are incurred ahead of the income, and are known with a greater degree of certainty. (Exceptional industries which get paid in advance such as management education and training tend to become over-supplied!) In other words, a budget, although usually specified with great precision, mirrors the degree of uncertainty under which the company is acting and from which its eventual profit will derive.

The dictionary definition of *forecast* is: what is believed to be most likely to happen in future. It is axiomatic that we cannot foretell the future; if my readers could, they would not need to buy business books but could put their knowledge to good use at Ascot races or in the Salle des Jeux at Monte

Carlo. On the other hand life would be impossible if the future were totally unknown, because they would not know when to get out of bed each day, nor even in which direction the bedroom floor lay! The inherent nature of the future is that it is neither totally known nor unknown, it is *uncertain*. The degree of uncertainty varies widely: when dawn will break tomorrow is highly certain, whether and when the trains will run to Ascot races is less certain, what will win the 2.30 race is highly uncertain.

In a business context it is most important to be able to distinguish between what is known about the future with relative certainty, and what is less certain (or 'more risky'). A forecast is not an attempt at fortune-telling. A good and actionable forecast is one which gives the best and most objective analysis of the inherent risks in the future, because as shown in Chapter 1, the profit arises from the proper management of risk.

A target, at least in the sense it is used in this book, is different again. A *target* is what we would most like to happen and will strive to achieve. Success in business requires both objective analysis and emotional optimism. 'Ah, but a man's reach should exceed his grasp, Or what's a heaven for?' as Robert Browning put it. Certainly the business Halls of Fame are peopled not with the cautious but with those who had the drive and vision to try for the impossible and win. Optimistic targeting is conceivably a precondition to growth. Trouble starts when laudable optimism becomes mandatory company policy through using targets as if they were budgets.

To go back to XYZ Widgets and their 1994 budget in Chapter 2; what if management had set a budget for 90 million sales, but had targeted to try for the 100? As the company visionary might have put it: 'statistics may prove we *probably* cannot sell more than 90 million next year, but I am damn *certain* we will not if we don't try.' If they then failed on the target but hit their budget, we have seen that they and their financial probity would have survived 1994. As we have also seen, any sales that luck, hard graft or enthusiasm gave them above that budget level would generate disproportionately good marginal profits. Some of these could have been ploughed back immediately into generating yet more sales and consequently profits. So even if the over-optimistic target was not reached, the outcome would have been so much better than what had happened to them by the end of Chapter 2.

THE STRATEGIC IMPORTANCE OF THE FORECAST

As already pointed out, in most businesses internal costs are more accurately known and more easily controlled than income which has to come from autonomous customers. A required level of profit is therefore more often missed through inadequacies in sales revenue than through poor cost-control.

A successful business plan demands the best information available for forecasting sales. The starting point is to take an objective view of the business environment from which sales have to be generated. Will they be easier to make next year or harder? Is competition likely to get weaker or stronger? What is the climate of opinion among the customers, are they optimistic or pessimistic about their future? What are the relative chances of making sales of 90 million units, 100 million, 110 million? What difference will a price cut or a price rise make? In other words to develop the best, most accurate, most objective forecast of the market for the period of the planning cycle. Chapter 9 is devoted to a generalised approach for doing this.

Given a realistically achievable level of sales income, a budget must then be constructed to allocate costs in such a way as to provide the required level of profit. This can usually be done in more than one way: for example, by planning to sell a larger volume at lower margin or a smaller volume at higher margin. Under expected market conditions, which of the alternatives seems the most feasible, or least risky? Of course, in some circumstances there may be very little room for manoeuvre on required levels of profit; but if there is no way at all in which costs can be managed to make the required profit from a level of sales which we believe the market will accept, then our company is not viable, and will sooner or later go out of business. Chapter 2 should have indicated that in general it is better to budget low and over-achieve, than to budget high and miss. The alternative approach of starting with a profit figure and working back from it to derive a sales forecast ('backing into the strategy') is a recipe for disaster.

To caricature what seems to happen all too often in practice, imagine the boss of poor XYZ Widgets constructing his company budget. He starts by calling his Financial Director: 'Figgis. How much profit must we make next year?' Figgis who has just spent a scarifying morning at the Merchant Bank knows the answer to this only too well: 'Not less than 10 million ECU, J.B.'. 'Understood, and how many widgets must we sell to make 10 million?' Not quite so easy, and Figgis has to call up his cost formulae on his PC: 'At today's prices, 1,465,273 units.' JB then calls his Sales Director: 'J.B. here, Jim. Your sales forecast for next year is a million and a half. Get your boys and girls to make out a detailed sales plan for that, will you?'

Unless some minion in the sales department has the temerity to challenge all three of his top bosses, XYZ has now imposed on itself a necessity to sell

1.5 million widgets, backed by a marketing plan based on the previous year's prices, margins, and method of approach, perhaps with a small cautionary allowance for inflation. No discussion of what the demand for widgets will be out there in the market, whether in next year's conditions it might be easier to sell less (or even more) at a different price ratio against the competition, and if so whether the necessary capital could be funded from a different source on more favourable terms?

'Backing into the strategy' by converting a profit need into a sales volume by the application of an historic cost-structure adds to the risks of failure without offering any compensating benefits in terms of increasing rewards. Indeed its greatest weakness is that it does not admit the existence of, let alone assess, the source and degree of risks inherent in the period being planned; and it sets out no alternatives for action should the single strategy put forward not come to pass exactly as laid down.

Given that any scenario for the future is uncertain, any plan, however carefully laid, may come to grief. No blame for this glimpse of the obvious need be put on the planners. However, as Chapter 2 demonstrated in great detail, if a business unexpectedly discovers in mid-year that it will be seriously below budgeted profit, it is highly likely to react in a way that will make matters worse. Planners are at fault if they fail to identify in advance where the plan is most sensitive to failure so that these factors can be monitored with care to give as much advance warning as possible of impending trouble. Further, the plan should have identified what the most likely effects of such failure would be, so that contingency plans can be worked out in advance to minimise early the effects of any disaster.

In other words, a successful business plan is not a budget nor any single set of figures, but a detailed evaluation of the source and size of the rewards and risks in the market situation, with a basic strategy for dealing with *all* the most likely of them. This strategy has to be flexible and robust enough to comprehend any minor and forseeable variations which may arise, and also to contain outline contingency strategies to deal with major, but less likely, crises. Naturally 'The Budget' always has to be set, preferably based on but slightly below the central forecasts of sales; but it should be backed up with a set of financial implications worked out for the best and least favourable circumstances that might arise. The more likely something is to happen, the more detailed the plan needs to be to deal with it.

One such source of alternative circumstances, which should always be considered but is often totally ignored, is potential competitive activity. For example, I have many times seen marketing plans which would indeed build considerably improved sales and profits, if only they could be implemented under conditions where all other things were equal. But in a market which is relatively static in size, any increased sales must come at the expense of other suppliers, who get hurt and retaliate. Sometimes one does so with sufficient power and accuracy to leave the original aggressor not only surprised but worse, rather than better, off. Such a situation may end up in a price-war which neither supplier intended and from which nobody, not even the customers, gains any long-term benefit.

Laker Airways actually died from this syndrome. There was no doubt (back in 1977) that there was considerable potential to increase traffic over the Atlantic by lower fares. A scheduled airline to holiday destinations at significantly lower price could stimulate new business from discretionary travellers. But the new Laker Skytrain was so cheap that it not only encouraged new vacationers, it also switched regular business travellers away from the established scheduled carriers. This took Laker Airways out of the charter sector where it had always been able to make a fair business into head-on competition with PanAm and British Airways who had no choice but to retaliate. Comparable low fares, with their well-known frequent schedules and reputation for reliability, brought their customers back in droves. Long before the Courts resolved Laker's accusations of 'predatory pricing' and 'collusion' it was all over. A 'niche' strategy designed to build business more slowly but less at the expense of the market leader would have reduced immediate profit but might have helped preserve Laker Airways for the future.

PROJECTION OF CURRENT TRENDS

Besides the potential confusion with budgets and targets, the word 'forecast' is often used synonymously with the words 'projection' and 'prediction'. Yet all three have different meanings, which should be clearly understood by their business users.

A *projection* (also called extrapolation) is a mathematical term with a precise meaning: the continuation of the current trend. A projection is a very useful aid to forecasting, because it helps to understand how we arrived at the current position, where we are headed and how far we might get if current trends continue. Projection can be done graphically by eye; although this is not very precise, as can be demonstrated by giving a group of people each the same set of points (such as ten years' annual sales) and asking them to project the trend forward. Unless the given points all lie on a straight line, the highest and lowest projections are likely to be some way apart even only two or three years ahead. Figure 3.1 perhaps exaggerates the problem, but the upward exponential, the levelling-off S-curve, the life-cycle hump and the cyclical wave-form are all legitimate extensions of the original line!

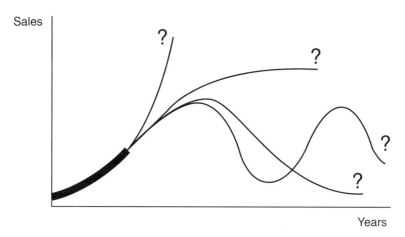

Fig. 3.1   The problems of extrapolation

Luckily, these days even the simplest statistical software package offers the PC-user a range of straight-line and curvilinear projections which remove the guesswork and artistry of traditional scissors-and-paste methods. Trend lines can be fitted and projected under pre-determined mathematical conditions and backed with statistics which measure the precision with which the line represents the data. Unfortunately this very precision can leave a sense of false security. A projection is not a forecast but an aid to one, or at best is a forecast based on a single dubious assumption: that current trends will continue unchanged.

Endless experience shows that although current trends rarely change suddenly and drastically, the rate of growth or decline tends to accelerate or slow down. Figure 3.1 shows how hard it is to determine which way or how fast merely by inspecting the past. This is for many reasons: saturation points are reached, technologies change, Governments make laws which affect the issue. All of us take action to try to speed a trend if favourable or to block it if not.

Peter Drucker quotes an example (*Harvard Business Review*, May 1985): 'Around 1909, a statistician at the American Telephone and Telegraph Company projected two curves 15 years out: telephone traffic and the

American population. Viewed together, they showed that by 1920 or so every single female in the United States would have to work as a switchboard operator. The process need was obvious, and within two years, AT&T had developed and installed the automatic switchboard.'

Nowadays, most new desk-top PCs are delivered with a basic software package entitled something like 'Janet and John get down to business'. This often includes a program labelled 'forecasting', where the user feeds in a few past years' monthly sales and (bingo) a 'forecast' is shown on the screen, perhaps even graphed, thereby saving a hard-pressed manager hours of painful calculation. But, alas, these programs rarely explain how they work and are usually projections based on simple moving averages with perhaps exponential smoothing for magic (see Chapter 9).

Their limitations can be exposed by asking them a simple question, such as: 'I propose to double my price, now what will I sell?'. If the program can offer only one forecast irrespective of the marketing environment it must be just a projection, and the description 'forecast' a misnomer.

THE MEANING OF PREDICTION

A *prediction* can be defined as a personal view of the outcome of a single future event. Predictions are the professional territory of the fortune-teller, but they have their place in business, not only among those companies who employ (and evidently find helpful) consultant astrologers. The nature of a prediction is that it implies certainty with no alternative possibilities ('you *will* meet a tall, dark stranger'). There is the story of the young lady, emerging from the last of a line of crystal-gazer's booths at the seaside and saying to her friend: 'That was a waste of money. They all said the same thing!'

The future of a company will be influenced by a number of events for which there is no back data to project nor hard evidence to assess, and so we have no alternative for planning purposes but to make a prediction. For example, our chief competitor either will or will not bring out a new line next year. This would make too big a difference to our sales and our marketing for the possibility to be ignored, but without industrial espionage we have to guess, based on what we know about their circumstances and policies. We may be right or wrong, but have no choice but to make the prediction explicit, put a probability on it, and where the chances are significant work out their consequences and an outline counter-strategy.

Predictions, like projections, are not in themselves forecasts (or at best very inadequate ones), but often form part of the input needed to make a forecast.

FORECASTING FROM PROJECTIONS AND PREDICTIONS

To say that 'our sales next year will be 1.5 million units', and say no more, is to make a prediction, not a forecast. It may or may not turn out to be right, but in either case gives no help to the management team in developing a strategy to achieve or to beat it, nor to protect the organisation against any unexpected disaster, nor to improve the basis of future forecasts.

A better forecast statement might be something like: 'our sales next year will be 1.5 million units, plus or minus 5 per cent, providing:

- our competitor does not launch a new product
- levels of sales tax do not change
- our new production line comes on stream next August as scheduled
- our price and promotional strategy is in accordance with the marketing review dated 5th November.

In this case, it will be quite clear to those who have to take action (such as scheduling production, budgeting cash-flow or setting targets for the sales-force) what is the natural range of variation anticipated and exactly what are the basic assumptions on which it is based. If the factory is late we will not be able to make enough. If the competition launch a look-alike we cannot expect to sell so much. If we cut our planned price or our advertising, this will affect sales up or down.

To arrive at a forecast in this sense will almost certainly require making projections of past sales, but they will need to be modified in the light of informed judgment of changes in future conditions. Some of this will involve making predictions (for example about future tax rates or competitors' plans). Chapter 9 will examine the approach to sales forecasting in more detail.

To recapitulate: for survival all decision-takers must understand the difference between targets and budgets, and must base the latter on the most realistic forecast possible about future market conditions. If conditions seem favourable, it is legitimate to target high, but budgets should be derived from a level of sales that is highly likely to be achieved even if optimism does not prevail.

The future is not unknown but uncertain and the degree of uncertainty is a measure of the risks which have to be managed in order to make a desired profit. A budget is a financial plan expressing the intentions of a business for making this profit. An essential input to the plan is a detailed market forecast under which the likelihood of making various levels of sales income can be evaluated.

Such a forecast is not a single figure, but something more complex. It implies uncertainty and a range of possibilities as a result of explicit assumptions. It is likely to have been made on the basis of factual market and company data, amplified by the knowledge and opinions of those most concerned with its implications. It should be available to all who have to implement the business plan so that the assumptions can be properly tested and the danger points continually monitored so that if anything goes wrong counter-action is initiated before it is too late.

4 MARKETING AS AN APPROACH TO PROFIT

THE RISE OF MODERN MARKETING

To execute the corporate plan and to achieve the business objectives as discussed in Chapters 1–3, the top management of a company has to allocate their resources to perform the various specified tasks. The resources are of two kinds only: people and money (or Capital and Labour in traditional economics texts), which will be discussed in Chapter 15. The tasks are many, some internal to the company, others aimed at the external environment. Almost all the external tasks can be comprehended under one function – *marketing*. It is therefore vital to have a clear understanding about what marketing is, what it can achieve and how it sets about doing that.

It is unfortunate that the uninitiated often regard marketing as 'a fancy word for selling and advertising'. Even many business people see it as no more than a set of communication techniques such as advertising, sales promotion and P.R., useful only to brand leaders in mass consumer markets.

Certainly, these familiar techniques of consumer marketing were first exploited by 'household name' companies in fast-moving consumer goods, who had become successful through owning excellent production and distribution facilities in a world desperately short of goods after World War II. When supplies first began to outrun demand in the 1950s, these operators found themselves having to defend their market leadership against heavy competition.

They did this by using the newly-developing techniques of market research to switch the focus of their operations from the product to the consumer. They began to adapt (and design from scratch) research-based products that fitted the needs of consumers, and used mass media and public relations on an unprecedented scale to communicate that what people really wanted was now in the shops.

As the retailers began to comprehend their importance to suppliers and became pro-active in their relationships, product managers had to develop new techniques of 'trade marketing' such as selling-aids, merchandising schemes and sales promotions. Many of the new products and marketing ideas originated at this stage in the USA and were adapted to UK and European markets, particularly by the big advertising agencies whose reputations depended a great deal on spotting trends and recommending them to their clients.

Later, the approach of consumer-orientated marketing was adopted by other (up to then) more protected businesses, almost always at the point where supply outran demand and competition consequently became heavy enough to eliminate the weak and squeeze the margins of the strong. Successively: household durables, travel, retailing, consumer services, media, motor cars, finance. More recently customer orientation has reached parts of the business-to-business sector and (the most recent recruits) the professions.

As each new sector comes on stream, techniques have to be selected with care and often need to be adapted. But the approach has always worked and helped the early adopters in each newly-distressed market sector to survive and take over (or push under) the laggards.

Marketing techniques continue to be developed and modified to meet changing conditions, but as business communications have speeded up (and the leading practitioners all become multi-national) new ideas now arise all over the world and successful innovations spread extremely quickly.

THE FAILURE OF 'PRODUCTION-ORIENTATION'

Water is a free good at the well and an almost priceless treasure to the stranded traveller in the Sahara. Marketing theory is based on the proposition that a product incurs only costs and has no value at its point of production (and that any figure in the balance sheet labelled 'work in progress' which is above scrap value could become wishful thinking overnight). A product gains value only if someone else wants it, it incurs income only when it is sold, and it makes a profit only if the price acceptable to the buyer exceeds total attributable costs. Buyers, not sellers, make markets.

Few businesses discovered this blinding glimpse of the obvious before the 1950s because the commercial environment in the 'bad old days' obscured it. Until the industrial revolution, production was largely small-scale and local and a producer usually managed customer relations in person. If your new shoes hurt, you took them straight back to the village shoemaker to put right. The industrial revolution created new problems, such as the technology of mass-production, the logistics of distribution of large quantities of goods and the financing of world markets. The latter were taken over by new specialists, particularly by wholesalers/retailers/agents and by merchant banks, leaving producers to concentrate on production.

During the 19th century, manufacture was mainly in the hands of those who had invented a new process, or had protected access to a source of cheap raw materials, or had the luck to inherit a going concern. They sold their output in bulk, free on board, to any middlemen willing to pay a price which more than covered the costs of production. While this continued, the producer would concentrate on keeping his machines turning, and needed to pay little attention to the ultimate destination or price of the product. Occasionally, if the product was sticking, the distributors would put pressure on the producer to 'do some advertising' to try and convince the final users that this was exactly what they wanted.

Sometimes this worked, and many of the great industrial fortunes were founded in this way. In the expanding commercial world of the 19th century there were many opportunities for large-scale entrepreneurs and the rewards for the enterprising and individualistic 'robber barons' were high. But the risks were high too. For every Benz, Leverhulme, Nobel or Rockefeller whose operations still flourish and command respect today, there were thousands of unknown bankruptcies.

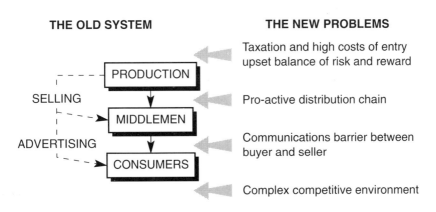

Fig. 4.1 The problems of production-orientation

Changes were taking place, but the problems created by two world wars linked by a deep and long-lasting world recession obscured the underlying trends and forced business management to concentrate on some enormous tactical problems. But by the middle of the 20th century, it was becoming clear to many of us that fundamental changes in the business environment had made the old ways too risky.

First, the rewards of success had diminished: governments were intervening and raising taxes on business profits. The technology of mass-production meant that the costs of entry into a new market were too high for individual firms and could not be financed without guarantees of substantial shares of profits to the lenders of capital. On the other hand, the penalties of failure (namely bankruptcy) had changed not at all. This upset the balance of risk and reward against the entrepreneur.

Second, instead of just reacting passively to the suppliers, taking what they offered and pricing it as they suggested, the distributors began to realise that they themselves owned the customers. They began to use their strength to increase their share of the final price of the product. The 'rise of retailer power' became particularly obvious in mass-market packaged goods throughout Northern Europe and the USA.

Third, the logistics of mass-production, which meant that products sold all over the world had to be produced in a few enormous high-tech factories, imposed an increasing distance between producer and consumer (not only through geography but also substantial socio-economic and 'lifestyle' differences); thereby creating a communications barrier between the decision-makers at the potential supplier and their potential customers.

Finally, the business environment had become more complex, and buying decisions were now affected by a variety of general economic, social, technological and legal trends, buyers had access to supplies from many countries and used alternative channels of distribution when it suited them.

All this meant that the craftsman cobblers who stuck to their lasts lost their business to the low-cost mass-suppliers who kept in close touch with the latest fashions in footwear and owned shares in the major stores in city centres.

MARKETING AS A PHILOSOPHY OF DOING BUSINESS

Marketing in the modern sense is not just a set of pretty techniques but rather a 'philosophy of management' or approach to getting and retaining profitable business. The most succinct yet comprehensive definition of marketing is that used by the Chartered Institute of Marketing (the largest professional marketing body in Europe) and already quoted in Chapter 1:

The management process responsible for identifying, anticipating and satisfying customer requirements profitably.

Chapter 1 posed the question: 'what in one word is marketing about?' and discussed the wrong answer: 'profit'. The profitability of a company or brand is the responsibility not just of the marketing department (unless perhaps the CEO is also the Marketing Director) but of *everyone* in the firm who has any say in sales revenue or costs. It is enlightening to talk to the staff at all levels in companies where this is realised.

The correct key word is *customer*. The specific role of the marketing function in generating profits is to look at the operation from the perspective of the customer (who supplies all the money earned by the firm), and to organise the resources of production, distribution and promotion so as to satisfy a pre-determined customer need.

The axiom of such 'customer-orientation' is that profits will be higher and more certain than if the company is 'production-orientated', producing what it thinks it is good at and afterwards seeking someone who might be willing to buy it.

Marketing is about customers, and if each business decision-taker looks at the effects of alternative courses of action on the customer as well as on the company, then he or she may well take more effective (and ultimately more profitable) decisions.

THE MEANING OF 'CUSTOMER-ORIENTATION'

It is now almost trendy to pay lip-service to 'customer-orientation', but not all who do so understand what it really means. For example, as part of a welcome reappraisal of policy, British Rail has taken to addressing as 'customers' the people who they used to call 'passengers' or 'travellers'. But to use the word in this context suggests a fundamental misunderstanding of the mechanics of the travel business.

If I buy a chocolate bar, it is probably because I want to eat it, and I am then indeed a 'consumer' of the product and a customer of its supplier. If I buy a ticket from a carrier, it is not because I want to spend several hours in an aeroplane, train or coach but because I have at a certain time to attend a conference in Prague or visit my Glasgow depot or swell the numbers at Grandmother's birthday celebration. The 'product' I am buying is therefore not the journey but my arrival at the destination.

While comforts and entertainment on the journey may be welcome, they are inevitably secondary in importance to the frequency, reliability and speed of the schedules. Most airlines appear to miss this point when they attempt to attract the business traveller by the rarity of their wines, pulchritude of their cabin staff and luxury of their executive lounges in which to while away their delays. These undoubted product benefits seem better suited to vacationers who may well be prepared to spend their time and money on the most pleasant travelling experience available.

A pan-European survey (OAG Business Traveller Lifestyle Survey 1992) showed that the top three factors influencing choice of airline for business travel were: 'most convenient schedule', 'effective security precautions' and 'reputation for punctuality'. In other words, business people will first check competitive schedules against the necessary arrival time (which is usually not under their control). If they have a choice they are most likely to book the airline which offers the most punctual flights, and good security. Whether a flight was good or bad, and so whether the airline should in future be put higher or lower on the traveller's repertoire is more likely to be judged after the event by when they reached their final destination than their degree of comfort while in the air.

Airlines may well agree, but claim that delays at airports are not under their control. Partly true, but do they concentrate their efforts on relatively easy to control in-flight service? The rush-hour scrums at Heathrow and Kennedy suggest few airlines are as good at matching check-in facilities to customer demand as the average supermarket, and the very efficiency of some 'lost-luggage' systems suggests that they get plenty of practice.

THE 'CUSTOMER-ORIENTATED' PRODUCT

The above somewhat petulant asides are not intended to build empathy with the well-travelled reader but to point out that satisfying the need of a business customer is rarely a simple matter of handing over a widget, even a top-quality one. Round the widget there has to be an invisible halo of associated services. Perhaps a guarantee of performance, a friendly technical help-line, a where-and-when-you-want-it delivery service, a reassuring supplier image, flexible terms of payment for regular customers and so on.

The widget has by law to be 'of merchantable quality' of course, but this is no more than the ante to enter the widget market. Customers will not repeat-purchase from a supplier whose goods fail to meet specification. But it is comparatively rare to have a fully-protected and unique design or process for which no competitor can provide a substitute adequate for most customers. The more similar the competing core products become, the more the final choice of supplier will depend on the buyers' response to the elements in the surrounding halo.

WHO IS THE CUSTOMER?

Another frequent misconception of the marketing approach is to take too broad a definition of 'customer', thereby indicating a basic lack of understanding of the nature of the buying process and making it difficult to design either products or approaches with strong appeal to the market.

In 1872, when my grandfather had to leave school at the age of 10 to help support his widowed mother and large family, a neighbour apparently gave the advice: 'Get into the boot and shoe trade, Jack. Everybody wears shoes and you will never be out of a job'. He did so, and with such success that by the age of 30 he owned his own shoe shop, which he proudly claimed in later life to be: 'the first shop in the City of London to fit electric light!'

Yet both young Jack and the neighbour must have been aware that of the many and quite small shoe factories in Victorian London some prospered while others closed, that cheap mass-produced shoes were beginning to flood into Britain from Italy, from Eastern Europe and from the burgeoning industry of the USA. Further, that while rich, young, fashion-conscious women spent large sums every year on shoes, thousands of their own neighbours in the East End of London replaced their one pair of boots only when worn out, and there were more than a few who could afford none at all.

It is difficult to deduce by looking at a photograph nearly a century old why J. Stutchbury's shoe shop in St. Paul's Churchyard flourished in a highly competitive market, but the chances are that the proprietor did not expect to entice every passer-by, but selected his stock and invested in the very latest display techniques with a highly specific and well-understood type of customer in mind.

'Going into boots and shoes', or (to move on a century) into franchised convenience food or telecommunications or semi-conductors or leisure facilities or corporate health-insurance is of itself no guarantee of success however large or fast-growing world consumption is expected to be. Big markets are not usually homogeneous but segmented. Success more usually comes from targeting a small sub-sector with a specialised need in common for whom a product can be tailored with a strong and preferably unique brand appeal; rather than from offering basic commodities designed to offend nobody and consequently to have only a weak appeal to anybody.

Fig. 4.2 Market segmentation and high-tech merchandising circa 1901

Yet when asked 'who are your customers?', too many business people, even if in a marketing role, give vague generalisations: 'architects', 'the textile industry', 'managers of pension funds', 'large fleet-owners', 'senior decision-takers in big companies'. Cross-examination often fails to narrow or clarify that description meaningfully.

Yet nobody can invent a product, design a sales presentation or create an advertising campaign that will motivate a whole industry or even all senior managers within it. Some firms and specific people within them will be much better prospects than the rest, and marketing effort designed and branded with them in mind will be far more effective, and cost-effective, than some vague or bland generality. The importance of targeting as a key to success is discussed in Chapter 6, and branding as an approach in Chapter 11.

To recapitulate: marketing is about customers. Knowing who they are and what they need are the first and most basic steps to making a profit from them. This does not mean that it is not important to know how to make such a product, or unnecessary to have the resources to distribute and promote it, only that these skills and resources should come second in the priorities of management. To accept marketing as a philosophy of doing business implies that better and more easily achievable profits come by working from a customer need back to the product than from starting with a product or process and then looking hopefully for buyers.

5 THE BUSINESS BUYING DECISION

THE LIMITATIONS OF CONSUMER MARKETING IN A BUSINESS-TO-BUSINESS CONTEXT

As reviewed in Chapter 4, the philosophy and approach of customer-orientated marketing was first developed in mass-consumer-goods markets, and only later adapted to other situations. As a result, a great deal of the 'revealed wisdom' and indeed most of the published information about marketing is derived from or at least concentrates on consumer goods and services. (An honourable exception has to be made in the case of Aubrey Wilson, who almost singlehandedly created in Britain a disciplined approach to industrial marketing through his books based on his pioneer work in Industrial Market Research and consultancy.)

The consumer view of marketing is acceptable as far as the general philosophy goes, but is less helpful when dealing with actual marketing techniques in non-consumer markets. This chapter will not try to adapt consumer marketing concepts, but review from 'zero-base' the fundamentals of a successful, profitable marketing approach to any business market, namely: who business customers are, and what is known about the nature of the business buying decision.

The similarities and differences between 'consumer' and 'business' (formerly called 'industrial') marketing are not well understood. As two business academics working in collaboration in Manchester and Lyon Business Schools put it: 'we view most of the traditional approaches to industrial marketing as inadequate, both academically and practically . . . particularly [through borrowing] from consumer marketing concepts such as the Marketing Mix and applying them simplistically.' (*Strategies for International Industrial Marketing* by P. W. Turnbull and J.-P. Valla, Routledge 1986.)

BUSINESS-TO-BUSINESS VS. CONSUMER MARKETING

When I was an examiner for various professional Diplomas in marketing, I would sometimes set as part of a question: 'discuss the differences between consumer and industrial buyer behaviour'. I was frequently disappointed by candidates whose answers could be summarised as: 'companies always behave rationally, consumers act on impulse'. I hoped that such simplistic generalisations had not been gathered from teachers or text books.

Marketing to businesses differs from marketing to consumers in three fundamental respects, in ascending order of importance:

a. The buyers are using their company's not their own money.
b. Potential customers in a business market are typically numbered only in hundreds or even dozens within one country (and probably only a few thousand in the whole of Europe).
c. Any non-trivial buying decision is taken not by one person (or small family unit) but by a large group (the *Decision Making Unit* henceforth referred to as the DMU) the members of which have different roles to play and degrees of influence on the outcome.

On the other hand, consumer and business marketing are similar to the extent that all buying decisions are made by *people*; and, further, that the decisions made by companies are made by people who when not in their roles as business executives take decisions for themselves and their families as consumers. Their demographics, personalities, aspirations and psychological processes inevitably remain the same in both roles. Consequently, both consumer and business buying decisions are complex processes, involving a number of factors: both tangible ('rational') ones such as price and product performance, and intangibles ('irrationals') such as personal prestige or security, and product or supplier image.

Certainly, much consumer purchasing behaviour can be seen to have a highly rational basis; consider the care that children take in assessing the merits of alternative ways of laying out limited pocket money, or the systematic research and testing carried out by a car enthusiast between the delivery of one model and the order for the next. Even a purchase partly conditioned by considerations of brand or user image may be a reasoned one. A young man who chooses a model of car with a 'macho' image may do so because he believes it will both enhance his standing with his peer group and his attraction for the opposite sex. An emotional decision perhaps, but surely not irrational? Even classic impulse purchases such as chocolate count-lines are usually made within a limited (so-called) *repertoire* of brands which each buyer has found by experience can acceptably satisfy a need, and who will have a corresponding list of brands which are never bought even when on offer or dominant display.

	Business-to-business	Consumer
Potential buyers in market	Hundreds	Millions
People in Decision Making Unit	9–10	1–2
Money	Company's	Own
Decision Process	Complex, Multi-stage	Complex, Multi-stage
Factors affecting	Tangible/ rational *and* intangible/ irrational	Tangible/ rational *and* intangible/ irrational
Marketing approach	Mainly direct and personal	Mainly at a distance and impersonal

Fig. 5.1 Typical business and consumer markets

Similarly, while companies scrutinise and debate their major purchases, tangible product characteristics such as specification and rational issues such as efficiency can sometimes be over-ridden by emotional or downright irrational factors. Consider the large mainframe computers expensively bought, housed and staffed during the 1970s and made obsolete during the 1980s which were never used beyond a fraction of their capacity; or the corporate headquarters buildings designed by trendy architects and filled with specially-commissioned works of art which are never visited by the customers or financiers who might be impressed. The decision-takers may have enjoyed being at the forefront of technology or indeed contributing to architectural history, but their decisions did nothing to help maximise the profitability of their operations.

Marketing emphasises the obvious point that, except in law, businesses never buy or sell anything. The selling effort and the purchasing decision are the responsibility of the people working there. Business-to-business marketing is therefore about *interactive personal relationships* between the staffs of suppliers and of their relatively small number of identifiable present and potential customer firms. 'Such relationships are often stable, complex and long-lasting . . . the major concern is with the management of relationships between suppliers and customers and the processes of interaction between them . . . buyer and seller companies are both active participants in the market.' (*International Marketing and Purchasing* ed. P. W.Turnbull and M. T. Cunningham, Macmillan 1981). A Marketing Director might well expect to meet or entertain all his or her biggest business customers in the course of the year.

This is very different from a typical consumer market where the potential customers are numbered in millions and so have to be dealt with at a distance through the intermediaries of market researchers, retail distributors and mass-advertising. Consequently, some of the classic techniques of consumer marketing such as blind product testing, point-of-sale promotion or mass-television advertising are not usually applicable to business markets, or at least not without considerable modification.

HOW THE DECISION MAKING UNIT OPERATES

It is not sufficient to target individual potential customer companies. Within each of these the marketer has to identify the members of the relevant DMU, by role, by job title and ideally by name. Only then can a marketing strategy be developed, based on an understanding of their individual needs and of the most effective channels of communication with them.

Sales-forces are well aware that most companies have Purchasing Officers (or complete Purchasing Departments) who have the task of locating and contacting possible suppliers. They may often conduct all the negotiations, and will certainly try to give the suppliers' representatives the impression that they are the only arbiters of the final decision. However, while such *Purchasers* are indeed part of the DMU, their actions are influenced and even directed by others.

Most of these others can be designated as Authorisers, Specifiers or Users. *Authorisers* tend to be Senior Management especially Finance Directors or CEOs, who set budgets and agree whether or not a given purchase can be made against them. Final authorisers are therefore involved in large numbers of decisions but only at a strategic level, in effect ratifying or vetoing plans worked out in detail by others.

Specifiers may sometimes be the ultimate users, but are more often R&D staff, engineers or external technical analysts able to summarise the company's needs and the characteristics of the goods or services that will satisfy them.

The final *Users* will certainly be consulted both at the specification stage and after the purchase has been made, and may well have identified the need in the first place.

There are signs of a fifth role emerging in the decision, particularly in larger companies, namely the *corporate specialist* or consultant. The specialist acts somewhere between authoriser and specifier and is empowered to oversee, advise and even to modify the whole operation in relation to corporate policy. For example, companies appoint Energy Managers, Total Quality Managers, Consultants in Ecology and Guardians of Corporate Relations. Their requirements may be included in purchase specifications. They may also be able to veto a supplier who would cause problems in their area of specialisation, for example: because of difficulty in disposing of contaminated packaging; or because they use undesirable production techniques; or have overt relations with countries which the buyer wishes not to be seen to support. Bigger companies employ individuals for this purpose or even whole departments, smaller ones may prefer to use outside consultants for such specialised purposes.

Each of these five roles is likely to be taken by a different department, and often not by an individual but by a group, including senior and junior members of staff. Interactions between them can be complex, and while few may have the power to say 'yes' to a proposition, all are important to a supplier because many may have effective powers of veto.

For example, if before the purchase of new machinery the work-force believe (perhaps through hearsay from other factories) that a particular machine tends to cause accidents, the Works Manager is likely to object to its choice (even if the rumour is untrue) in case it causes an industrial relations problem.

Recent multinational research indicates that an average of 9 people influence a typical industrial buying decision in Europe, with a range as wide as 3–20. The more important the decision, the more people are likely to be given, or to demand, a say.

At one extreme, fundamental decisions such as the relocation of offices or a new pension scheme (and certainly a change in supplier to the staff canteen!) is liable to require consultation with the whole staff at all levels. Re-equipment, adoption of a new technology or other major capital transactions will necessarily involve several departments in depth (with perhaps the

Customer Country	Supplier country				
	Average	France	Germany	Sweden	Britain
France	10	20	7	5	7
Germany	8	7	15	6	5
Italy	6	8	4	3	8
Sweden	10	10	6	15	9
Britain	9	8	8	6	15
Average	9	11	8	7	9

Fig. 5.2 Average number of persons involved in purchasing decisions
Source: Turnbull & Valla

appointment of a project team to mastermind the transaction). At the other extreme, the need for routine re-purchases of a minor raw material might be flagged mechanically, with the purchasing officer checking alternative suppliers or negotiating prices only at annual intervals. Most users are permitted to do their own shopping up to a cash limit, although in hard times executives in more and more companies complain that even a box of pencils requires three signatures on the order!

1. *Identification of need.* The factory floor – 'Our No. 4 grinder is worn out. Please may we replace?'

2. *Authorisation of Search.* Chief Executive – 'Go ahead, within a budget of x'

3. *Specification.* Engineering – 'We need a machine with a capacity of n units per hour which can accept brass, aluminium and mild steel'

4. *Corporate check.* Specialists – 'Are there any overall corporate implications?'

5. *Search for Suppliers.* Purchasing Department – 'Do you wish to tender to this specification?'

6. *Choice.* All the above

7. *Authorisation of Expenditure.* Finance Department – 'Are you within budget?'

8. *Monitoring.* Specifiers and Users – 'Did we get what we want? Is it working properly? Are there any problems?'

Fig. 5.3 A typical buying sequence for capital equipment

Figure 5.3 shows an example of the interaction and sequence of events for a typical minor capital transaction. All these stages of consultation take time, and in certain cases lead to major changes in requirements and/or budgets before reaching a final choice. The important implication is that suppliers will not usually be approached until point 5, by which time several key decisions have been taken (such as the exact specification) in which some suppliers might with mutual profit have been involved.

Purchasing Officers usually work to a detailed brief laid down elsewhere in their company, and so negotiations with them by supplier sales forces tend to concentrate on price and terms of delivery (where the supplier may not have much in the way of competitive advantage) rather than matters such as product performance, tailor-made or optional extras, and service options (where the supplier probably will).

All this leads to great diversity in decision-taking, even within a customer sector. For instance, a seller of pension funds may negotiate with a specialist Pensions Manager in one firm, and a non-expert member of the Board in another apparently similar one. In both cases the Proposal will have to take account of the conflicting needs of many other people, whose views may be made known to the seller only at second-hand, and who may not be passed all the information supplied.

By contrast, a car-hire firm may find with one customer that most hirers are given wide autonomy in choice of car and supplier, in another they hire to individual choice but within published company guidelines on price, in a third all hiring is done centrally by a specialist Transport Manager.

Clearly different marketing tactics will be appropriate to each case. Different suppliers in the same market may sensibly decide to use different marketing strategies by designing their offer to appeal more strongly to one type of customer rather than another.

THE TRIGGERS OF BUYER BEHAVIOUR

Before this often-complex buying process takes place, a firm has to be aware of a *need* and it has to have the *opportunity*, *means* and *will* to satisfy it. These can be called the 'triggers of buyer behaviour' which will differ from market to market.

In almost every market some of the triggers can be influenced by suppliers, but changes in most of them will be due to circumstances entirely beyond the control of either buyers or sellers. Such factors which are important but cannot be directly influenced must therefore be identified and included in any market forecast. But the effects of factors which are under a supplier's control, even if less important, are vital to the marketing effort simply because they are all the supplier has to help achieve an objective.

For example, a firm will not seek the advice of a patent agent unless it discovers that it could run into trouble over patents, is aware that such specialists exist, has the funds available to pay for the advice and considers the degree of risk justifies the trouble and expense. Not a simple combination even in a trivial case, and one which leaves patent agents in a somewhat passive, deterministic situation!

What creates such a combination of circumstances? Figure 5.4 gives a simplified model of business buyer behaviour. Consider the market for a good or service, product X. Customers (and potential customers) are businesses which buy X, and supply markets Y and Z (which could be other goods or services and selling either to other businesses or to domestic households). Customer firms for X are in business to satisfy the needs of *their* customers. Their experience of supplying the Y or Z market leads them to believe they will *need* a specific mix of input goods and services (including X), and set each year a procurement budget in the light of their forecast sales income and the profit targets laid upon them by their suppliers of capital.

Their *means* to satisfy their needs for service X will depend on a large number of external factors which vary greatly from market to market. Central is the likely demand from buyers of products Y or Z. This in turn depends partly on the presence and marketing efforts of alternative suppliers of Y and Z (e.g., imports), and partly on the business climate in which all these companies will have to operate.

'Business climate' (often called the Total Business Environment or TBE) by business economists includes the effects of economic, social, technological and institutional/legal trends. For example, in years expected to be recessions, most businesses keep inventories low, and purchase inputs only to keep pace with booked orders for finished goods, while in good years they manufacture ahead of orders and build up stocks of raw materials in case of shortage. Changes in customer technology or new institutional demands (e.g., for consumer or environmental protection) may affect the patterns of purchasing.

The *opportunity* for buyers to satisfy their needs for X will depend mainly on the marketing efforts of all the competitive suppliers of X, such as specification, price, availability and promotion. They too will be operating in the same TBE.

The *will* to take action depends usually on an individual in the company championing the cause and creating a climate of opinion so that others believe in it too. This usually means that the course of action has to be to the personal advantage of key people at various levels whose motivations will differ.

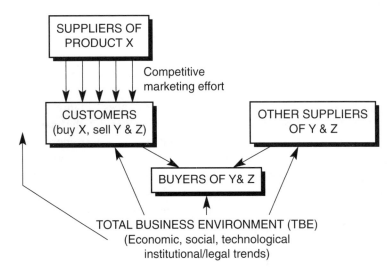

Fig. 5.4 The triggers of buyer behaviour

CUSTOMER MOTIVATION

Wolfe's Law of Business Decisions states that: 'a firm takes such actions as will tend simultaneously to maximise the prestige of top management, the security of middle management and the rewards of junior management.'

In other words, junior executives, who do most of the legwork which precedes a deal, are likely to show most enthusiasm for propositions which will enhance their pay and prospects.

Their bosses, the middle-managers, will be responsible for selling any deal within the company and for making it work afterwards. They have already progressed some distance up their chosen career ladder and are likely to have outside responsibilities such as dependants and mortgages. They will be more concerned about the chances of something going wrong for which they would be blamed than with any potential success in which many other people would claim a share. Consequently, they will prefer to support propositions which are non-controversial and safe, rather than any which might eventually generate more sales or profits but which bear a degree of risk.

Top management, on the other hand, may feel relatively secure (or at least protected against disaster financially) and hence disinterested in immediate rewards which are penally taxed. They are more likely to initiate and ratify propositions which offer the chance of enhanced personal prestige within the industry or the outside world of the business community, media or Government. Hence the sponsorships of avant-garde art and opera which impress rather than sell and take-overs which astonish more by the sums of money involved than by the commercial synergy they create.

Wolfe's Law was identified from experience many years ago, promulgated only for the enlightenment and entertainment of colleagues, and has not been published before. While an extreme over-generalisation, and not intended to be taken entirely seriously, this Law has often helped to illuminate otherwise inexplicable corporate behaviour. More seriously, it implies that to be successful, any sales proposition to a business must not only meet the buyer's overtly stated needs 'good for sales/productivity/costs/profits/etc.', but in addition it ought to offer a varied set of tangible and intangible incentives for the members of the DMU.

To recapitulate: business decisions are made by groups of people, including all levels, differing specialist roles and varying degrees of influence, both positive and negative. Central to successful business marketing is a good understanding of the structure and interactions of the whole DMU, the motivations of and the most cost-effective means of communicating with its various members. At the least, the supplier can reassure the authorisers and users that a particular brand is a sensible and reliable choice. At best, it may even be possible to persuade the specifiers and specialists to insist on a set of requirements which can be satisfied by only the one supplier!

Finding out about the structure of customer DMUs and the triggers of buyer behaviour is one of the most important tasks of Market Research, which is to be dealt with in Chapter 7.

6 IDENTIFYING TARGETS FOR MARKETING

THE MEANING OF TARGETING

Chapter 4 showed that the fundamental of marketing is the customer and Chapter 5 that the 'customer' for a supplier is not really another firm but a group of its employees who take its buying decisions. The ability to design an effective and cost-effective marketing campaign depends on the supplier first seeking out firms which already buy and use the product category (or could shortly be persuaded to start to do so) and then identifying in each case the members of the DMU, understanding the triggers of their buying behaviour and the means by which they can be influenced. This chapter will examine how to obtain this knowledge through business intelligence and market research.

The point about targeting is that in any market, some sales will be easier to obtain than others, and that marketing effort will be more cost-effective (i.e., profitable) if it is concentrated where it will do most good. No one expects anything like 100 per cent of a market; 10–20 per cent is a more usual figure even for a market leader. In other words, it would be theoretically possible to be market leader even if 80 per cent of buyers never bought. Hence any part of the marketing effort is wasted if it lands on firms who will never buy from this source for any reason or ones who need to purchase only rarely or very little. It is well worth investing time and money before planning any campaign to identify, and target, the most likely prospects. Even spending 10 per cent of the marketing budget on research can be justified if it raises the effectiveness of the rest by as little as 12 per cent. It might do that if it identified say 25 per cent of a prospect list as showing no potential and which could therefore be eliminated from the marketing plan.

A good starting point is to define the kind of customer base that the supplier would like to serve, bearing in mind the assets available to provide the service and the reality of the market-place. For example, which can we supply most efficiently, a small number of large orders or a larger number of small ones? A parallel but not identical question is, will the customers be mainly big or small firms, and is our product an important or peripheral part of their inputs? Is it in the nature of the business to sell 'one-offs' or will most business come as repeat orders, and if so will the buyers need the product regularly or only occasionally? In summary, will an individual target customer be important to us, and will we be important to them? Will we have to be in contact regularly, only now and again or just the once and that's it?

In many cases the targeting might appear to be obvious: target agricultural machinery to farmers, ready-to-pour concrete to construction firms. But this is rarely the whole story. All except the largest and richest farms contract-out their combining, so that the contractors are a big part of the target for harvesting machinery. Construction firms do what their customers specify. Local authority works and housing departments sometimes specify brick where poured-concrete is technically more appropriate, because they wish to avoid problems with councillors who might fear voters' complaints that their town is being turned into a 'concrete jungle'. So part of the target for the concrete industry is local authority architects and the politicians who authorise their work. Targeting is not just defining an industry but selecting that part of it with best potential.

However, in most cases naming a single industry is of no use. Many goods and services are sold to a wide range of users, for example: handling machinery, controls, telecoms, lubricants, vitamins, solvents, stationery, insurance, legal advice and so on. In these cases, industrial sector will be a much less useful indicator of sales potential than perhaps some combination of size, technology, degree of capital-intensity, possession of an internal specialist department, number of locations, type of industries they serve and so on.

Contract Research and Development, for example, will be of greatest value to companies, whatever industry they may be in, which do not have their own internal department. Companies which do have one are more likely to use outside R&D only on a project basis for overspill or for rare technologies. Very expensive plant (like the combine harvesters or tool-making equipment) will have its best potential among very large users, or specialist sub-contractors.

Some in a group of apparently similar firms will therefore be highly likely to buy a particular product, others perhaps highly unlikely. Defining a target means in effect identifying what the first group have in common with each other and how they differ from the second. Setting a target means adopting a workable definition of current and potential users and then identifying the actual members of it.

USING THE CORPORATE DATABASE

Probably the easiest part of targeting is to compile a comprehensive list of companies which already do, or potentially could, buy a particular product. Every firm with something to sell knows the names and addresses and probably a great deal more information about its current customers. It will also have a record of lapsed customers and a list of enquirers and other contacts who have not yet placed an order. How accurate, up-to-date and comprehensive those records are will vary greatly for many reasons. Improving the corporate database is discussed in Chapter 8.

In every case, strategic market analysis should begin with the names of known customers. Internal records ought to show what products, how much and how often each has bought. Can we classify each of them as heavy, light but regular, and occasional buyers? How do we define these terms? Are there any clues which tell us what triggers an occasional purchase, or the gaps between? Has anybody changed category recently, do we know why?

In addition there may well be on file in the sales or accounts departments facts such as their credit rating, size, the nature of their business, the purpose for which the products were used, mechanical or other technological information, the names of the buyers and other executive staff, their customer industries and so on. How well do we know each of our customers and what else would we like to know? How do the heavy, light/regular and occasionals differ? Does any of this information answer any of the questions already raised?

It should already be a matter of routine to update and search this database for such patterns and to supply missing items. Certainly it is worth compiling a substantial dossier of facts and gossip about every customer of significance for tactical reasons alone. Making these dossiers available to all who have direct contact will help to improve routine customer relations and to anticipate potential problems and opportunities.

Strategic examination will suggest where more potential sales might best be sought. In some cases this is obvious: a manufacturer of textile machinery will have compiled a census of textile producers. Here targeting will depend on obtaining early warning of who will expand, update, replace, change technologies or start up and who will shrink or close down. Normal trade intelligence, 'keeping one's ears to the ground' and routine service calls may be sufficient. Are the service engineers briefed to keep their eyes open and to ask pointed questions and report back? If the prospects in the established market seem poor, for example in an irretrievably declining industry, targeting will be diverted progressively to a search for opportunities for diversification.

Where the goods or services are sold to a range of industries, then the target is not obvious and has to be defined in other but identifiable terms. A series of indicators of potential are needed: firms with the most 'points' can be expected to have the greatest potential. The list can be used as a brief for 'desk' research of readily-available sources to pick up extra names and addresses, for example through trade directories, professional associations, trade fairs, editorial references and advertisements in trade media, commercial list brokers, personal contacts, response to couponed advertising and so on. The effectiveness of business information networks is discussed in Chapter 8, and the compilation and regular updating of a substantial list of good prospects should be possible for all but dominant market leaders and extreme specialists who should be in contact with their whole market already.

ASSESSING THE POTENTIAL OF PROSPECTS

Additional sales can be generated both by selling more to existing customers and by gaining new customers. One advantage a business market has over a consumer one is that the number of possible customers is usually small and even fewer are significant because of the so-called '80:20 rule'; that is, that in surprisingly many cases about 80 per cent of sales come from only about 20 per cent of the customers. Many companies therefore can achieve a sensible rate of short-term growth by adding only a few extra large customers each year either by growing existing small buyers or by recruiting new large ones. Most would in any case prefer to concentrate marketing effort where the returns will be highest, instead of indiscriminate comb-canvassing, or expensively pioneering larger numbers of relatively small buyers unless they happen to be extremely cheap to service.

A first long list of candidate companies which appear to be in the right market then needs screening to identify the minority with the highest potential for immediate attention. An early filter of potential can be gained by comparing the known characteristics of existing large and small buyers and matching them with the prospects list. This will indicate where further research must be done, but there is usually a limit to the amount of meaningful data that can be collected from published sources at reasonable cost. This is the point where a switch from desk to *field* market research is necessary and likely to prove cost-effective (see Chapter 7).

MARKET RESEARCH TO HELP TARGETING

The lists can be used to draw representative samples of large and small existing and prospective customers as defined. A researcher can be commissioned to make exploratory visits to examples of each of these four types of companies, and to interview as many people as possible of those who take part in the buying process for the product. The object is to find out:

- the company's usage of the product type – quantity, frequency, purposes, suppliers, means and opportunity to increase, etc
- who are the DMU – job specifications, job titles, authority and role in the purchase (authorisers, specifiers and advisers, buyers, users) how they all interact, their needs and motivations and the various 'triggers of buyer behaviour' described in Chapter 5
- the way in which suppliers are short-listed and the criteria on which the final selection is made
- the type of information each member of the DMU needs, the sources they use to get it and other possible means of communication with them.

All this is expensive per firm researched, but trying to save money by narrowing the scope at this stage runs the risk of accidentally eliminating what might turn out to be the most crucial factor. In any case, quite small numbers are sufficient in the first instance to gain an impression of which types (if any) of the existing customers might be persuaded to increase their buying either by our taking share from competing suppliers or (less likely) stimulating greater usage of the product type or even substituting it for other products.

It would also suggest which types of non-buying companies have either the largest potential or the easiest business to obtain. And, in all cases, it should give pointers to how the extra sale might be made, in terms of who has to be persuaded, what might persuade them and the best means of doing it.

After such exploratory research it will be possible to quantify on a larger scale the hypotheses which have been generated. The probably substantial cost of this could be justified if the more accurate data gained would increase the cost-efficiency in targeting and marketing. In other words, if considerable sales potential appeared possible but the cost of obtaining the facts seemed too high, it would be sensible to commission a second stage of research with more companies in the sample but concentrating on those firms and issues shown in the exploratory stage to be of greatest importance to marketing strategy. If necessary, cost could be further controlled by limiting the number of personal interviews and substituting perhaps a mixture of cheaper telephone calls or mail to deal with some of the simpler issues.

APPLYING THE RESULTS

The results of such *targeting research* can in themselves directly help marketing planning. For example, a cargo airline wanted takers for the marginal capacity left after serving its regular heavy users. Research showed that the best target segment for new users of air freight would be companies who occasionally exported goods which were highly perishable, highly fashionable, or expensive and delicate; because in these cases shorter transit time, less handling, lighter packaging and cheaper insurance more than offset the higher freight costs per kilogramme. Most such companies sold over long distance too irregularly to interest professional export agents, and so might be persuaded to go direct to an airline. The research also showed that there were usually only two parties to the DMU, authorisers who agreed the expenditure (often after the event) and despatchers who actually did the work and decided which deliveries went by which method.

It appeared there would be no difficulty in persuading authorisers, such as financial or distribution directors, of the facts that for long distances air was preferable to sea and road. The problems were to be found among the users, namely despatch departments, often located far from headquarters, where long-serving staff were unfamiliar with the logistics of air freight, resistant to any changes in their way of working, and had in any case long been on excellent terms with the agent of a shipping line who took all the paperwork of occasional export orders off their hands.

This research encouraged the airline to develop a more user-friendly booking system and to back it by a two-pronged campaign stressing cost-efficiency to authorisers and explaining how to do it ('just use your normal packaging and call this number') to despatch managers.

THE IMPORTANCE OF THE REGULAR BUYER

One group should be top of every target list: existing customers, especially the handful of key accounts which probably provide more than half of total sales income. Any sales person will confirm the easiest sale to make is a repeat purchase by a satisfied customer. Maintaining the loyalty of and then growing these customers is usually the most cost-effective use of marketing funds.

Unfortunately, client service generates less adrenalin in management than pioneering, and in most companies the person who lands the big new account is given a bigger salary and faster promotion than the one who keeps the big old account happy and loyal year after year. Yet wresting customers from competitors is a long and expensive process and even those with a good track-record have many more failures than successes. A new business operation may take a long time to pay off.

This is not to say that gaining new business is not an essential part of company growth and should legitimately be allowed for in the budget: only that it should not be funded by taking money away from giving existing customers proper service, and that investment in any specific new prospect should be proportionate to the value of the business multiplied by the likelihood of getting it (see Chapter 16). Having the data to make such calculations objectively is one of the side-benefits of targeting research.

PROBLEMS IN TARGETING

Every business is different, and some will not be able to take this approach. For example, office stationery is bought by hundreds of thousands of businesses in any one country and total turnover is not always a good indicator of their need for envelopes, paper and cassettes. A few giant prospects may be targeted, but many such suppliers gain their turnover from a large number of small orders. The task of identifying and profiling these mini-customers as recommended above would be too expensive even if feasible.

Such a case is much closer to a consumer than a typical business market, and the approach to it can be adapted from classic mass-marketing, for instance by the use of intermediaries for distribution, and the cost of communication with their customers through mass-advertising in national media is likely to prove justifiable.

At the other extreme are products which are bought at long and irregular intervals. Specialist builders of hydro-electric dams must be pleased if even the most satisfied of customers repeats in any one century; and the sellers of armaments have to take into account that a carefully nurtured relationship with a potential government buyer in a third-world country can be terminated with extreme prejudice at any time if the competition manage to make their sale to the opposition party first! Lists of target buyers are here less important than lists of future opportunities, but the same techniques of business intelligence can be used to gain advance information and assess its chances, with luck, ahead of the competition.

To recapitulate: targeting is the essential first step towards a successful and profitable marketing strategy. The first stage is to profile existing customers, who themselves form a vital target. Then the company database supplemented by a variety of desk research can be used to generate a list of companies with apparent potential for new business. Priorities should be assigned to each according to their known characteristics.

---

1. Supplier's needs and limitations
   - Target market share
   - Capacity number of customers
   - Capacity size of orders
   - Few large or many small or mix?
   - Can we accept a dominant customer?

2. Order characteristics
   - Once only or repeat business?
   - Frequency
   - Important input or peripheral?
   - Lead time or short-notice?

3. Significant customer characteristics
   - Industry
   - Geography
   - Production technology
   - Size: turnover, employees, number of sites
   - Specialists in-house?

4. Decision Making Unit
   - Purchasers
   - Authorisers
   - Users
   - Specifiers
   - Corporate advisers

Fig. 6.1   Check list for customer targeting

But purchases are made by the employees of these candidate customer companies, and field research is usually necessary to identify and profile the members of the DMU and determine the triggers of their buyer behaviour. Such research will usually be expensive but is likely to justify its cost through increased efficiency in generating new sales.

The result of proper targeting is to know as objectively as possible: *where* there is potential business, *who* takes the key decisions, *how much* it is worth and the *chances* of getting it. This enables marketing effort to be concentrated hard-headedly where it stands the greatest chances of being successful and to be set at levels of expenditure where the overall return will be profitable.

7 MARKET RESEARCH: THE HOT-LINE TO THE CUSTOMER

ALL YOU REALLY WANTED TO KNOW ABOUT RESEARCH BUT WERE AFRAID TO ASK

Chapter 6 has illustrated the kind of information needed to target customers and to develop marketing strategies, and suggested that market research would be needed to obtain much of it. Later chapters will indicate that market research can also help in several other parts of the marketing effort such as customer communications. Most suppliers of fast-moving consumer goods have had market research departments for decades, and become addicted to regular supplies of data about markets, competitors, distributors and consumers. Research is part of their furniture of management, and more to the point is no longer the first item to be axed at budget time (perhaps only fourth or fifth!).

However, this is not yet the case in many business companies (in Britain, for example, membership of the consumer-dominated Market Research Society is nearly ten times that of the Industrial Marketing Research Association despite the latter's wider base for recruitment). Management of these businesses may not be fully aware of the benefits to be gained, or may in the past have had experience of an inappropriate or badly-conducted project or may not even be sure how to set about getting what they want at a price they can afford.

This chapter will therefore review the benefits and limitations of market research from the point of view of a non-specialist business user. It will not go into technical details about how to *do* research: it is part of the thesis of this book that specialised disciplines should be delegated to qualified experts. What the buyer and user of research needs to know is:

- what research can and cannot do
- where to use it and where not
- how to select, brief and motivate a specialist

- how to understand the results, assess their validity and apply them.

This chapter is therefore subtitled: 'All you really wanted to know about research but were afraid to ask'.

MARKET RESEARCH? IT'S A WASTE OF TIME!

In the pioneering days of consumer research in the 1950s, when every presentation had to be a missionary sermon, there were five standard objections to doing research, which are still alive and well in parts of industry.

One is that research takes too much time. Certainly a typical major project needs 8–12 weeks, and should not be hurried. I have been involved in many studies which were designed, conducted and reported in 48 hours, but these were generally journalistic or public relations exercises where the fact of doing the research was far more important than anything it uncovered. Indeed one of the ways to deliver 'research' so fast is to cut out (or postpone until after the event) all the quality controls and checking procedures. Commissioning research at the last minute may only add to the risks of an already fraught situation, and it may be even be better to do without and continue the project on judgment (as it presumably has been up to then!). If the results are going to be important it is wise to give the researchers adequate time as well as enough money to do the job properly. Research should be built into the critical path for any new project or planning cycle.

When I was a director of a research agency, clients would often telephone to ask how much a project they were planning might cost and how long it would take. Rough back-of-envelope figures were usually accepted in the spirit they were offered. However, when at a later date they requested an official firm proposal, if the price turned out a little higher they would usually come up with the money with only a slight grumble. But if the time needed was a couple of weeks longer than the guesstimate usually all hell broke loose: the client had enough trouble in delaying action until the originally quoted time. This is a special case of the well-known syndrome: 'If I needed it tomorrow, I would have asked for it tomorrow!'

Another general objection is that research is expensive. Certainly large projects cost large sums and good research costs more than bad research. If budgets are tight, it is better to keep research costs down by confining it to situations which are of highest importance, and to topics which can be actioned. The project which is a certain waste of money is the one which is not implemented!

Very big companies can afford to do a certain amount of research speculatively: 'We do not know what we will do with the results, but it might be interesting to find out.' Everyone else should treat research like a normal business expense, not to be undertaken unless its benefits can be justified in cash terms. If a project costs x, what information will it provide and what will we do with it? How will this affect the rewards and risks of our operations? Is that worth more than x to us?

Market research in most of the developed world is a highly competitive market and the published profits of the successful practitioners are nothing to get excited about. Hence the price of research depends largely on its costs of production, so that cheap research is usually of poor quality, and the buyer should be highly suspicious of any quotation which is exceptionally low. Indeed anyone not an experienced buyer of research will find it a good rule to take the middle of three quotations: the lowest supplier may not have understood what was involved and may need to cut quality in some way or ask later for more money. (An exceptionally high quote may simply be a polite signal from the agency that they do not want the job.) There are exceptions; for example, syndication enables the costs of one survey or research service to be shared by several users willing to accept identical data. Any such arrangements should be made clear to all parties by the agency.

The third general objection is that 'we knew all that already'. This is sometimes used as a put-down for uppity researchers: the writer used to be tempted to preface presentations to certain clients with: 'Here are the six problems you told us to find out about. Before I show you your customers' answers, please will you give me yours?'. It is in fact usual and desirable for research to confirm the beliefs of those with first-hand experience of the situation, although it should add to their confidence by expressing them in concrete terms. Indeed, if any findings are contrary to commonsense, it is wise to ask for them to be checked! However, if research always confirms its buyer's prejudices and never gives new insights there may be something wrong with the original briefing. For instance, 'research to find out' which is the best of several alternative advertising strategies is always of more use than 'research to prove' that current policy is right. If it confirms it, you knew that already; and if it does not, you will not have found out what to do instead.

When a young advertising agency researcher, I always hated to be used as a 'tie-breaker'. The agency said the new idea was brilliant, the client disagreed and the battle raged round the boardroom until someone said 'let's research it!' Whatever I then did, however skilled and objective my technique, the result would either torpedo my colleagues or flatly contradict a valuable client. If implemented, the research would leave one party still believing he had been cheated; and, if not, it had wasted time and money without doing anything to help client's sales or relations with the agency.

The fourth objection is that a company can find out all they need to know by using their own secretarial or sales staff. The professional researcher who is told by a client that 'our reps can get all that stuff' cannot help wondering how a salesperson will find the time to elicit information during a routine sales call for which a trained interviewer would need at least 45 minutes. And indeed whether someone well known as a supplier's representative would be given the same answers as an independent stranger offering confidentiality under the Code of Conduct? Further, is anyone who is objective enough to collect and pass on without argument comments critical of his employer's products, terms of business and service entirely suitable to hold a job in sales?

Company staff are not trained in research, they are not free of charge and they should not have enough spare time for lengthy interviews and analysis. Of course (as enlarged on in Chapter 8) all staff should be trained to look out for and pass on market intelligence, and liaison staff should routinely collect simple factual data from customers (such as changes of key staff or brand of machinery used), but this hardly constitutes market research which should cover a range of related topics such as attitudes and should sample non-customers as well. Market Research is a skilled specialisation. When needing a new factory, a manager will not hesitate to send for an architect, or when suing a supplier will brief a lawyer. Amateur market research can do as much harm to a company as amateur brain-surgery to an individual!

The final general objection is the most complex one that market research is misleading. There are indeed many cases of spectacular research-based failures, of which the case of Ford Edsel (the 40-year-old car which is now a museum piece) is still one of the most frequently cited. Some failures happen simply because research is ignored or over-ruled. As a clue to the case of Edsel, legend has it that hundreds of possible names were checked, yet the company launched the car bearing the name of a nephew of the founder Henry Ford, which was not even included in the research. Certainly some lessons must have been learned because all today's Ford cars are fully-researched at every stage and are successful.

Research can cause failure if it is misinterpreted. Researchers are on safer ground when they present findings about customers and markets than when they draw conclusions about marketing action which may depend on other data which they do not have; and users will get more useful research if they make sure they brief their researchers thoroughly. Research is an aid to decision-taking, and potentially a highly cost-effective one, but not a substitute for it. It always requires the addition of other information and hard work by the human brain before any decision can be taken.

Research itself can fail through circumstances beyond anyone's control. Business decisions are intended to affect the future. Research is not a crystal ball and can only find out what people did, bought or said they wanted yesterday (or more usually at last purchase). A change in the marketing environment such as a new competitive product or a recession can invalidate any conclusions which are based on the assumption that the future is going to be like the past. A sad example is a research programme at the end of the 1980s by a large textile manufacturer in a third-world country whose conclusions gave encouragement to re-equip for growth. These were invalidated almost immediately after implementation by an unforeseen change in Government policy which permitted large-scale import competition compounded by an exceptional drought severe enough to destroy most of the country's chances of generating any wealth for at least a year. A positive scenario was changed to disaster, with dire effects on prospects for profits, employment and growth, about which the survey could give little further help.

A research project can also fail because it was done badly. Not surprisingly, most such failures happen because either the wrong questions were asked, or the wrong people answered them, or the wrong people did the asking. Most of the rest of this chapter will concern itself with ways of avoiding these types of built-in failure.

RESEARCH AS AN INSURANCE POLICY

Research cannot guarantee success. It is best looked upon as an insurance policy against failure, and the more serious the risk of failure in the market the easier and cheaper it is for research to spot it ahead of time. A new synthetic source of food was found so universally nasty on so many dimensions that work on it had to be stopped after only one consumer product test!

The analogy with insurance is an instructive one. When the late Ray Willsmer was director of a group of charter airlines, he overcame their resistance to research by pointing out that one of the largest single items on every year's budget was insurance (covering a fleet of Boeings is not cheap) and pointing out that nobody had ever suggested cuts or doing without. 'If we believe it is worth spending all this money each year to make sure we have all these seats available, should we not be spending at least an equal sum in finding out whether there will be that many bums needing to sit on them next year?' This is not to say that a company's research budget should equal its insurance premiums but that similar thinking should guide both.

The 'high-risk–high-reward' entrepreneurs of Chapter 1 are in least need of research, and are in consequence least inclined to use it. They have a point in that research not only eliminates obvious failures, it sometimes throws out potentially successful but unconventional ideas too. Sony claim that had they used research as their sole guide, the Walkman would never have reached the market. Entrepreneurial businesses tend to confine themselves to research on a small scale as a *generator* of ideas, and do any testing of them live in the market-place. On the other hand, a concept-test gave Sir Clive Sinclair, the highly successful entrepreneur, warning that his 'C-5' electric car would be a failure and indicated how its drawbacks might be overcome. He rejected it because it recommended a fundamental change in his company's usual marketing approach.

But for a market leader, a serious failure is unthinkable not so much for its costs but because of its domino effects over the whole operation. As Chapter 3 showed, it is this type of business which first developed market research and still gets the most value from it. In companies where all new ideas and any changes to established successes are pre-tested, a failure serious enough to damage a sound reputation with the customers becomes extremely rare. Failures still happen because research is neither magic nor an exact science, but a new product which survives thorough small-scale pre-screening to highly visible market test will very rarely make spectacular losses and if withdrawn it will only be because it fails to reach a required level of profit.

Research has another down-side in addition to its demands on money, time and skill. Users should be aware that well-researched businesses lose some of the benefits of high creativity along with its risks. Their products, advertising and indeed strategies tend to become safe but mainstream. Companies playing low-risk–low-reward will be grateful to make this trade-off. Yet the researchers working for the market leaders are likely to collect similar data, and competition between them may degenerate into a war of attrition between almost identical 'best' offers to customers. Consequently, there is a risk that guerilla tactics by new entrants with high creativity and little to lose can carve small but painful 'niche' shares from the leaders' market.

WHEN NOT TO DO RESEARCH

While managers sometimes run unnecessary risks by failing to do necessary research, much money is wasted on researching the trivial, the inevitable, the unresearchable and problems for which adequate data are already available. Research is also sometimes used as a form of delaying action. A difficult or unpleasant decision can be shelved for three months simply by calling in a research agency: ('Sorry J.B., the data on the potential for extruded widgets won't be in until end-June!').

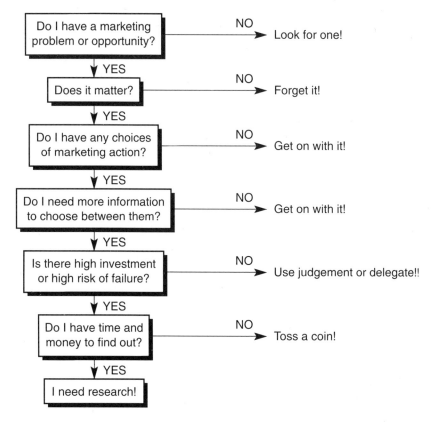

Fig. 7.1 Defining a need for research

The check list in Figure 7.1 should be applied whenever research, or indeed any major marketing decision, is in prospect. If the answer to any one of the six questions is 'no', research is unnecessary or at least of low priority for scarce funds. Contrarily, after six 'yesses', it should be clear to all concerned that they are in a situation where research is essential. They will also understand what needs to be found out, what will be done with the information and also have a good idea of how much money it is worth investing to solve the problem.

THE RESEARCH APPROACH

Given all these pitfalls, how does a manager who is not an expert get the right research done? Most problems in market research projects, as in most types of marketing activity, get built in at the very beginning through lack of a clear objective from the buyer or adequate understanding by the supplier of what was wanted and why. Getting this right has to be the responsibility of the buyer, who can use a proven approach to research which works equally well with business or consumer markets, for goods or services, and in any country. Figure 7.2 shows the sequence.

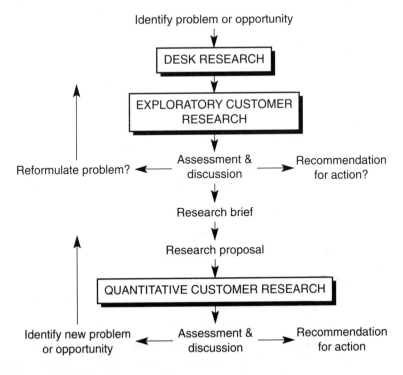

Fig. 7.2 The research approach

The start is to define as specifically as possible the apparent problem or opportunity. Before commissioning expensive new external research, it is sensible to examine what is already known from in-house and published sources (known as secondary or 'desk' research). Chapter 8 will discuss the consequences of the 'information explosion', which means that nowadays a great deal of information relevant to a business problem can often be gathered quickly and cheaply. Next, contact should be made with customers on a small, exploratory scale to discuss the problem objectively and from their perspective, often a highly illuminating activity. It may be possible to do this using in-house facilities, or more usually through external specialists in 'qualitative' research. This used to be called 'depth' or 'motivational' research, terms no longer appropriate because what is usually needed is an extensive review of the customer's behaviour, knowledge and opinions rather than a probe in depth into his or her psyche as was once fashionable.

At this point those who have to take decisions and those who have collected the data should assess the situation together. There are three possible outcomes. On rare occasions, enough information may have already been gathered to support an immediate recommendation for action. Sometimes the problem has to be redefined (for instance, what was suspected at the factory to be a weakness in product performance might turn out to be an awareness problem among the customers). If so, a second round of desk and exploratory research may be advisable. Most usually, it is found that the problem and what is and is not already known about it can be defined more closely, leaving an 'information need' to be satisfied before taking action.

The information need forms the basis of a brief for full-scale research. This will usually need to be *quantitative* research (meaning research which provides assessable statistical answers) because most business decisions are quantitative in nature: 'How shall we divide the marketing budget between advertising and promotions?'; 'Is the demand for product x sufficient to support a second production unit?'; 'How many customers will notice if we replace raw material y with a cheap substitute?'.

Even if all work so far has been done in-house, this is the point where a professional research agency must be called in. No company can nowadays afford to maintain its own full-time all-purpose field research department. Apart from a few highly specialised product-testing units, almost all the companies who once had large-scale market research operations have closed them, floated them off independently or made contractual arrangements with an outside agency.

A competent researcher (as discussed below) will be able to respond to a

Brief with a Proposal which stands a good chance of being actionable and cost-effective. The buyer should discuss the details to make sure that the researchers fully understand the problem, and are recommending the most effective and economical approach.

The survey is then commissioned, and its results should ideally be presented in person by the researchers and discussed with the users to make sure that all the relevant information has been reported and its meaning and limitations properly understood. Unless there has been some unforeseen problem, it will now be possible to make recommendations for action and to make them with confidence.

The data then become part of the company database, and later re-examination may well point up further problems and opportunities thereby simultaneously increasing the value of the research to the user and incidentally making more opportunities for work for the agency.

This approach is lengthy, but going straight to the quantified stage without desk and exploratory work runs the risks of paying good money to duplicate existing data, or missing out the topics which are of greatest importance from the customers' point of view or ending up with data which are neither actionable nor relevant to the real problem. On the other hand, the natural temptation to take a premature decision after the desk and exploratory stages should be resisted because it will add to the risks which research is supposed to reduce.

It should be clear that qualitative and quantitative are complementary techniques, not substitutes. Research suppliers who suggest the opposite probably have a specialist's axe to grind. In almost any situation it should be quite clear which is more appropriate; if there appears to be choice of technique this is probably because the objectives are still too vague. This is not a matter of cost. Qualitative of necessity needs expensive and lengthy face-to-face interviews with individuals or groups, but uses only a few. Quantitative surveys can often collect simple facts through relatively cheap telephone or mail contacts, but need hundreds of them. As it happens, business-to-business research agencies report that the average cost per project commissioned tends to be about the same in each case.

Qualitative is exploratory, provides ideas, gains insight into a problem. It suggests to creative people which lines to explore and to researchers which questions to ask in quantification. Quantitative research provides hard numbers and is a necessary preliminary to taking expensive or risky decisions. Most major research projects need both, and in any case quantitative research should not be undertaken in a new area without qualitative exploration. Sometimes a quantitative survey throws up new and interesting ideas in addition to its principal objectives. These will often repay qualitative follow up, such as re-interviewing respondents in companies which show unexpected changes in their behaviour.

USING RESEARCH AGENCIES

Chapter 15 will deal with the selection and control of outside marketing suppliers. As far as research agencies are concerned, it is more important to choose one which is good at research than one which happens to know a lot about your particular market. (You are qualified to teach the agency about your business, if necessary, but not about theirs!) Companies who are regular buyers of market research should employ their own in-house specialist who will be competent to take such decisions, to manage the research budget, perhaps do feasibility studies and some exploratory work, and indeed to avoid most of the problems described in this chapter. It is not hard to justify investing say 10–15 per cent of the market research budget in a small specialist advisory unit in-house.

The basic liaison between research agency and buyer is based on a written Brief and a written Proposal. The buyer's Brief ought to consist of:

- a definition of the marketing problem
- a summary of what is already known about it
- a review of the alternative courses of action contemplated
- a statement of the information need
- an indication of the amount of time and money available to fulfil it.

Without all this information an agency is likely to waste time by putting up proposals which cover irrelevant topics or duplicate existing information; and which are either too lengthy and expensive or inadequate in scale for the problem.

A good Proposal should be expected to contain:

- a review of the background (to prove the researchers have understood the brief)
- choice of research technique (e.g., telephone interviews), with justification
- recommended size and design of sample to be contacted (e.g., Chief Engineers in 200 textile manufacturers stratified by turnover, region and specialisation)
- outline of the information to be collected and the method (e.g., by means of a draft questionnaire)

- nature of fieldwork and its quality controls
- analysis and reporting format
- price and timing
- agency terms of business.

Such a proposal forms the basis for contract between buyer and agency, and its acceptance and any required amendments should always be put in writing.

For major projects, it is desirable to approach more than one research agency, but soliciting too many alternative approaches will confuse the buyer without guiding the final choice. Indeed buyers known to create work with little chance of success by tendering widely for small jobs are likely to get only perfunctory treatment from the most reliable agencies.

Research agencies are professional profit-making businesses, and good relationships are best built up over time by using only a small number so that each has to compete but can expect a fair amount of work at a profit if it does a good job. By doing so, you will have reassurance of their skills in research and the agencies will gain first-hand experience of your way of working, market and customers which will save you having to brief every project from scratch and will make their ideas and interpretations increasingly relevant and helpful.

ERRORS IN RESEARCH: WHAT CAN YOU RELY ON?

Measuring and reducing sources of error in market research is a highly technical subject, and much nonsense is written particularly in the context of political polls in newspapers. Research users should always ask their agency to supply estimates of the accuracy of any data they supply. A claim that the work is 'error-free' is the hallmark of a charlatan.

Most errors in sample surveys can be classified under three headings: *sampling error*, *bias* and *human error*. All three are likely to be present in any survey. They can be detected, estimated and minimised, but cannot be eliminated. They are minimised by using researchers of the highest possible skill and by allocating enough time and money to do the job properly. They are detected by validating findings against other data such as sales figures, published market data and earlier surveys.

The easiest to estimate is *sampling error*, because there is a great deal of statistical theory about it. Sampling error is not a 'mistake', it is the natural variation which arises from taking a small sample instead of a census. This is a 'random' variation, and so any figure can be either too high or too low. The bigger the sample the less the sampling variation. Ten coins tossed together will not always come up five heads, they often show six or four and occasionally all ten or none, while 10 000 tosses will produce very close to 5,000 heads.

Unfortunately the error is inversely proportional to the *square root* of the sample size. If a proposed size of sample delivers a level of sampling error unacceptable in view of the importance of the decision, to halve the error implies multiplying the sample size (and probably its costs) by four not two. Consequently most quantified surveys use a few hundred interviews which provide sampling errors of around five per cent of the total sample. Larger samples are recommended usually because of the number of sub-samples that have to be examined separately (such as categories of size of firm, industry group or product usage characteristics).

Bias is any *systematic, non-random* error. It is independent of sampling error and likely to be much larger. Bias can happen at all stages of a survey: design (e.g., by checking only leading brands); questionnaires (e.g., by asking leading questions); samples (e.g., by interviewing only purchasing officers); respondents (e.g., by the tendency of minor members of a DMU to exaggerate their influence on a decision); interviewers (e.g., by using untrained people such as salespeople or students); reporting (e.g., by selecting only the results that fit the client's prejudices).

Most of the expensive and time-consuming procedures of the highest-quality research agencies are designed to minimise bias: piloting questionnaires, personal briefings for interviewers, training/supervising/back-checking fieldwork, routine checks on the office work and analysis. Buyers should welcome such quality controls, and be suspicious of agencies who do not mention them in their proposals.

Human error can be more drastic in its effect and harder to detect because it is usually more subtle (such as using American billions in European reports and vice versa). The best guard is to validate the results against other data and common sense. Is an estimate of total consumption in a country commensurate with known domestic production plus imports minus exports? Does the claimed rate of purchase per buyer per month square with their usage in output or their known orders? How does the survey price per tonne compare with what we have been selling at? Any apparent serious anomalies should be raised immediately with the researchers. There may be an obvious reconciliation, or there may have been a correctable error, or the survey itself may have a bias. It should be remembered that human errors at the analysis stage (which are often incorrectly described as 'machine errors') can be corrected quickly and cheaply. Serious errors at the data collection stage (such as flaws in the sample, questions, fieldwork) cannot be corrected *at all* after the event.

One of the topics for discussion at proposal stage always has to be the trade-off between cost, size and quality of the project in the context of the importance of the problem. If the price-tag on a proposal runs above budget, the sophisticated research-user will always sacrifice number of interviews or range of topics in a project in favour of quality of sampling and of data collection generally. However, the cost should be commensurate with the size and risks involved in the decision. Choice of pink or green paper on a leaflet used once does not need 2,000 random interviews. But should a decision to change the specification of a market leader or to launch a two million ECU advertising campaign be taken on the strength of four token group discussions costing 4,000 ECU? ('Don't worry J.B., we researched it, and it's fine!').

APPLICATION OF RESULTS

Field surveys are the most expensive side of market research because of the high cost of contacting representative samples of business decision-takers. Taking short-cuts in sampling usually results in biases which invalidate the findings. Researchers in consumer markets are usually more aware of this than business researchers. Making research cost-effective depends largely on knowing why it is wanted. The technical details of research design can be left in the hands of specialists, in-house if possible, otherwise from an agency proved by results to be reliable.

Research to find out 'just for interest's sake' is an expensive luxury. Like all marketing activities, research projects should have 'action-standards' set for them. Figure 7.3 shows six good reasons for doing research, and for which the research profession has over the years developed effective techniques.

Research can help achieve any of these objectives, if made specific enough, but it cannot usually do more than one at a time. It is not logically possible to develop a hypothesis and test it from the same data. Research to provide reassurance after a decision is taken, or to demonstrate a known fact is not usually very action-orientated and poor value-for-money compared with stimulating ideas, gaining insight into a situation, or helping to make better choices among alternative marketing tactics. Research provides better value for money when done to guide decision-taking, and the earlier it is done the better the value, preferably before ideas have hardened and options narrowed.

Research objective	Marketing action
Find out/Describe	Understand current behaviour and attitudes of customers
Track	Quantify trends in market
Demonstrate	Prove a known fact Provide reassurance that a course of action is right
Develop ideas or hypotheses	Stimulate creativity Guide R&D Design more research
Quantify a hypothesis	Make choices for action
Monitor performance	Evaluate action

Fig. 7.3 Reasons for doing research

Oddly enough, the application of research results should not be a problem. Under the approach put forward in this chapter, research is never started unless the results are really needed: by the time they arrive the decision-takers should be screaming for them, and the researchers should know enough about their purpose to be able to present their findings in an action-orientated form. Companies where the usual reaction to research is 'So what?' or 'Yes, but what can we do about all this?' almost certainly either fail to plan their operations properly or do not communicate them to the researchers.

A colleague, now head of an international research organisation, swears to the genuineness of a telephone call he once had from the Director-General of (let us say) the Widget Founders' Association. 'Mr. B., I have great pleasure in informing you that our Development Committee met yesterday and voted £5,000 as our Industry Market Research Fund for the year. Further, they unanimously agreed that your firm should be commissioned to spend this sum.' 'Thank you very much for your confidence in us,' responds B. 'How would you like us to spend the money?' 'Oh, we leave that to you, you research chappies must have a good idea of what you can find out about the market for widgets!'

To recapitulate: market research is the fundamental of customer-orientated marketing. Its most complex technique is the field survey, the hotline to the customer, a way of bringing the customers' needs into the boardroom ahead of taking any key marketing decision. Use of market research is no guarantee of marketing success, but an insurance policy against serious and expensive failure. Investment in research should be concentrated where the risks are highest or the sums at stake are largest.

Research techniques can be left in the hands of reliable professionals provided they are given fully detailed briefs, and sufficient time and money to do their job properly. The buyer and user of research is solely responsible for identifying the marketing problem or opportunity and the alternative potential courses of action before calling in the experts. Despite the lack of guarantees, the chances of getting reliable, relevant and actionable data can be greatly increased by using the well-proven three-stage research approach of *desk*, followed by *exploratory* followed by *quantified* research.

The first of these stages is of particular importance in business-to-business markets and Chapter 8 will deal with the role of the company information unit and the building, updating and use of the corporate database.

8 PROFIT FROM THE CORPORATE DATABASE

KNOWLEDGE AS A SOURCE OF POWER

Nam et ipsa scientia potestas est (all knowledge is power) said Francis Bacon (1561–1626). Today's hard-pressed business manager may feel like responding to the daily flood of queries from superiors and subordinates in the words of an anonymous but classically-educated information manager: *Quomodo sciare non sanguineus gipsi sum* (How should I know? I'm no xxxx fortune teller!). But help is at hand, and to complete this near-syllogism in dog-Latin, *De illegitimis nil carborundum* (reputedly from the Royal Navy and meaning 'don't let the bastards grind you down'). As the need for business information has grown, so has the supply. We are living in the Information Age, and there is a very great deal of useful up-to-date information available quickly and cheaply to those who know where and how to find it.

This chapter follows the review of primary/field research in Chapter 7 with an examination of the sourcing and management of business information for the purposes of secondary/desk research and of the power available from creating a Marketing Information System. Just as consumer researchers have long ago been forced by the numbers of people in their markets to develop skills in sampling and questionnaire design, so have industrial market researchers been forced by their generally lower budgets to collect and make good use of published data wherever possible. However, the way they do this has changed greatly; the days of 'sending somebody to look this up in the public library' are long gone. The biggest single change in market research since the 1950s is arguably the amount of business information that is readily available at low cost from a wide range of official, academic and commercial sources.

The companies and the management within them who can best access the relevant parts of all this available information will be the ones with Francis Bacon's power of knowledge. The more they know about the current situation and trends in the market, the marketing options available and their likely effects on the customers, the better (i.e., less risky, more profitable) their decisions will be. They will also be able to spot the problems and opportunities before their competitors do (and perhaps even more important to themselves, ahead of their own colleagues) and in time to do something about them.

EXPLOITING THE INFORMATION EXPLOSION

Science had to face this problem long before. The first scientific journal to disseminate new discoveries was published in 1665 and others followed until there were too many for any scientist to keep abreast. But as specialisation grew, a scientist would not need to see everything anyway and needed some way of isolating the few articles relevant to him. Therefore in 1830 the first abstract journal was launched to summarise the 300 then in print and to point scientists towards those papers most useful to their own work. 150 years later in 1980, there were over 100 000 scientific journals and 2,000 abstracts, creating the new problem of abstracting the abstracts.

For business the problem is already even worse, because of the even wider range of interests. To the scientific journals must be added 70,000 other journals, 200,000 new books published each year (90,000 of them in English), leading to an estimated three thousand million titles in print. The chances are high that the fact one wants is in there somewhere; the chances of finding it unaided seem somewhat lower.

The 'information explosion' has come upon the business community more quickly than the scientists. Even 30 years ago, external information needed by a commercial company was so scarce that most of it had to be gathered by expensive field market research. A company would store any published data it stumbled across in a 'company library', staffed by a professional librarian who daily scanned the business and trade press and the catalogues of publishers, universities and government departments for relevant items. Occasionally such items were found and clipped or sent for and squirrelled away in case of need. Usually a single room and a card index sufficed for storage and retrieval. Enquirers at the library would be handed a file or two and told to come back if they needed more.

Twenty years on, the 'information explosion' was well under way. The increase in the amount of commercially useful information accessible 'off the page' or 'down the wire' was such that no company could afford the money or space to buy and store it all in-house, just in case someone might need it some time. 'Libraries' were in any case no longer appropriate because information was usually out-of-date by the time it had been typeset;

and most companies were within easy reach of excellent business libraries in business schools and the better Trade Associations and Public Libraries when they needed one.

Information Departments were now staffed by professional Information Officers, skilled at identifying sources and bringing data in on request. They held in-house only such reference sources as were in constant use, and would respond to 'ad hoc' enquiries by searching on-line databases and telephoning primary Information Providers or other useful contacts. The basic problem had become that instead of too little information, such a search would often turn up too much for the users to cope with; and new problems had arisen of reliability and comparability of sources, and the summarisation of raw data into actionable information.

FROM INFORMATION CENTRE TO MARKETING INFORMATION SYSTEM

Where do we go from here? As the 1990s progress, the information user will be expected to manage more and more of his or her own data, but will be able to locate most of them from a computerised Marketing Information System which has collated relevant in-house, published and field-research data and made them all accessible through a user-friendly on-line search system. The information specialists will have moved behind the scenes to feed the database, to be approached in person when the answers are not found through the usual channels.

It will be a change of function for the new Data Managers to give their company's management direct access to the data they want rather than finding them for them as the Information Officers did. This means that they have to be made aware of the company's information needs. Management should therefore include the data specialists in all marketing planning discussions, to give them advance warning of new topics, and to encourage them to put forward at once any information which already exists, thereby reducing the costs of expensive field surveys.

But good information managers will know that they should not wait to be asked (in case they are not!) and will have to learn to be pro-active, on their feet round the departments asking if decision-takers can find what they want in the form they want it.

MAKING THE MOST OF CORPORATE DATA

The Marketing Information System therefore has constantly to be fed with useful, accurate, timely and cost-efficient data. Where will they all come from? The starting point has to be the nearest to hand and cheapest sources.

	1970s	1980s	1990s
Title	Library	Information Centre	Marketing Information System
Location	Market Research	Communications	Data centre
Purpose	Acquisition Storage Reference	Location Dissemination	Satisfying needs for information pro-actively
Staff	Librarians	Information Officers	Data Managers
Key equipment	Catalogue Scissors	Telephone Photocopier	Modem Feet
Besetting problem	Too little information	Too much information	Integration Summarisation
Mascot	Squirrel	Truffle-hound	Chameleon

Fig. 8.1 The changing role of the Information Department

All companies have, and most under-exploit, a most valuable marketing asset: their own company data. Various departments continuously collect and store data on the internal functioning of the firm (production, distribution, purchasing, cash flow etc) in order to monitor and control operations; and also data on the external world (orders, deliveries, payments, complaints, enquiries, etc) in order to service the customers. The market research department carries out surveys of customers and often keeps general market and economic data.

Such departmental data are often not consolidated, and those who compile them have usually lost interest in them by the end of each financial year, just at the point when there is enough information to be worth strategic analysis. Paper records are often thrown away after a further year.

However, with electronic record-keeping now the norm, there are fewer problems in combining past data from different sources into a single archive database which can be re-analysed for strategic purposes.

This will usually require putting data into a common form which might in some cases demand minor changes in input format. For example, orders recorded by the sales department are usually classified by sales territory, because they are used to control and reward their staff. For strategic marketing they would be more interesting if analysed by size of order, product mix bought, customer industry, new/repeat purchase and so on. This is sometimes difficult to do after the event unless essential information is included at source.

Air Canada was once one of my clients, and in the days when econometric modelling (see Chapter 9) first became an economic proposition for business, I proposed that they built a model of trends in transatlantic travel to help forecast future demand and to test the sensitivity of business and vacational travellers to marketing activity such as promotional fares and advertising. There was plenty of published general market information on the world travel market, social and economic trends, competitive activity and so on. We needed only Air Canada's own sales data. I visited their Center for Operational Data in Montreal and was amazed at the scope and power of the computerised database.

For every Air Canada flight all over North America and overseas they knew for each passenger where the journey began and ended, how much baggage they carried, their sex, class of travel and fare, whether they were alone, accompanied or part of a group, and whether they booked direct with the airline or through a travel agent. They even knew if they needed a vegetarian, Kosher or salt-free meal. There were several years' records to sample: a market modeller's dream.

'Marvellous,' I said, 'please can you extract for me numbers of travellers and average fares for five years by month, for all your transatlantic flights, comparing passengers originating in each European country and originating in Canada?' 'No trouble at all,' they said, 'all except that last thing. We do not keep on file where the ticket was bought, as it makes no difference to running a flight which of the bodies are outward and which homeward bound! You could get that only from the original ticket counterfoils, which are all supposed to be tied up in bundles somewhere down in the basement. The guy at the desk can give you a key.' So after one glance at uncountable thousands of dusty tickets I went home and the model was never built.

If at the time the database was computerised to improve the efficiency of tactical operational control, Air Canada's Operational Research boffins had considered the possibility of its later use for strategic business and marketing planning, a few minor and inexpensive modifications to the input data would have paid large dividends.

Yet the same is true for any company. For instance, if it is possible to cross-reference and compare over time such data as cancelled orders, complaints and late payments it might be possible to identify ahead of time where trouble will strike, when and why. Comparison of the characteristics of customers who buy a single product and the range in depth might identify types of customer with unsatisfied potential for sales, or new developing market segments worth pioneering. When different parts of the data are collected in different departments it can be difficult to match them up, but the rewards for doing so will be worth the work and political inconvenience of co-ordination.

To give an example from a consumer field, the Marketing Director of a large UK canned goods company once asked me: 'My market share is going up according to Nielsen [a syndicated research monitor of sales through grocers], and going down according to TCA [a syndicated monitor of household purchases]. Please tell me which of the two is wrong so that I can fire them?'

Reconciliation was not obvious and required validation against client's ex-factory sales, total production statistics from the trade association and total consumption figures from the government's National Food Survey. Inevitably these all used different time periods (four weeks, two calendar months, six-week journey cycles, quarters, whole years) and different units (tonnes, cases, cans, pounds weight, ounces per head per week). Production figures also had to be adjusted for imports and exports.

The key to the apparent discrepancies in the figures lay in the fact that the two continuous research sources measured different aspects of the market with neither covering the whole. TCA missed any consumption outside domestic households (in caterers, schools, prisons, etc) and Nielsen ignored any sales not made by grocers. Therefore it would be unreasonable to expect them to coincide in values, but why should they show opposite trends?

The answer turned out to be a new marketing problem for the client. At the time, new outlets for canned goods were opening (such as cash-and-carry warehouses) and some traditional fresh food shops such as greengrocers were trying to defend themselves against the big supermarkets by stocking a range of canned goods as well as fresh. In consequence the grocery trade, particularly the smaller outlets, were losing their share of the total market for canned goods. The client was concentrating his selling efforts on the biggest sector, the supermarkets, and indeed was doing very well there as

Nielsen correctly showed. But they had missed out to the competition in what turned out to be a tactical opportunity in new stockists, as shown correctly by TCA.

So the answer I had to bring back to the Marketing Director, in the spirit of the original question, was 'There is nothing seriously wrong with the research data themselves, only with the interpretation and action taken. How about firing your research and sales managers instead?' Had they looked at all their sources of information together (as they now do) they would have spotted this change in market structure early enough to exploit it; perhaps by a one-off 'commando' sales drive offering a bonus to new stockists in cash-and-carries and fresh food outlets.

EVERYBODY'S CONTRIBUTION: BUSINESS INTELLIGENCE

As the previous chapter showed, market research is the formal and assessable collection of data by trained professionals. But a great deal of useful information can be gained regularly and cheaply through informal Business Intelligence.

Everyone from time to time comes across facts, gossip and contacts which could be of interest to their employer. Wise managements encourage their staff at all levels to pass it on. For example, the sales force should collect specimens of competitors' products and sales material (and fill in a 'competitive activity' section on their regular reports; to avoid the embarrassment of leaving it blank they will start looking!). New employees (even junior ones) should be debriefed about their previous knowledge of the market and contacts with suppliers, competitors and customers.

Representatives should be appointed to attend all major trade fairs, conferences and seminars, not as a 'jolly' but to collect, summarise and pass on what happened. Companies which send large numbers of top people to an important event at a prestigious watering-hole and nobody to anything else may miss vital news. A visit to competitors' stands at a Trade Fair on a quiet afternoon may come up with a stack of literature and all kinds of useful ideas. Editors of trade magazines should be cultivated, because they try to see everything and know everybody. While they never divulge information given in confidence, they naturally collect quite a lot of non-confidential information which is not published because they rate it as not 'newsworthy', but which might be of great specific interest. (Of course, you will then be under a strong obligation to give a 'story' in return when asked!)

There should be a mechanism for all such Business and Market Intelligence to be collected and evaluated. Naturally, not all the rumours will be true, but if relevant they should be put on file pending confirmation, and if the topic is important it may be worth cross-checking. A warning should be given here to take care not to cross the line between the legitimate gathering of intelligence and industrial espionage. The law and the ethics are discussed in Chapter 17.

As an example, British Telecom routinely carry out 'market research' among their own large sales force by inviting groups to form a 'sales feedback panel'. A professional (external) market researcher holds regular group discussions in which sales people discuss informally and without personal attribution issues relating to business customers' attitudes, competitive activity and the way in which the company approaches them. British Telecom believe in this way they gain the maximum of information without overloading the sales process with information gathering, and avoid the 'filtering' likely to occur when sales people report officially to their boss. Any matters of importance can be cross-checked by formal market research.

THE GROWTH OF THE ON-LINE INFORMATION PROVIDER

Besides in-house data, market research and intelligence, we need a variety of external data. Where is all this information to come from? How do we tap into the 'information explosion'? The proliferation of sources of commercially-useful data is due to a number of factors. One is the trend to 'open government', and data once treated as state secrets have been declassified by government departments and collated internationally by bodies such as the European Commission and United Nations. Universities and research establishments are now more interested in commercial research, and perhaps the sponsorship money it brings. Pressure groups such as trade associations find information an excellent device for gaining publicity. Media specialising in business news have proliferated to cover the world, and their proprietors offer free market research data to attract advertisers.

These trends have been aided by the growth of computer power to store, access and analyse data in almost unbelievable quantity, and the fast long-distance communications networks which have been set up to transmit them.

A good example is Tradanet, a dedicated system set up to connect the computers of retailers and their suppliers so that they can transmit automatically price-lists, orders, delivery notes, invoices, payment advices and complaints. It is a spin-off from the adoption of the European Article Numbering system whereby every product, supplier, distributor and location can be identified by a unique number, which, through barcoding, can be read electronically.

WH Smith, a very large UK retailer, claims that transferring to Tradanet all their routine liaison with major suppliers has eliminated five million of the pieces of paper they handled every year. Further, that one of their suppliers who used in effect to close their accounts department for six weeks each year to process the WH Smith Christmas order can now complete the work in ten working days. Tradanet works internationally and can equally well be used by non-retail businesses if registered with their national Article Numbering Association. Its virtue is that it translates between most widely-used computer languages automatically. The number of alternative systems of this kind is growing.

The huge but unmanageable mass of data that has rapidly become available to business has created an opportunity for a relatively new service, the commercial On-line Information Provider. These do not usually generate data (or only of one specific kind), but collate and make readily accessible the data from a range of other sources. The father of them all was 'Lockheed' in the USA which in the late 1970s began summarising into computer memory every story in every edition of most newspapers in the USA. twenty-four-hour access was made available to subscribers by telephone line to terminals located originally in public libraries, universities and the newspapers themselves. The subscriber was able to type in proper names or other 'key words' and the database would offer a catalogue of all mentions of the subject in the press as far back as the database went. The enquirer could reduce the number of references where necessary by adding further selection criteria and then print them out in full. This task is an impossibility even for a team of humans working for months, yet the computer typically takes a few minutes from start to finish.

Since Lockheed, many such databases have come on-line, such as a full listing of university and medical research theses, the British Library catalogue, articles in professional journals and the daily business press in the world. Specialist services for marketing are now available, although inevitably concentrating on the consumer side. In 1980 there were about 400 on-line databases, by 1990 over 4,000.

Much of the work of secondary research can now be carried out by on-line searches, which will either bring the data straight to the searcher's desk, or else provide the names and addresses of the original sources all over the world from which full data can be ordered. Such published information can be fed into the corporate database for later reference by all users. The most sophisticated corporate databases actually allow users direct access to the on-line Information Providers (with, of course, passwords and other safeguards, to prevent some passer-by printing-out the whole of Encyclopaedia Britannica!).

I became better informed overnight and saved much time when my Information Department began circulating each morning the headlines of all relevant articles in the whole of the day's business and industry press; and before meeting a new client could personally key in his name and company to the database and review everything that had recently been written about them. ('Good speech you gave to the International Conference, if I may say so, Sir; and what is this I hear about your potential take-over of XYZ Widgets?')

The multiplication of these sources has created the need for yet a further breed of specialist: 'information brokers', known in the USA as 'database surfers'. Few of these exist at present, but they are information scientists specialising in access to on-line databases who in effect supply companies with the services of an external information department on contract. According to the London *Times* (6 November 1992) over 80 European surfers have formed their own on-line network, called Eirene, to share skills and workload.

BUILDING AND MANAGING THE MIS

Most businesses, except for the very smallest, should already have some of the skills and specialisations necessary to create a Marketing Information System (a more user-orientated description than 'corporate database') and may even have an approximation to it available.

The MIS needs to be fed regularly (daily?) with information from five sources:

1. in-company data
2. commissioned and syndicated market research
3. business intelligence
4. selections from generally available published sources
5. external on-line Information Providers.

The running of the database itself and liaison with the departments which provide the in-house data require skills in Information Technology. Most larger companies will have IT specialists in their computer systems department.

The function of identifying and liaising with outside sources requires information specialists. Many companies will already have an information function within the market research or corporate communications departments. Indeed, there are few companies so small that they cannot today justify employing (and funding) at least one qualified Information Officer. Such people usually save their employers many times their own salaries in the course of the year in the speed and economy with which they locate data, let alone the potential savings in field research and from stealing marches on the competition through early-warning of news.

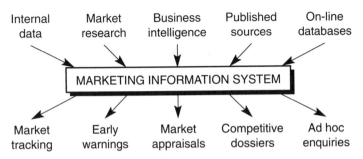

Fig. 8.2 The marketing information system

Putting these skills together and making them readily accessible is more difficult, and may in the first instance require an external specialist. The magic which will put a MIS on every desk-top is called videotex: software which enables non-technical people to access interactively information contained in a (possibly distant) computer.

This is the system which drives the ticketing systems of airlines and hotels, links many companies' warehouses and branches to head office and permits local stockbrokers and forex dealers to do their job even if far from the financial centres, currency exchanges, and big dealing-rooms. Minitel is a domestic form of videotex to be found in millions of homes in France which has developed from an electronic telephone directory to offer a range of services such as messaging, home shopping and home banking. Other countries have its most primitive form, teletext, broadcast behind their TV programmes for decoding on the TV screen.

Some companies already have such an installation, and an inspection of a live system is the best way to realise how powerful a computerised MIS is. Big computer companies not surprisingly pride themselves on their systems. Digital, for instance, have a system so comprehensive that their managers cannot only use it to look up rail and air timetables, they can actually reserve tickets from the screen on their desks.

Perhaps a more difficult problem is the political one of security. The database is a very valuable asset which cannot be replaced quickly or cheaply. Once everyone relies on it, the system going down for any reason will quickly bring normal operations to a halt. It will therefore need to be secure against the hacker or the industrial spy and protected against an accident or a virus or a disaffected employee. Several people will have the job of putting new data into the system, and some of them will also need to edit them. It is vital that the database is properly protected from ignorance, carelessness or malice, but without making routine work difficult. Complete computer security is almost impossible, but it is worth the cost of expert guidance to develop procedures which give the maximum protection with the minimum of nuisance.

To the extent that knowledge is power, the manager of the on-line MIS will be the person with most of it. Certainly, those users who are most skilled will have big advantages over those who are not. It is therefore likely that the MIS has to be a staff function reporting directly to the CEO, thereby taking it away from the more traditional line function of the information centre reporting to market research, communications or even sales. Further, parts of the data will have to have restricted access, although too many gateways and passwords will hamper those who most need the information.

USING THE MIS:
SCANNING THE MARKETING HORIZON

As already explained, a good MIS alone or in combination with field research will be able to answer many of a marketing manager's questions as they arise. But besides reacting to 'ad hoc' questioning, the MIS is more useful when used to search systematically for problems and opportunities *before* they impinge themselves on the company.

The best use of an MIS (as it is of marketing research in the widest sense) is to track trends in the business environment, the market and the company's place in it, relative to customers' needs and major competitors' activities. All market researchers should regularly scrutinise their database to provide:

- early warnings of marketing problems
- possible new marketing opportunities
- consistent monitoring of the effects of the company's and its competitors' marketing activity
- dossiers on each major competitor.

Emergency warnings should be sounded for any sudden and unexpected changes that appear in the situation. But even if trends are steady, it is good policy to encourage the researchers to prepare and circulate regular market reviews (perhaps quarterly, because anything more frequent may not get read), and to make them present and discuss the key findings face-to-face with senior management. Such meetings will provide better value and stimulate more creative thinking if done outside the pressure of specific problems, where somebody is usually on the defensive and likely to throw smoke-screens round the data. Such discussions will also keep the researchers up-to-date with management's plans so that their contribution will become more relevant and the database expanded in line with future needs.

Competitive dossiers are a particularly helpful marketing tool. By collating hard information and gossip from sales, research, the trade press, trade fairs and the personal knowledge of staff, a picture can be built up of each competitor. Their size and financial structure, methods of operation, the strengths and weaknesses of their products, character and background of key staff, specimens of their advertising literature, and so on. All marketing staff should be expected to study this under the heading of 'know your enemy'. Over time they become skilled in anticipating the competitor's moves and changes in strategy and how it will react to ours. Such events as a management re-shuffle or the news of a relocation can be evaluated, and any likely good or bad effects anticipated. Many of the nasty surprises that businesses suffer at the hands of competitors might be anticipated, and competitors' major mistakes could be exploited, instead of copied as has sometimes been known to happen: 'XYZ have just cut their prices by 20 per cent/modernised their house-style/taken a 10,000 square metre stand at the Frankfurt Messe – we had better do the same!'

To recapitulate: profitable, low-risk decisions depend on accurate, timely information about the market situation and the consequences of alternative courses of action. The best way of keeping everyone informed of what is going on in the market place and how the company is performing is a Marketing Information System, available interactively on-line on managers' desks, and fed with internal company data, market research and relevant external data from a range of commercial information providers.

Besides answering queries as they arise and giving emergency warnings of any impending crises, it should also be used to track our own and competitors' marketing activity, and to provide the data for regular systematic market reviews and building dossiers on the activities of leading competition.

The market tracking data also forms the starting point for the annual sales forecast and budgeting exercise, the subject of the next chapter.

9 GETTING THE SALES FORECAST RIGHT

THE ARGUMENT SO FAR

Chapters 1–3 discussed the relationship of profit to risk, and suggested that the essence of successful management is a good understanding of the size and nature of the risks being faced. 'Planning' is not just a matter of raising resources and allocating them once for all to a set of tasks in the hope that enough income will arise to cover them, but rather a set of contingency plans that envisage a variety of outcomes. The key to doing this is a *forecast*: defined as an objective assessment of the degree of uncertainty in the external world in which the business will have to operate, and of the likely effects of favourable and unfavourable factors which might arise during the planning period.

Chapter 4 described the philosophy and approach of marketing: that risks can be lowered and profits made more certain if the product on offer is produced, distributed and promoted with the needs of specific customers in mind. Chapter 5 identified some of the known characteristics of business customers and the 'triggers of buyer behaviour' of their Decision Making Units.

Chapters 6–8 explained that the fundamental act of marketing is identifying the target customers with best potential and then learning as much as possible about their relevant behaviour and attitudes. This is the task of field market research harnessed to the power of the 'information explosion'.

This chapter will explain how such information can be turned into a forecast which will lead to a business plan likely to remain reliable and robust under a variety of circumstances. Readers whose forecasts never go inexplicably wrong should skip this chapter. Chapter 10 will follow the forecast through into the creation of a marketing strategy.

THE NEED FOR A ROBUST FORECAST

The handicap that many businesses lay upon themselves is that their sales 'forecasting' is carried out either by some purely mechanical projection process (such as by exponentially smoothing recent monthly sales or by running a not-well-understood forecasting programme and taking the output at face value), or – worse still – by writing long-term corporate plans which demand every year for financial reasons pre-determined and equal rates of growth of both sales and profits (as opposed to Return on Investment which is a quite different thing).

Neither of these cases takes into account known market conditions or even the possibility that they might vary from year to year. So the strategy put forward will often turn out to be inappropriate, or as we say in this book 'risky'; thereby (as caricatured in Chapter 2) leading almost inevitably to lower profits, over-reaction and even greater difficulties in subsequent years. How can a business get out of this vicious circle? How can reality be brought into a forecast in time to affect the plan?

The forecast is the first step in formulating a business plan, and it must therefore be generated some time ahead of each new financial year. Most companies will already have forecasts from previous years, which are assessed, adjusted and rolled forward at regular intervals. Not too often, it is to be hoped, because if plans are constantly changed planning itself becomes meaningless.

I have worked with companies which up-date their forecasts and fine-tune their budgets as soon as they see the sales figures every month: 'You've got to be right on the ball at XYZ!' This provides an environment in which strategic management is impossible: every time a plan is ready for implementation, the wind changes speed or direction slightly and the plan has to be readjusted accordingly. Once they have learned this, line managers soon cease to make more than token efforts towards the future and live from day to day. They protect themselves by adjusting their own short-term forecasts so often that they become self-fulfilling. (For example, by using 'most-recent-12-months' as the running forecast. It does not change enough from month to month to look suspicious and can be guaranteed to be absolutely spot-on each December!) 'Stop-Go' management policies quickly remove momentum from a business (or an entire economy, come to that), leading to drift, and eventually to crisis.

THE FORECASTING SEQUENCE

A forecast therefore has to take account ahead of time of a variety of possible minor changes in circumstances, so that a plan can be developed which will be robust enough to survive them. This implies that to avoid self-fulfilling forecasts, and to prevent carrying forward flaws in the system, the original annual forecast should be evaluated from scratch at least once a year, and a new 'zero-base' forecast produced. Figure 9.1 suggests a system for doing this, which can be applied in most companies, even if they do not yet have computerised Marketing Information Systems as discussed in Chapter 8.

---

1. Gather data (monthly or quarterly readings) of sales and related variables for as far back as possible.

2. Identify:
    -   Seasonality
    -   Longer cycles
    -   Random variations
    -   Trends
    -   Discontinuities and other changes in trend.

3. Relate the trend to outside influences and to company marketing strategies.

4. Extrapolate the trend (i.e., assume first that current trends continue).

5. Make some assumptions about the future of relevant outside influences, and alternative company marketing strategies.

6. Modify the extrapolated trend under the alternative assumptions.

7. Discuss the assumptions and their implications with all concerned. Play 'what if . . .?'

8. Make and publish 'The forecast':
    -   The agreed best estimate with its underlying assumptions.
    -   A descriptive written scenario.
    -   Alternative (contingency) estimates under best and worst assumptions.
    -   Action standards for variation (i.e., how far can you permit actual to depart from forecast and for how long before you change the forecast and re-budget?)

Fig. 9.1 A sales forecasting sequence

The sequence is in three parts, steps 1–3 backward-looking, steps 4–7 forward-looking and step 8 synthesising the results. All the authorities on forecasting agree that the soundest basis for anticipating the future is a thorough analysis of the past. Before attempting to look forward it is essential to understand as much as possible about the current situation and how it was arrived at. The better the corporate database, the easier it will be to do this. In most cases, sales (and everything which affects them) will vary widely by month and by year, but there will be an underlying trend partly obscured by identifiable patterns, such as seasonal and other consistent cycles, by known oddities such as the effects of strikes and natural disasters and by inexplicable but measurable random variations. What the forecaster needs to do is to strip these short-term variations off, so as to expose clearly the trend.

CYCLICAL INFLUENCES

Seasonality is not confined to the ice cream and Christmas tree markets. Every business needs to take it into account. I worked for a short while for a company, medium-sized in its market, which supplied a business service. Head Office insisted that each subsidiary divided its annual sales and profit targets into 12 equal monthly instalments. However, in our not unusual case, few of our business customers would sign new contracts or even ask for quotations in the period around Christmas. Consequently our sales and profit situation was always poor in December–January, our Board meetings fraught, and we spoiled our festivities by working far into the night trying unsuccessfully to find attractive seasonal sales propositions.

On the other hand, in spring and early summer, when customers were reviewing their needs and starting their annual plans, sales were easy to make and instead of working hard to exploit the opportunities we all hit our targets early each week and went home to tend our gardens. Naturally neither we nor Head Office saw the inanity of our system quite so clearly at the time. But had we put in a proper planning system based on a market review, rather than just trying to placate an unrealistic financial controller, we might possibly have produced for him better or at least more reliable results.

Besides seasonality, some businesses are also affected by longer cycles, of which the commonest is the (approximately) five-year world business cycle which has been tracked by economists for over 100 years. Except when distorted by major wars, most of the past peaks and troughs can be identified clearly, and while they did not occur exactly like clockwork and some were more dramatic than others, most of the turning points were (or could have been) anticipated from published figures to within a few months as much as two years ahead.

All markets are affected to some extent by general economic trends, and so a business forecaster needs access to a good economic forecasting service. Luckily there are many available, some even free of charge. When I ran Thomson Group Marketing Services we had an economic forecasting group consisting of an executive with an assistant and an on-line terminal who had a splendid track record of spotting changes in economic trends some 18 months ahead even during crisis periods. The economist (I suspect over-modestly) claimed that all he did was subscribe to all the academic and commercial forecasting services he could find and averaged the lot!

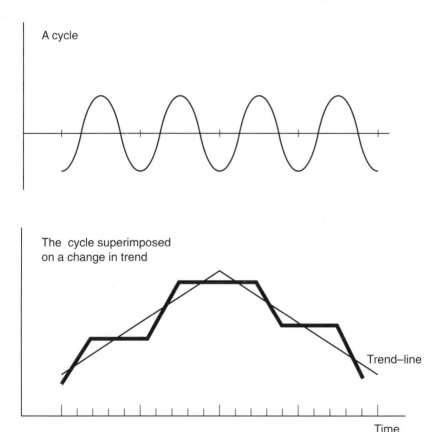

Fig. 9.2 Economic forecasts

Interpretation of some services may be difficult if they show forecasts of such items as Gross Domestic Product only at current prices, and do not separate out their different ingredients such as the business cycle, inflation and the underlying trends. This means that the visible effects of short-term booms and slumps are changed when the trend changes from up to down. Figure 9.2 shows this in simplified terms. When an economy is growing, the booms show up as extra rapid growth and the recessions as a levelling-off. When an economy is in decline, the recessions show up very clearly (this is when business talks about 'slump') and the booms may seem no more than a breathing space. Readers might try lining up Figure 3.2 with their own economy over a 25-year period in which there should have been five world economic cycles and at least one change in trend. They may also find it instructive to try to identify when their government changed party!

Cycles are common in agricultural production and hence in farm-gate prices and they are reinforced by official action such as the EC's Common Agricultural Policy. Those who build schools, train teachers, print textbooks or supply machinery for sugar confectionery will know how World War II started recurrent 20-year baby booms which will continue to distort European demographics and directly-related markets well into the 21st century.

THE COMPONENTS OF CASH SALES

The most important figure to forecast for budgeting purposes is, of course, *cash sales*. Movements in past data often look illogical, but help can be gained from analysis. Sales in money are the product of volume sales and selling price, and volume sales are the product of total market volume and share of market. The trends will in most cases become much clearer and more explicable if *market size, market shares and market prices* are examined separately and multiplied together afterwards. These three components of money sales are all likely to be less volatile than their product; and because each one is affected by different factors, its movements are likely to be easier to understand if studied on its own.

The items listed under each heading in Figure 9.3 are only examples. Each market will be affected by a different combination, and even if the whole list appears relevant they will not all be of equal importance in their apparent influence on market trends. They can be identified by analysis of past years, ideally by using regression analysis (programs available in most good statistical software packages).

Of great importance to marketing planning will be which elements do and do not appear in the lists. If changes in price or promotion have affected recent market shares not at all or to a lesser extent than distribution and size of sales force, this is a clear pointer to where the lion's share of next year's

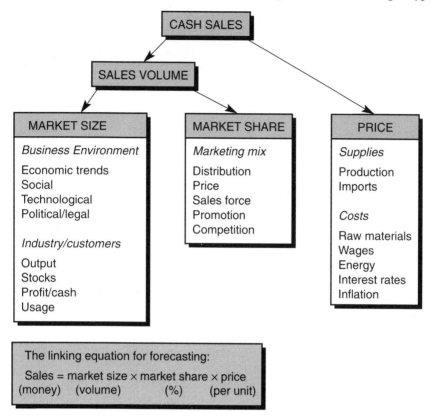

Fig. 9.3 *The components of sales*

marketing budget should go. If the key indicator of market size turns out to be customers' stock levels or cash-flow, then these should be monitored with more care in future, perhaps monthly, and if necessary, extra market research funds should be allocated to do it.

Many of the elements which most affect sales will not be under the supplier's control, particularly external economic and technological factors, and competitive activity. These cannot be ignored, but have themselves to be forecast using a combination of analysis of past data, field market research and business intelligence.

For example, if competitor A act as price leader in the market (see Chapter 12), it will be very important to anticipate their price changes. This may mean identifying and checking on their main suppliers of raw materials (e.g., by buying from them ourselves occasionally), scanning the trade press for news of any industrial relations problems or negotiations they have been having with the trades union, asking the sales force to give early warning of signs of pressure from or interest in imports, asking a friendly customer to pass on A's latest published price lists.

THE ROLE OF EXTRAPOLATION

Chapter 3 explained that an extrapolation or projection (the past extended forward) is in effect a forecast under the assumption that there will be no changes in trend. The mindless use of such projections is highly dangerous, firstly because trends (whether upwards or downwards) are almost never steady but tend to go up or down faster or slower, so that future circumstances will not be the same as the past. Next year is much more likely to be either better or worse for us than it is to be exactly the same as this year, and we may already have a good idea which. Secondly, we will be taking action to try to do better next year than this. If we plan to cut our price or raise our advertising spend, will this not raise sales above trend, and if so should not our forecast take account of it?

Thirdly, extrapolation at a constant rate quickly leads the forecaster into Wonderland. Fifteen per cent more sales may not seem an unreasonable increase in a good year. But setting a target of 15 per cent annual growth implies that we expect sales will double during a five-year plan. During those five years, at least two will have prospects below average (by the definition of an average); can we expect to catch up in the good years? Will the customers be able to absorb twice as much of our product five years hence? How will the competition respond to this policy?

This is not to condemn the use of projections: they are easy to do and give a clear indication of where we are heading. But they should *never* be used as 'the' forecast, only as a valuable step towards one.

Recent data can be extrapolated by eye using graph-paper-and-ruler, but it is better to estimate trends by centred moving-monthly-averages (centred because the past 12 months' sales tell you not where you are now but where you were at mid-year), or by exponential smoothing which gives greatest weight to the most recent data, or better still by least-squares curve-fitting. Any member of the marketing staff with some statistics can do this by looking up the formulae in a book on business statistics or much more quickly on a PC with a statistical package. However, before handing it over, this person must be quite sure what the software has done to the original data, and should not extend the extrapolation too far ahead, as it is in the nature of all fitted curves to mislead by quickly heading towards the ceiling or the floor.

ASSUMPTIONS AND PREDICTIONS

We should by now have summarised and charted all the facts we have about the market and our own sales in the past, and which we also believe to be important (preferably because we have so demonstrated). We must now summarise all that we believe (or even better, can demonstrate) about the future. This will come under four main headings: ourselves (what do we plan to do?), our customers (what do they want, what are they likely to do about it?), our competitors (what is our best idea of their intentions?), and the external market environment (what will happen, what may happen, what will or may *not* happen?).

Where there is enough hard statistical data this can be done by the same analysis and extrapolation as we have used on our own sales, for example trends in the world economy and in the total market. More usually, there will be no such basis, particularly where the behaviour of particular individuals or small groups is concerned. Will there be any change in business taxes or interest rates, and by how much? Will any competitor launch a new brand? How strong is the loyalty of our best customers? What are the chances that any of them will go into liquidation or be taken over by our competitor's best customer?

We cannot know such answers for certain, but we can make an assessment from published data, business intelligence, our own past experience and the views of any experts to whom we have access. For example: 'on average XYZ have launched a new product only once every three years, yet they put one out both last year and the year before, neither exceptionally successful. We reckon the chances of yet another to be small, say 10 per cent.' If this is a crucial issue to us, perhaps we might put our corporate ear a bit closer to the ground for some confirmation.

In this way we build up a set of explicit and written *assumptions* about relevant future events over which we have no control. These are predictions of a kind (see Chapter 3), but are best expressed as relative likelihoods of the alternatives ('oil prices: up more than 5 per cent, 1 chance in 10, steady 6 in 10, down more than 5 per cent, 3 in 10'). These can be used to modify the projections up or down on judgment, or for those expressed numerically it may be possible to incorporate them in a mathematical modelling process to be described later.

By putting together assumptions and modified projections, we build up a picture of what is most likely for the coming year, a 'central scenario' in futurologists' jargon. Indeed we might wish to have several such, because there is always some chance that even the most likely assumption might turn out wrong and we need to take a view about what might happen to our sales. As a minimum we ought to look at the combined effects of the most pessimistic assumptions (combining Murphy's Law that 'anything which can go wrong probably will' with O'Toole's Corollary that 'Murphy was an incorrigible optimist'); and contrast the result with the most optimistic view of what might happen if all the red warning lights turned green together.

The closer the outcomes of the best and worst scenarios, the less inherent risk there is in the situation and the more confidence with which we can implement our plans. If they are a long way from the central scenario (particularly on the downside), we are facing a risky situation, and need to take care, particularly about anything involving new investment.

THE FORECASTER'S WALKABOUT

While there may have been consultations about specific topics with experts and other outsiders, everything else so far could conceivably have been done within the marketing department. But before finalising any company's sales forecast, it is wise at this point for the forecaster to go out to discuss the work in draft with others who either will have to act on it (heads of production, distribution, sales, finance) or who might have relevant information (including some quite junior staff and outsiders such as the advertising agency).

This is for several purposes:

- Vital information may be missing. 'Half-a-million cases of product 123 next year? No chance! Didn't anyone tell you I have to close the Eindhoven plant for three months to fit new effluent-scrubbers before somebody prosecutes!'
- There may be differences in opinion about the assumptions. Forecasts which are not believed tend not to happen. There may be need to modify, explore new scenarios or at least add more explanations
- There is more than one way in which the company can respond to the market, and the outcomes of all sensible alternative strategies should be explored before finalising a plan. Those who have to implement them should be encouraged to play 'what if . . .?' with the scenarios. Some

outcomes will cause more trouble, some opportunities be seized more easily than others, and it is better to know which in advance

- Departments will have to collaborate, and will be better able to do so if they understand what is going on and work to common assumptions about the future. People who have been consulted at the planning stage feel committed to the plan (even if their views do not prevail) and will work harder to achieve it than if it is handed down to them on a tablet of stone from on high.

It is worth including in the walkabout everybody responsible for profit, meaning all who take or influence decisions which affect either revenue or costs. No forecaster wants the embarrassment of having to withdraw and rework the forecasts after presentation because some elementary fact was not taken into account, or to be overruled for unexpected reasons which turn out not to be really valid.

THE FORECAST DOCUMENT

Only after all this work should the forecast be finalised and widely circulated. As discussed in Chapter 3 it will not now be a single figure but a slim document (too fat and it will not be read). It will contain:

- The agreed best estimate of sales, but with its underlying assumptions stated explicitly
- A descriptive scenario of the coming year, with forecasts of factors and events most likely to affect sales
- Alternative (contingency) estimates of the outcome under best and worst assumptions
- Action Standards of how far and for how long actual can be allowed to deviate from forecast before action has to be taken such as changing the forecast or ditching the plan.

A forecast produced in this way will be carefully scrutinised, believed, implemented, and best of all kept for reference to be used as a map to guide the organisation along its agreed journey. This could be said to justify the inevitable amount of time and work needed to set the system up. Once in place, the monitoring system will keep the database fed as a matter of routine. Forecasts in subsequent years will be easier and faster to check and up-date. As time progresses, comparison of final outcomes with initial forecasts will show up any consistent weaknesses or missing items, so that the accuracy of and general confidence in them will gradually improve.

ACTION STANDARDS AND CONTINGENCY PLANNING

The action standards are particularly important, because future sales will inevitably suffer from random fluctuations to at least the same extent as the past, and which should not be allowed to cause over-optimism or panic. Moving from 5 per cent below trend one month to 5 per cent above the next is no reason on its own to deduce that there has been a change in the situation or need to modify the plan; next month's figure may be back down again.

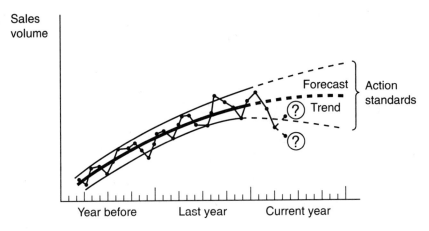

Fig. 9.4   Action standards for a forecast

Analysis of the past will show how much noise there is in our system which we will have to continue to tolerate. But suppose last month's sales lie outside this limit? Rather than taking immediate and ill-considered action which might have to be countermanded next month, it is best to remember that such a deviation happens naturally about once a year and on its own should act as no more than a warning to be investigated. Is the drop across the board or just a delayed single large order? Does it relate to known factors such as weather conditions or strikes? Have any competitors (or ourselves) taken any recent action which might have affected the issue? Is there anything worth researching?

If next month is back to normal we heave a sigh of relief and carry on. If still outside the limit we may then decide that we are genuinely off course and must take action. But by now we should have some idea of what we are up against, and in many cases there will be a contingency plan at least in outline that we can implement without panicking.

CUSTOMER ATTITUDE SURVEYS

At this point experience suggests several readers may be saying to themselves, 'I do not need all that process, I just get my sales force to ask their customers. They ought to know what they are going to buy next year!' An excellent thing to do: it gets the sales force thinking, it gives them a talking point for their next visit, it shows concern for the future of the customers and may even persuade some to commit themselves to future orders.

But a basis for a forecast? Most customers know what they now *think* they will need, but they may know less about the future of the market than you do (you at least know about the coming price hike and the new product); and they may not want to show their hand because buyers have to assume that anything they say to a seller is part of the negotiating process. Further, what figures will the sales force pass on? It cannot be guaranteed that the apple-polishers who exaggerate their sales potential to demonstrate their enthusiasm to Head Office will exactly compensate for the old hands who underestimate on the cynical assumption that their future targets for bonus will be set as a multiple of their own estimates.

Such survey data should be considered as a measure of customer or sales-force confidence, and as such are a useful input to the forecasting process, not a substitute for it. If you are optimistic about next year and the customers are pessimistic, your sales force is in for a rough ride irrespective of the true state of affairs, and it is as well to know this in advance.

ECONOMETRICS AND ALL THAT

Other readers may be saying that there seems too much hand calculation and personal judgment in the approach described. For those who have a reliable database which contains several years of monthly or quarterly readings of sales, prices and other related market and economic variables, there is the option of building an *econometric model* of their market.

This is a mathematical equation (sometimes a set of them) which explains sales or some other 'dependent variable' in terms of the level of or changes in a number of independent marketing and economic variables. Multivariate analysis, usually multiple linear regression, generates the explanation by identifying the best fit to the data by least-squares in multi-dimensional space. It rejects variables which have shown no consistent relation to sales in the past and adds or multiplies the remainder at different weights to select the combination which explains as much of the changes in the past data as possible.

As a simple illustration, such a model might be:

Volume sales next quarter = Base level + a × change in customers' declared profits in last quarter + b × expected change next quarter in our price relative to market average + c × percentage share of last 12 months advertising expenditure + seasonal factors.

Here a, b and c are constants derived from multivariate analysis of past data. The equation will be supplied with some statistical diagnostics to show how well it explains past sales, and what degree of random variation can be expected about any projections. Such a model can be used for four purposes:

1. *Understand the structure of the market.* In this case that customer profits and our competitive price and advertising are more important than any other factors
2. *Evaluate past activity.* For example, what did last year's price cut and advertising campaign actually achieve, and which was more cost-effective?
3. *Make projections* which take into account all the independent variables, so as to forecast the effects on the market of variables not under our control such as customer profits. What sort of sales will we have if our customers are squeezed by high interest rates?
4. *Simulate the effects of alternative marketing strategies* to short-list those with best potential (a more objective and confidential way of playing the 'what if?' games). If the customers are likely to hold off, how much do we need to cut price to maintain a given level of sales? Suppose our competitor doubles their advertising spend, are we better off in profit terms if we match them or keep our head down?

Building such a model is an expert econometrician's job, and may take time and money even if a good database is already available. However, running the model and updating it regularly can be carried out quickly and cheaply by any competent statistician. Originally developed to forecast national and world economic trends, econometrics have been applied to commercial problems since the 1960s, but became commonplace only during the 1980s when PCs made the computing power and software cheap and readily available. There are several textbooks which explain the benefits and limitations and there are many easily-understood marketing case histories in the excellent 'Advertising Works' series (UK Institute of Practitioners in Advertising every two years from 1981).

Useful though models can be, there is no magic in them, and the *Garbage In Garbage Out* rule applies. The output can be no more accurate than the input data. Although multivariate, the forecasts are still projections which assume that the market will react in future in the same way as in the past, which is often but not always true. They must still be treated as an *aid* to better judgment, not a *substitute* for it.

Today's computer is not a 'brain' but a machine which can do enormous amounts of boring routine arithmetic faster and more accurately than a human can. It therefore permits more complex analysis of business data. But interpretation of the output and planning action on it still requires judgment. It is a better use of human skills and experience to apply them to the computer's work than to guess their results in the first place. But the projections of an econometric model, however sophisticated, should be scrutinised, and if thought necessary adjusted for non-quantifiable factors on judgment before being treated as 'forecasts'.

EXPERIMENTAL MARKETING

Yet other readers may say that far from needing econometrics, they have little or no hard data at all (perhaps a new product, a new company or a new market). A rule of thumb is that for every year to be forecast, there should be three years' back-data. For example, not even seasonality can be reliably estimated with less. In such cases, the operating risks must be assumed to be high, and the strategy developed accordingly, with a high degree of flexibility built in from scratch. It may be possible to find analogies (e.g., other countries, parallel new launches, similar companies) which help to deduce the parameters of success and failure against which progress can be measured.

Once started, it is possible to ncrease the rate of supply of useful data by the 'hot-house' methods of *Experimental Marketing*. For example, if the operation is divided up in some way (e.g., geographically or by user industry), different parts of the market can be given different marketing treatments, thereby identifying the causes of success and failure much more quickly. Modellers can also benefit from experimental marketing, for example the response of a market to advertising can be estimated much more accurately if one group of customers are subjected to a much higher rate and another group to a much lower rate than the rest.

To recapitulate: 'Forecasting is difficult,' Sam Goldwyn is reported to have said, 'especially about the future.' Sales forecasting is a technique of marketing intended to identify and eventually reduce the risks in a situation. Many profit failures happen because management either do not know enough facts about their market and customers, or they do not take enough precautions against the risks inherent in the situation, and in consequence act on an unrealistic view of the future.

In 1988, a market research firm, Yankelovich Clancy Shulman, forecast to Beecham that a new cold-water detergent, Delicare, would win between 45 per cent and 52 per cent of the US market if backed with $18 million of advertising. The product was launched and achieved between 15 per cent and 20 per cent. Beecham sued for $24 million in damages, but settled out of court without making the full details public. But for matters to have gone as far as a full national launch with apparently no regional testing or contingency plan for undershooting target, whether or not the forecasting technique was at fault or not, it would seem that the forecasters and forecast users must have been at cross-purposes in some fundamental way.

Sales forecasting is not a branch of fortune-telling, and its output is not a single number. It is an objective analysis of what has happened in the past and why, leading to a quantified view of what is most likely in future. It has to be based on explicit assumptions, and should also include contingency evaluations of alternative better and worse scenarios. An agreed forecast with its action standards can be used as a basis for monitoring future progress and will give early warning of trouble.

10 FROM BUSINESS OBJECTIVE TO MARKETING STRATEGY: THE MARKETING AUDIT

OBJECTIVES, STRATEGIES AND TACTICS

Chapter 3 pointed out the hazards created by using jargon words with different meanings as if they were synonyms; it illustrated them by attempting to distinguish the concept of a 'forecast' from the concepts of budget/target and projection/prediction. In a similar way some business people (and many politicians) appear very confused between Objectives, Strategies and Tactics. This chapter is devoted to this issue, and will discuss these three concepts (plus two others, the Marketing Audit and the Resources Budget) in the context of making a Business Plan.

The simplest definitions arise from an analogy with geography: an *objective* is the destination to which one wants to travel; a *strategy* is the choice of means of transport: a *tactic* is the route actually taken; a *marketing audit* is the map which gives the information needed to choose the most suitable means of transport and the most efficient route, a *resources budget* is the price of the ticket and the food for the trip.

Clearly these are five different concepts, yet not totally independent of each other. If the chosen means of transport is a bicycle it is unrealistic to set a destination the other side of an ocean, it is inefficient to choose a route straight over a high mountain, the journey is likely to be even more precarious if the map is the wrong scale or out-of-date and it may never be completed if there is no money for a puncture repair outfit and a packet of sandwiches. If there are unexpected problems (such as a blocked road), it will usually be easier and cheaper to modify the tactical route (e.g. make a detour), rather than to change the strategic mode of transport (e.g. to charter a helicopter).

To translate back to business terms, a company might set as its objective to grow in turnover or in valuation on the stock-market; or to defend its market leadership against competition; or to get itself taken over; or (in at least one real case) to help its Chairman win a peerage.

If the chosen objective is to 'maintain market leadership', alternative strategies for consideration might include technological leadership based on an intensive programme of R&D; or exceptionally responsive customer service based on customer research; or undercutting competitive prices by exploiting the economies of long production runs and the benefits of bulk-buying raw materials. Choice of strategy would depend on whether the Marketing Appraisal revealed desire among customers for technical improvements, or weaknesses in competitors' customer service, or high market price-elasticity; and on whether the Marketing Audit confirmed that there was a likelihood of the R&D department providing convincing product improvements in the immediate future, and whether there were significant latent cost savings available on the production side.

If the 'low-price' strategy was chosen, tactics to implement it might be to set a base price near market average but then to offer larger discounts for quantity than competition could match, and to promote them by mailings to existing customers and heavy advertising in trade magazines. Reactions to the discounts and the promotional material might need to be pre-tested in some way, and they may need to be modified during the year if competitors over-react to them.

THE NEED FOR MEDIUM-TERM PLANNING

Not all companies have plans beyond their next financial year. In many ways such businesses have to operate as if the world was coming to an end on the 1st of January the year after next! Yet they will buy (and borrow the money for) new capital equipment. By writing down an asset over (say) seven years, the company has made the assumption that the asset will be commercially useful and profitable for that length of time.

In other words, all companies have a long-range plan implicit in their capital budgeting, but do not all make its implications on cash budgeting explicit. This seems to add to the risks attached to the capital.

A successful company should seek to lengthen its planning horizon and plan explicitly for the period over which it writes down its expendable assets, typically between three and 10 years. If circumstances are so volatile that this is not sensible, then it could be said that capital assets should be minimised (for example by short-term leasing). The benefit of medium-term planning is that objectives can be set which will remain unchanged during the period of each plan (unless some major and unexpected and therefore traumatic event takes place in the marketplace). The same strategy could then be kept from year to year with only fine tuning, while the tactics might well have to vary considerably to take account of changing market conditions. Such long-term strategic consistency permits great synergy between the work of different parts of the operation and builds up a 'fly-wheel' effect on customer images and loyalty.

By contrast, a company with no longer-range perspectives and so does not know where it really wishes to go), whose 'objectives' are really only strategies and whose 'strategies' are therefore only short-term tactics will see the need to change course far more often and will be likely to abandon its best marketing ideas long before they have properly registered with the customers, let alone become worn out.

THE CORPORATE BUSINESS OBJECTIVE

When making a business plan, the starting point must be to decide the destination. Setting corporate and business objectives is not a task for the marketing department because they will involve considerations other than customers, such as internal industrial relations, corporate finance and the relations of the company with any parent or subsidiaries, the business community and the general public. However, to the extent that the whole organisation will be involved in achieving the objectives, it is wise for corporate planners to consult with marketing (and other management) on their feasibility and likely costs before finalising them. Marketing management should from time to time tactfully remind them of this.

Corporate and business objectives will usually consist of three separate parts:

1. What the corporation believes its function to be and its place in the business community. (This is fashionably called a 'mission statement'. For example, the mission statement of Microsoft Corporation Inc. is 'a personal computer on every desk and in every home'.)
2. Who is the target customer and what is the customer need to be satisfied?
3. Financial goals stated both qualitatively (in words such as grow, dominate, defend, diversify), and in quantitative terms (e.g., desired turnover, profitability, rates of growth, return on investment).

A plea should be put in for simplicity. Gerald Levin, Chief Executive of Time Warner (a complex group) said: 'There has to be a fairly simple identity that drives a company, and when you get too far away from it, you begin to have problems.' Good objectives should also be realistic enough to be achievable, sufficiently generalised to be applicable to all functions of the company, and to maintain their validity for a substantial length of time during which business and market conditions may vary considerably. As was pointed out in Chapter 9, some years are more conducive to survival and growth than others and which are going to be can sometimes be pre-determined by good forecasters.

When long-range planning first became fashionable, I was seconded to a team creating a corporate plan for a New York-based business which had never before had one. I found myself in the delicate position of being the most junior person present, yet the only one who had ever actually written a long-range plan. There were some very high-powered financial consultants on the team who (basically to facilitate raising capital for expansion on Wall Street) demanded as financial goals that each part of the organisation should attempt to grow by 15 per cent every year in both turnover and profit.

While this was offered as a desirable 'target' (in the jargon of Chapter 9), I was almost certain that if it was adopted by the holding board of the group, all their operating subsidiaries would be expected to budget accordingly each year. This of course would commit them all to plan to quadruple in size within a decade; which seemed a tall order when many were already estab-lished leaders in highly competitive markets. Luckily nobody thought it necessary to specify *volume* growth, only money, and the rates of world inflation forecast for the next few years were going to mitigate the degree of over-optimism. But I did take my career in my hands to argue that the word 'average' should appear in the adopted financial objective because it was possible that in an international and diversified group each year some subsidiaries might inevitably do better or worse than others. This would not matter to the group if the overall total averaged out on target.

The team saw the logic, but did not consider the point particularly important. However, they were kind enough to humour me and the objec-tive which was finally agreed committed each subsidiary only to an *average* of 15 per cent growth of turnover and an *average* of 15 per cent growth of profit over the period of the Plan. I have often wondered since how many local Chief Executives spotted the loophole and used it to plan to have some years of growth and some of consolidation, thereby perhaps avoiding sacking all their key staff to preserve margins every time they faced a short-term squeeze of turnover.

THE MARKETING AUDIT

Once the objective has been decided, the next need is for a good map of the territory so as to choose the most appropriate route and means of transport to get there. A most effective map can be drawn by means of a Marketing Audit. The term audit has of course been drawn from accountancy to describe a process which looks at an operation as comprehensively, objectively and precisely as possible. A *marketing* audit looks in two directions:

1. internally at the assets and resources the company has at its disposal
2. externally at the competitive market and business environment in which it will be operating.

Chapters 6–9 dealt with the methods available for looking at the customers, competitors and the business environment generally, and pointed out the need for a Marketing Appraisal containing both accurate and detailed descriptions of the current situation and also meaningful forecasts of the opportunities and risks in the immediate future, and offered advice about preparing one. It must be backed up by an audit of the company's *internal assets* which can be applied to marketing.

ASSET-BASED MARKETING

'Classical' marketing, as described in Chapter 4, starts with a customer need and works back to a product and marketing approach to satisfy it at a profit. Such an approach created and sustained most of the successful international business giants from the 1950s onwards. But it had a side effect of leading competitors onto the same high ground in their markets where they conducted wars of attrition at increasing cost. The obvious escape route of diversification into new markets also led to problems. Market research easily uncovered many customer needs, and a company which tried to satisfy them all soon found itself moving in many directions at once, including some in which it had neither resources nor expertise. Such over-diversified companies ran into trouble through over-stretched resources and unprofitable sidelines.

The way ahead was first put forward in the late 1970s by Hugh Davidson (and is summarised in his *Offensive Marketing*) as *asset-led marketing*. This is a supplement to, not a substitute for, customer-orientation. Alongside the search to identify customers and understand their needs should run an examination of the assets of the company and ways to use them more

People	Skills, experience, motivation, organization, direction, knowledge areas, communications, speed of reaction, outside contacts, training quality, philosophy, creativity
Working capital	Amount, availability, utilisation, location, credit lines
Operations	Relative modernity, exclusive elements, shop secrets, flexibility, economies of scale, efficiency in use, capacity utilisation, added value, quality of service
Customer franchises	Brand names, trade or buyer franchises, unique products/services, patents, superior service skills, access to third-party resources (joint ventures or agreements)
Sales/Distribution/ Service Network	Size, skill, coverage, capacity utilisation, productivity, relations with external distributors
Advantages of scale	Market share, relative and absolute media weight, purchases/leverage, geographical/international coverage, sales/distribution/service (above), specialist skills due to scale (e.g. market research)

Fig. 10.1   Check list of types of asset.
Source: Davidson, *Offensive Marketing*

effectively in the market-place. This then provides a benchmark against which any new market, product or customer need can be assessed: can it be satisfied using our assets, and will it let us use them more effectively than we do at present? It can also act as a brief for the research: we have these skills and resources, how can we exploit them more fully?

Figure 10.1 gives Hugh Davidson's own check list of possible sources of assets. Alternatively, each separate operation can be scrutinised individually in terms of what it does now and what it might do if pushed. For example, what is our achievable *production capacity*: not the total for a whole year, but how much could we guarantee to produce how quickly in response to an unexpected large order? What about sourcing raw materials if our usual supplier had difficulties? What is our rejection rate, and what percentage of total production faults are detected? How is our product quality compared with competition (is that what R&D say or the customers)? What are our strongest and weakest technical features?

Each question should be answered factually and assessed as objectively as possible in terms of what is known about the customers and the competition rather than what the organisation itself believes or wants. It may be useful to use an external consultant to direct the auditing process. Someone regularly engaged in such work will be able to cut through the problems of internal politics, provide objectivity and offer wider experience of technique. A useful and currently fashionable way of doing this 'benchmarking': making direct quantified comparisons with successful competitors, or similar companies in other fields or countries (especially Japan, see *Thurow*).

By assessing each operation in this way a list of *exploitable* assets can be built up, and at the same time a list of potential weaknesses against the competition that need scrutiny. Some of these will be more important in the marketplace than others. Ideally it will be possible to identify those of our assets which are key factors for success, and whether there are any missing assets which we need to acquire or key weaknesses for us to correct as a high priority. Any other asset or liability can be ignored or at least rated as a lower priority.

PRODUCT LIFE CYCLES

One aid to identifying assets is the well-known Boston Matrix, widely used by consultants, whereby products with high shares of high growth markets are classified as 'stars', those with high shares of low growth markets 'cash cows', low shares of high growth markets 'problem children' and low shares of low growth markets 'dogs'. The theory goes that the stars should be fed resources to exploit their position, until their market levels off and they develop into high profit but limited life cash cows which should be 'milked' to fund the launches of potential new stars. Problem children must have their problems solved quickly or else be withdrawn, otherwise they will develop into dogs draining cash from growth products and damaging corporate reputation.

Where these categories represent reality they give pointers to an appropriate strategy. But the definitions are vague and ambiguous (what rate of market growth counts as high?), and many products do not fit the categories too well.

A second good textbook template is the equally well-known 'product life

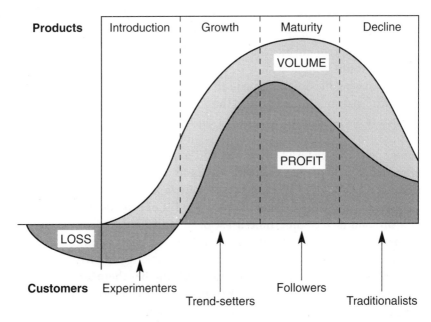

Fig. 10.2 Product life cycles

cycle' bell-shaped curve (Figure 10.2). According to this, a successful new product recoups its development costs early in its life, grows to a peak volume of sales, levels off in its maturity and then later declines, generating good profits until it reaches a cut-off point where it has to be withdrawn. A Boston 'problem child' is a product whose growth phase is too shallow to pay off its development costs quickly – a 'dog' is a product which never has and never will make a profit.

Studies of domestic consumers suggest there are distinct segments of 'experimenters' who almost as a matter of routine try new products, which then get taken up in volume by 'trend-setters', are passed on to 'followers' as the trend-setters move on to the next new wonder, and reach conservative traditionalists only after they have been on the market for long enough to become commonplace. There is some evidence that, judged by their buying habits, many companies fall into one of these four categories too.

While no theoretical system of classification will fit all situations, I have found that combining the Boston Matrix and the life cycle curve into the eight categories shown in Figure 10.3 can sometimes give more inspiration

Brand Share ▼	Product life cycle ▶ New	Growth	Maturity	Decline
High	INFANT	STAR	CASH COW	WAR-HORSE
Low	ABORTION	PROBLEM CHILD	DOG	DODO

Fig. 10.3 Product classifications in the market life cycle

about where a product is and what its future might be. The category names should be self-explanatory. Strategies for success should follow the high line until the product finally reaches its cut-off point where no further action can generate adequate profit. Any product falling into the lower line needs remedial action or removal. Even if your problem child is not star material, could it be turned into a cash cow before it reaches the dog stage?

But while some products fall into distinct life cycles (and in fashion-led markets such as 'high-tech' quite short ones), many others manage to survive for decades (and even cases such as newspapers for over a century), perhaps as a result of a programme of regular reformulations, up-dates and re-launches. It may well be that the length of the life cycle is as much in the hands of the supplier as the market. Strategists should at least consider whether a long-established product could be categorised as a 'war-horse' (provided it has not yet fallen into 'dodo-hood') and not be milked too fiercely. Instead, with its development costs paid and its capital written off, its life could be prolonged by a little up-dating and promotion. It might be thereby kept in substantial profit for a further lease of life, or at least until the development and market testing of a modern substitute.

DRAWING THE MAP: SWOT ANALYSIS

By this time the internal Marketing Audit and the external Marketing Appraisal will have between them generated a great deal of data, probably far too much for strategic analysis. The best approach to identifying the parts most relevant for strategic planning is the now widely-used *SWOT* analysis technique (Strengths, Weaknesses, Opportunities, Threats). These four headings summarise the key points of what is known and should not need to cover more than one page of paper each.

Strengths mean specific competitive assets exploitable in the market as identified in the Marketing Audit, Opportunities mean specific and positive changes in customer needs or the competitive market-place as identified in the Marketing Appraisal. Together they act as a small-scale map of the territory to be covered, with the original documents offering a larger-scale view when necessary.

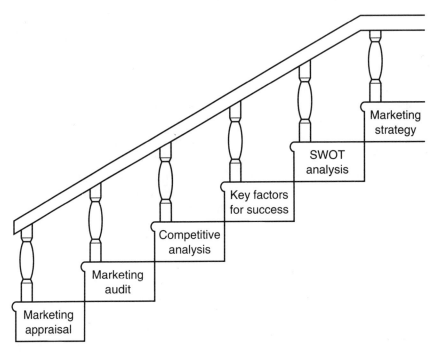

Fig. 10.4 Strategic market analysis
Source: Davidson Offensive Marketing

Figure 10.4 summarises the five preliminary steps that have to be taken in order to bridge the gap between setting a corporate objective and selecting a strategy to achieve it. If any step is missing, it will increase the risks of choosing one which is inappropriate, unachievable or unprofitable.

CHOOSING THE STRATEGY

The strategic planning team should use people with a variety of skills, including at least one marketing generalist and also the expert on the company database. They should at this point take the objective and the maps away for detailed study. There are almost always several alternative strategies which will achieve any objective, each with both advantages and disadvantages, each incurring costs.

The planning team should therefore identify such a range of alternative strategies, assess and cost them. Since in most cases the company will not be starting from scratch, the existing strategy will make a useful benchmark for the assessment: can we be more effective, can we be more profitable?

The key criteria for assessment of each strategy will obviously be *relevance* to the objective (can it get us there?), *feasibility* (are we able to implement it using existing skills and resources?), *competitiveness* (does it exploit our assets over the competition?), *cost* (can we afford it?) and *profitability* (is it worth the money?).

Just occasionally, none of the strategies on offer will match up to the criteria. This may be because the maps are in some way deficient, thereby identifying the need for more research. Alternatively the objective set may be unrealistic in some way when the team has to refer back to top management for 'clarification'; a tactful way of suggesting that they have either withheld vital information or have seriously lost touch with reality!

The choice of strategy will usually be inspired by considerable debate and wide consultation. Someone may have vital information which would otherwise be overlooked. If all who have later to develop tactics for its implementation are given a say in the selection of the strategy they are more likely to try their hardest (even if overruled, as was pointed out in Chapter 9 in the context of the sales forecast).

The final result will be a clear statement of: the *corporate objectives* for the medium term, the chosen *strategy* to achieve them and the outline *resources budget* available to implement it. This statement should be widely circulated because the whole company must work together to achieve it. A secret corporate strategy is not a strategy, just a secret! However, each department should be given guidance about how its function contributes to the total, how it integrates with the others, and how much of the budget can be allocated to it.

To recapitulate: setting corporate objectives is the task of top (general) management rather than marketing because they are determined by a number of factors which relate to the internal structure and goals of the company as well as to external market considerations.

Before setting the strategy, a *marketing appraisal* of the external environment and a *marketing audit* of internal assets have to be carried out. These need to be summarised by means of a *SWOT analysis* to determine the company's competitive strengths and weaknesses and the key factors for success in the market-place.

These all act as 'maps of the territory' to help identify and cost a range of alternative strategies. A wide range of internal opinion should be canvassed before agreeing which is the most relevant to the objective, feasible, competitive, affordable and profitable. The agreed strategy should be circulated widely to all those who have to implement it.

11 POSITIONING, BRANDING AND CORPORATE IMAGE

THE INTANGIBLES OF BUYER BEHAVIOUR

In Chapter 5 we discussed the business buying decision: how a company has to have not only a need but also the means, opportunity and motivation to satisfy it. The decision is usually made by a group of people with different roles who interactively decide which good or service best fits their collective need. In making that decision they take account of a number of factors (as they do when buying on their own account): some of them tangible such as specification, price and after-sales services, some intangible such as the reputation of the product or its maker.

This book does not attempt to discuss the tangible aspects of products, beyond reiterating at several points that to succeed in the market-place a product must be capable of satisfying some need of some buyers, and that what is on offer is not only the core good or service, but its packaging, delivery, price and a surrounding halo of services. Any product whose offer fails to deliver its promise to satisfy a need will not generate repeat sales. To grow and make profits, the product has also to satisfy the need *better than its competitors* in some way. The tangible aspects cannot be discussed usefully here because each market is different in its requirements and has its own technologies to cope with them.

This chapter discusses perhaps the most important *intangibles* which apply to the marketing of almost all goods and services, namely *brand and corporate image*, and the concept which links them with the tangible aspects, namely *product positioning*.

THE NEED FOR A GOOD REPUTATION

In the 1930s McGraw-Hill business magazines first produced perhaps the most successful ever and certainly the longest-running business-to-business advertisement, shown as Figure 11.1. Its point is obvious: a buyer commits not only the company's money, but also his own reputation and career. Even

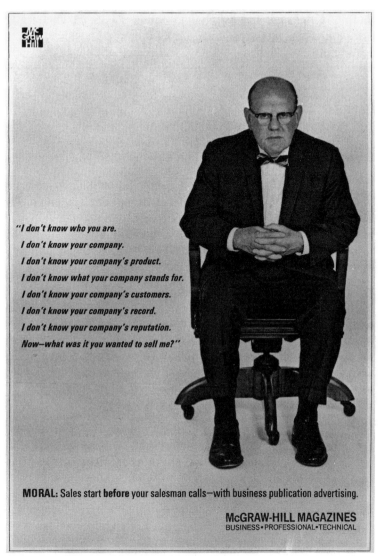

Fig. 11.1   The need for a good reputation
Source: McGraw Hill

if 'the deal' is good in terms of price, quantity and specification, a buyer has always needed reassurance about the supplier. How do they stand on fair dealing, financial stability, reliability for delivery and so on? Today's buyer also has a range of new items to check. Will the buyer be held responsible if his company runs into problems by dealing with a supplier who destroys rain forests, tortures laboratory animals, launders the funds of organised crime, exploits third world workers, is located in countries with undesirable political regimes?

Worse, as will be discussed in Chapter 17, besides their customers and suppliers, most companies must be prepared for interaction with a number of groups who may never buy their products but nevertheless have the power to cause problems and to divert their attention and resources away from achieving the corporate and marketing objectives, for example:

- Euro-, national and local governments
- political pressure groups and activists
- Trades Unions
- the media and other opinion formers
- investors and financial institutions
- universities and schools
- local communities where the company is located.

Most heads of companies are nowadays highly aware from what has happened to them or to others that they are continually at risk from a range of perils: natural disasters, human errors, financial and media predators, even international terrorists. Some kinds of risk can be anticipated and minimised by security precautions, insurance, good legal and financial advisers.

But, while the rest cannot be prevented, something can (and must) be done in advance to mitigate their effects. An embittered strike, accidental pollution of a river, a corporate raid on the shares, an adverse medical report in the media on a major ingredient, even a spectacular divorce by a key employee can have sudden disagreeable effects on a company's financial rating and even on sales. Yet when the victimised company tries to put forward its own point of view it is liable to make matters worse. Efforts at such a time will be seen as special pleading and can even reinforce the accusations they are intended to rebut: 'no smoke without fire!'. Hence reputation management cannot be started after disaster has struck but has to be treated as an on-going task by opening a dialogue with both friends and potential critics in times when there is no crisis.

ICI: THE PATHFINDERS

While companies occasionally used to do what was called 'prestige advertising' to promote their shares or to fend off government interference, the first attempt to create a favourable 'corporate image' in the modern sense was made in Britain by Imperial Chemical Industries in 1969. Research had shown that although awareness of their name was high throughout the British public, ICI were thought to be remote, cold and monolithic, concerned only with the manufacture of 'chemicals' whose nature was specialised and possibly dangerous, and whose use had nothing to do with everyday life.

ICI used mass-media, particularly television, to position themselves as 'the pathfinders': an enterprising and technologically-advanced company which spent much effort on improving everyday life through (for example) medical products, fertilizers, aids to reducing pollution and exploring new sources of energy. Tracking research showed that this campaign built ICI's reputation gradually over a decade, as the company with the best reputation in Britain on many dimensions such as being a good employer, a good investment, innovative and socially responsible. Its developments have maintained this position since. ICI modify their tactics to fit market conditions and their own objectives, but have continued such a strategic corporate image campaign in most years ever since. This is over and above advertising carried out by their many operating divisions to help sell to businesses a wide range of chemical-based raw materials such as feedstocks, plastics, pharmaceuticals and agro-chemicals, and the even more substantial sums used to promote Dulux paint and ICI's other consumer goods.

Many other companies now run corporate image advertising as a matter of routine, some have even set as their campaign target: 'match ICI'.

REPUTATION MANAGEMENT

While building a good reputation can be expensive, maintaining one need not be. The benefits of advertising consistently are that if a channel of communication is opened in good times and becomes accepted by customers and others, it will also be listened to in bad. It can even be used to pre-empt controversy and to defuse problems.

For example, Houston Light and Power in the USA used their regular customer communications channels to initiate a debate on nuclear versus other forms of electric power, so that when they announced plans to build a nuclear power station in Houston there was understanding of the potential benefits to the community and no political campaign to stop it.

Just as a good product is the essential basis of profitable sales, so the best (and essential) generator of a good corporate image is good corporate behaviour (see Chapter 17). For example, high and consistent quality products, regular innovations, good value, fair dealing with customer complaints, well-qualified, trained and motivated staff, consistently executed policies for dealing with employees, customers, local communities, government and the environment. If any one of these is seriously wrong no amount of promotion of the company can put it right and might only highlight the weakness.

Unfortunately in a competitive world, doing a good job is not enough. Positive action has to be taken to reinforce the position, and to involve the staff at all levels. Indeed, it is no exaggeration that if the product to be promoted is the company itself, the 'product manager' should be the CEO, and that unless the whole staff is properly briefed and motivated to reinforce the desired image a great deal of damage can be done unwittingly.

While highly-visible advertising is likely to be needed, this is only one aspect, and a variety of communication techniques will be needed. A good logo is just the tip of the iceberg. House-styling and stationery, condition of vehicles (and their drivers), the dress and demeanour of all staff that meet the customers and public, appearances at trade fairs, sponsorships of sports, arts and local events (or their lack), all make statements to the benefit or detriment of the company as a whole.

Although a planned corporate campaign does not 'sell' anything, it will generate climates of opinion (both inside and outside the company) within which the marketing effort can be carried on for maximum effect and minimum hindrance. A good corporate reputation will in the long run pay for itself by developing 'goodwill', an asset with a cash value on the balance-sheet, and something which will carry over onto the image of all the company's products.

PRODUCT OR 'BRAND' IMAGES

Rather more visible in its effect is the reputation of the product itself with its current and potential buyers. Marketers of consumer goods take the importance of branding for granted, as a necessary condition for maintaining loyal customers and for adding values not just to the product but to the whole company. Nestlé bought Rowntree-Mackintosh at four times asset value, largely to obtain their portfolio of highly respected international brand properties; Ford of Europe bought Jaguar cars at a premium price to gain credibility in the prestige segment of the car market.

Despite the fact that there are many examples of strong brands in business-to-business fields (such as American Express, IBM, Hoechst, ICI,

JCB, Mitsubishi, Shell, Union Bank, Xerox), business marketers are often less sure of the benefits of branding.

Branding is defined as the active and consistent projection of the qualities which differentiate a product or service (or the organisation which supplies it) from its competition. Chapter 12 will explain the differences in hard cash between selling an undifferentiated 'commodity' and an added-value premium-priced brand.

Economically speaking, branding reduces the price elasticity of a product compared with that of its immediate competitors. In other words, the supplier can obtain more sales at the same price or a premium price for the same volume. In addition a strong brand can have the benefits of:

- high customer loyalty and repeat purchasing
- easier sales negotiations and less acrimonious complaints
- easier cross-selling of the product range and any new introductions
- greater resistance to new competitive products.

A good product image can be built on any combination of factors, both tangible ones arising from the product specification and its built-in service benefits and guarantees; or from intangibles such as the supplier's business practices, long-established traditionalism, user prestige, and so on. However, it is essential that the image factors chosen are desirable to the buyer, can be readily recognised, and add value to the product. It is rare if not impossible to create a favourable image of a basically undistinguished product by applying 'advertising' as if it were a cosmetic.

BRAND IMAGE RESEARCH

As in most aspects of marketing, research can help by tracking the brand image of competing products among buyers and non-buyers. This can be done on a quantitative basis, typically by an annual 'U&A', or Usage and Attitude survey. This measures, among different customer segments, attitudes to a product group and the images of the leading brands on a list of relevant dimensions and relates them to purchasing and usage habits.

Analysis of the image scores which compares the brands among their users and non-users and by heavy and light users of the product category, will show how the market positions the brands in comparison with each other, their relative strengths and weaknesses, and which image dimensions appear most important in determining buyer behaviour.

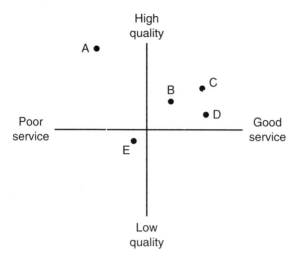

Fig. 11.2 A brand map

Interpretation is difficult because a brand image is multi-dimensional, but the typical 'brand map' can show only two at a time (as in Figure 11.2). Brand A can be seen to have a distinctive image on the two dimensions shown (although not entirely favourable), brands B, C and D are seen to be good but very similar, while E has a relatively weak or indistinct image on these dimensions.

There was once a fashion among ingenious researchers to show three dimensions at a time by sticking paper flags on sticks of different lengths into polystyrene ceiling tiles: but not much extra comprehension resulted! Computers now offer some very fancy graphics, but too much data at a time will usually confuse rather than enlighten the user.

ESTABLISHING AND COMMUNICATING THE PRODUCT IMAGE

It is important that all aspects of a product's marketing operation reinforce the chosen image. The real quality of a piece of machinery will be undermined if the instruction manual has printing errors or is hard to understand, if it is delivered in flimsy packaging from a badly-maintained company van, if the installation and maintenance is carried out by a poorly-trained, ill-mannered operative or if the customer service telephone is persistently busy.

Establishing a strong brand is an expensive and lengthy process, but once established can be economical to maintain. Media advertising is one of the best ways of building awareness and regularly and cheaply reminding buyers, potential buyers and their advisers of the distinctive features of the brand. Such 'image' advertising then acts as a backcloth against which the rest of the marketing effort can take place.

However, every part of the marketing mix must be integrated. If the advertising stresses product specification and the range of optional extras, the potential customers will only be confused if the sales presentation or the representatives at the trade fair major on the cash discounts and the low price of the basic version. If advertising has indeed built up a strong image of quality, it can be assumed that the enquirers are not in the discount market and price need not be raised until it is established what model best fits their need. Even when negotiation starts, the sale may well be more easily closed by adding extra options or guarantees than by raising doubts through eagerly discounting the list price.

PRODUCT POSITIONING

Marketing philosophy states that profit stems from satisfying a need of a customer. The more specific the need and the more precise the definition of the customer, the more unique the product design can be and hence the more certain the profit. *Positioning* is a statement of how a product best suits that customer and that need by differentiating itself from its competition. It is then possible to co-ordinate all marketing activity to reinforce the positioning.

In *Relationship Marketing* Regis McKenna states 'positioning begins with the customer . . . the market actually positions products.' He believes and gives many examples of the way that a successful positioning is a statement of the relationship of a product to its buyers. He quotes a colleague who asked the seven key people in a new 'high tech' single-product company in California 'what business are you in?'. She got seven answers, one described the company in terms of product applications, a second the high technology, a third the nature of the market-place and so on. The company had a 'good' product technically, but its actions were in conflict because there was no coherent vision of what business it was in, where it was heading or who it was trying to do business with. In other words, it had no coherent positioning.

To illustrate the power of good positioning, I would sometimes play a game at management seminars. I would read out a short list of well-known brands of consumer goods and services (as a crude example: Jaguar, *Financial Times*, American Express, Dunhill, Harrods) and ask the delegates to write down who they thought used that collection. For example: what nationality, sex, age, income bracket, occupation, family status, type of home, favourite drink, holiday destination and so on. The group members would usually come up with quite similar and surprisingly detailed portraits, even when we went on to apparently more arcane collections of brands (the secret being to use well-known names from markets where other people are likely to see or know what the user's brand is).

The point is that success in markets where a brand makes a statement about its user depends on everyone, users and non-users alike, knowing the competitive brand positionings. Any sudden and dramatic changes (even if technical 'improvements') could well undermine or even destroy the carefully-nurtured supplier–user relationships.

Yet in business-to-business if everyone in the buying company (or at least in the DMU) knows the competing brands, by supporting or opposing a choice, each will have to make a statement about what they believe their company is and their own role in it. The supplier who can say most convincingly 'we are your brand, you are our customers' has a strong advantage even over a competitor who is a bit cheaper or includes a little more active ingredient.

To quote McKenna again: he interviewed a computer engineer who had mandated the use of a certain Intel chip for his company's products. Had he evaluated it against all its competitors? 'No, we just tend to buy from Intel because we have a business relationship there, we know where they are going and we trust the company.' In fact, Intel's specifications are apparently sometimes inferior to competitors'. They have succeeded in positioning themselves as technology leaders in semiconductors through their unique processing technology and their key people who often serve as spokesmen for the whole semiconductor industry.

To recapitulate: to gain the synergy of integrated marketing activity, a product needs to be clearly positioned so that supplier and customers alike know who it is aimed at, what need it satisfies and how it is uniquely best qualified to do so. Positioning is the first stage in building up strong loyal relationships with customers. It depends not only upon a good product but also on a strong brand and corporate image. As a result, the customers will know which is 'our brand', the one whose supplier will understand our needs and look after us in time of trouble better than the competition.

All parts of the marketing mix have to be co-ordinated to the positioning and must reinforce the product image. Price and marketing communications are vital elements in doing this and will be discussed in the next two chapters.

The 'corporate image' of the company itself affects the reputation of all its products and also its financial ratings and its likelihood of becoming a target for attack by political pressure groups and the media. Image management is needed in good times as well as bad, but if successful can pay for itself by minimising the effects of disasters and in the long-run add to the investment value of the company through 'goodwill'.

12 PRICING STRATEGY

PILE IT HIGH, SELL IT CHEAP AND GO BANKRUPT!

A common myth about marketing, at least in Britain, is: 'The best way to increase sales is to cut prices – look at Tesco.' (This is a reference to a UK supermarket chain, one of the ten largest retailers in Europe, ostensibly founded on the principle of 'pile it high, sell it cheap'.) Surprisingly, this myth is believed by many business people as well as by politicians, the media and the general public. This chapter is not concerned simply to disprove it, but rather to explore the benefits of the alternative strategy to price-cutting, that of adding values to justify a policy of premium prices. It is not denied that price is an important element in the marketing mix, but it is not the only one and price should never be viewed in isolation from the others.

Many markets (both consumer and business-to-business) are dominated by one brand which acts as a price leader for its competition. Such a position is appropriate for, and can most easily be attained by, a supplier who enjoys considerable economies of large-scale production or distribution, or who has some incontestable advantage in formula, or who faces demand which is highly elastic to price.

Most other markets are more directly competitive, with several brands contesting the leadership. Such markets frequently degenerate to wars of attrition where competition tends to concentrate on price, with the result that all brands become more and more alike in product quality and pro-motional approach so that customers have less and less scope to use discrimi-nation. Eventually the whole category becomes a low-margin 'commodity market'.

The experience of many marketing practitioners is that for a supplier not endowed with the assets to become a dominant brand, a potentially more profitable strategy is one of brand-differentiation. Particularly so, where values can be added which are recognisably useful to a more discriminating segment of consumers and for which they are willing to pay a premium price ('charge high and give more').

These added values can be tangible or intangible and can relate to the core product itself, to essential related services, or to the image attached to the product, the supplier or its users. The higher the premium that can be charged the narrower the size of segment needed to generate a given profit requirement.

Identifying the characteristics of the segment and their needs for added values demands customer research and pre-testing; and to make them widely recognisable they must be consistently communicated and promoted to the target segment.

THE THEORETICAL ROLE OF PRICE

In economic theory, price is the main factor used to explain the links between supply and demand for a product. This is because the pioneer economists such as Marshall worked in the context of commodity markets and stock exchanges, where the 'product' is homogeneous, quantity supplied can readily be increased or decreased at short notice in response to changes in demand, and there are large numbers of both buyers and sellers in close contact with each other. In such cases, it is easy for buyers to seek the cheapest source available, and those suppliers whose costs of production are above that price respond by progressively withdrawing product until the market is under-supplied and prices rise. Consequently, all prices do indeed converge to levels which exactly clear the market.

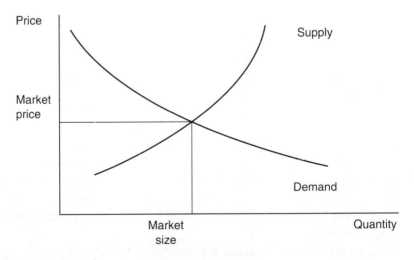

Fig. 12.1 Classical supply and demand

But, in typical business markets, buyers and sellers are separated geographically, either or both may be few in number, a lead time is needed to make substantial changes in supply, some products may be too perishable to be stored until needed, and at least some suppliers are likely to make efforts to ensure that they offer products clearly different from competitors'. The hypothesis of a single 'market price' no longer holds, and price-dominated marketing strategies are consequently risky.

PRICE CUTTING AND PRICE WARS

An inherent belief that price is the main determinant of buyer choice will lead a business to react to any sales-led crisis by 'discounting' to distributors or final customers or both. As shown in Chapter 2, unless sales respond, this compounds the disaster, in that continued low sales at the lower price will make an even smaller contribution to fixed overheads. But even if sales volume goes up, gross margins will remain squeezed and a higher total income will not be generated unless price elasticity is high (a concept to be discussed later).

Worse, the extra sales may be the result of 'pipeline-filling' by the distributors or by final customers stocking up ahead. Such increases may be only temporary, to be later compensated by a downward re-adjustment. Worse still, any significant increase in sales will come at the expense of other suppliers, and is likely to encourage retaliation by the most badly-hit competitor. This in turn usually leads to a general price war which quickly drives the weakest suppliers from the market, and leaves even the strongest on permanently reduced margins.

Such a price war of attrition can benefit only a supplier who already holds a major share of market and who also enjoys increasing economies of scale of production. Providing it has sufficient cash to survive short-term losses, such a company can use 'predatory pricing' to bankrupt the opposition leaving itself a near-monopolist. This will eventually be bad for buyers, and everyone else will be wise to avoid the war in the first place.

BUYER BEHAVIOUR AND VALUE-FOR-MONEY

In reality, as explained in Chapter 5, business buyers buy the cheaper of two items if (and only if) a whole lot of other things are equal. Much market research has concluded that most buyers make choices on complex grounds in which price is only one element. They are also concerned with the fitness for purpose, quality, availability and after-sales service of the merchandise and also with the reputation of its supplier. Firms who say they 'always buy the cheapest' usually have a 'hidden agenda' of assumptions which they take for granted about the choices available to them.

(Any reader who doubts this should consider his or her own behaviour on a non-trivial purchase such as a new pair of shoes. Would you buy the cheapest available if they were the wrong size, of poor workmanship, in a bizarre or out-of-date style, had to be collected in person from the factory, or came from a doubtful source such as a stranger on the street corner?)

In other words, people (whether buying for themselves or their business) usually want not 'cheapness' for its own sake, but *Value-For-Money*, a multi-dimensional concept. They may well seek a lower price, but take it only if satisfied about many other things. This behaviour can be summarised as an equation:

$$VFM = \frac{Quantity \times Quality}{Price} + Service + Image$$

Marketers planning to build demand through customer satisfaction therefore have the option of improving any of the five elements in the right-hand side of the equation. All are worth evaluating because price cutting may not always be the most cost-effective.

PRICE ELASTICITY AND PRICE CUTTING

The reason why price wars are so damaging is that if profits are to be maintained, a price cut must generate large sales increases. Figure 12.2 shows that for a product expecting to make a profit of 20 per cent on turnover, sales volume must increase by as much as one one-third in response to a modest 5 per cent price cut in order to maintain the same total level of profit – a tall order even in a buoyant and non-competitive market!

The underlying concept is *price elasticity*, an economist's measure of the sensitivity of a market to price. Elasticity is defined as the percentage change in sales following a one per cent price change, other things remaining equal. If sales go up by more than one per cent following a one per cent price cut, a market is said to be 'price elastic', if by less than one per cent it is 'inelastic' to price. The example quoted above from Figure 12.1 of a five per cent price cut producing a 33 per cent increase in sales implies a high elasticity of 6.7. In reality, few markets show elasticity above 2, and below 1 is most common.

Price cut	Gross profit margin			
	5%	10%	20%	30%
1%	25	11	5*	3
2%	67	25	11	7
3%	150	43	18	11
5%	–	100	33	20
10%	–	–	100	50

* On a margin of 20 per cent, sales must increase by five per cent following a price cut of one per cent to maintain the same Gross Profit. This implies a price elasticity of 5.

Figure 12.2   Price cutting: how much more must you sell to break even?

Prices in established markets are set by what the *buyers* will pay, not what it costs the sellers to produce. Analysis of costs of production will indicate to a supplier whether or not it is worthwhile competing in a given market, but 'cost plus' pricing is likely to be either uncompetitive if too high or under-exploiting the potential if not. Simple arithmetic based on Figure 12.2 will show that price cutting below what the market will bear is ineffective as either an offensive or a defensive marketing weapon.

Most businesses have an intuitive understanding of the elasticity of demand they face, which is indeed implied by any rational price strategy. For example competing with the leading brand by undercutting its price rather than adding product improvements is sensible only if the market is believed to be more responsive – 'elastic' – to price than to quality.

However, it is possible to quantify price elasticity directly, if enough hard data are available on recent competitive sales and price-changes; providing that the analysis is capable of disentangling the effects of price changes from those due to seasonality, advertising, distribution and so on. Econometrics is the most usual method, and as explained in Chapter 9, an *econometric market model* can be of great help in developing and evaluating alternative marketing strategies, for example, comparing the likely effects on sales and profits of alternative combinations of price and promotion in the light of past experience.

IS PRICE COMPETITION UNAVOIDABLE?

Some Marketing Directors may say that they realise the potential lack of profitability of heavy price competition, but cannot avoid it in practice. For example: 'I am sure my loyal customers would not be put off by an extra one or two per cent on the price of my product. But my salespeople are under constant threat of losing orders if they do not offer discounts, just so that their purchasing officer contacts can justify their role in the DMU. I would much like to improve my ROI, but not at the expense of my volume.'

THE VALUE OF PRICE RESEARCH

Is there another way? Can the mix of price and value be chosen so as to maximise simultaneously VFM to the customer and ROI for the supplier? An obvious help is market research. As pointed out above, much research has already been carried out into customer reactions to price. Among others, this has led to the conclusion that a price can be set too low as well as too high. (This is perhaps a glimpse of the obvious: which of us would eagerly respond to the offer of a solid gold watch for 50 ECU, or a Rolls Royce car for 500 ECU?)

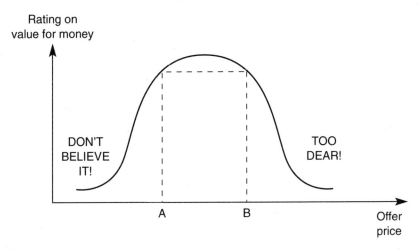

Fig. 12.3 A price/value curve

Figure 12.3 illustrates a typical price/value curve. While there must be a point which maximises value, this may be difficult to find and maintain in a dynamic market. Of greater importance is the essential bell-shape of the curve which indicates that a brand has the same degree of customer acceptance at price A as it has at price B. Assuming that both are possible from cost-plus considerations, a supplier who chooses the higher price B builds in a margin to provide for strategic product enhancements and tactical promotions to make it even more acceptable, which would be difficult at A.

Research of this kind is cheap to do, and is often thought-provoking. In some markets, price awareness is low, or even incorrect. A leading airline for years refused to quote in its advertising any fares to its long-distance destinations because management thought the sums were so large, until research showed that many of its best potential passengers knew only full-tariff prices and out-of-date ones at that, and when shown even basic promotional fares immediately revised upward their likelihood of making a trip.

In other markets, while customers are aware of prices, and even of ranges of prices, they may rank price lower than other considerations when making their final choice from a short-list chosen within a maximum budget. (For example, high-risk purchases where the penalties of making the 'wrong' choice are much larger that the benefits of getting a bargain, such as insurance, computers, machinery, safety equipment.)

Even more common are markets where there is a recognised 'Price Leader', usually the best known supplier. Buyers compare other suppliers' prices with the leader, and according to circumstances may sometimes buy something cheaper like a commodity product (perhaps when the need to be satisfied is a trivial one); and at other times may pay a bit more for something they believe will provide better quality or reassurance that they have made the right choice. We do this in our private lives when we buy supermarket gin for everyday, but a well-known brand when entertaining a customer or the boss. Or we may simply add prestige or reassurance by changing the source of supply: the 'Harrods bag' syndrome, whereby the apparent value of a conventional brand is enhanced when bought from a highly-reputable store.

The Price Leader therefore is responsible for the greatest influence on the price structure of the market: all competitors will set their prices in reference to it (at, above or below). Any brand with an inherent advantage of lower input costs or greater efficiency in production or distribution can match the leader at a lower price or in some way offer more or better at the same price. Alternatively, by pricing low, the leader can erect a 'barrier to entry' which inhibits new entrants.

CHARGE HIGH AND GIVE MORE: THE PREMIUM BRAND OFFER

Larger quantities are almost always a more profitable offer than price cuts. 10 per cent more for the same price, sounds more generous than 10 per cent discount. It also encourages buyers to stock up ahead, thereby improving suppliers' cash-flow and protecting brand-share. It will also cost less to provide unless the supplier has very low fixed overheads.

When marketing against an established leader, a temporarily convincing offer of better value for money can often be made by price-cutting or extra product. Yet while 'Extra Stock Free!' makes a powerful tactical sales promotion, its impact is likely to weaken if used so persistently that the offer price becomes the expected price. It is the thesis of this chapter that a permanently motivating and more profitable approach is to add values to the product and charge a premium price *above* the market leader – 'charge high and give more'.

How to do this will obviously differ from market to market and according to what is practicable for the suppliers. There should be many opportunities to up-grade the product specification: extra or higher-quality ingredients, a wider range of sizes, colours or flavours, a more fashionable or beautiful design, more convenient or ecologically-acceptable packaging, better or longer-lasting performance, enhanced safety or ease of use. In fact, any 'product-plus' that will be recognised by and useful to the buyer.

But value can be added to a product without changing its formula. The customer can be offered additional service, for example: guarantees (such as 'or your money back'), free or subsidised estimates, installations and repairs, round-the-clock ordering, help-lines and service calls, buy-now-pay-later terms. Anything which the buyer can interpret as 'if anything goes wrong, they will see me right'.

As was discussed in Chapter 11, it is also possible to add value by establishing a good image for the product and its supplier, which then rubs off onto the user. For example: sound business practice and probity, user prestige or connoisseurship, advanced technology or alternatively 'traditional values', even market leadership. Anything whereby the buyer will feel reassured that the choice has been the right one or that other people (not least the boss) will respect him or her for it.

Whichever single or combination of factors is chosen, the image must have three characteristics if it is to add enough value for a premium price to be charged:

1. Be recognisable to its users (and preferably to others as well)
2. Be useful in some way, tangible or intangible
3. Be known about by users and non-users alike.

If any of these is missing, it must be added or the buyers will not pay a premium. The first two can be achieved by customer testing at the product development stage, and limited trial ahead of launch. The third needs brand advertising, and possibly also corporate advertising for its supplier.

EXAMPLES OF ADDED VALUE STRATEGIES

There are many well-known examples of highly-successful premium-priced brands which have added values in a variety of ways. Rolls Royce aero-engines do it by borrowing the prestige and rarity of their cars; the *Financial Times* newspaper by high authority with its readership which is limited to business and finance; American Express by offering a range of services designed to help business travellers which are reinforced by consistent worldwide promotion.

It is significant that none of these suppliers is volume leader in its market, in which there are also plenty of operators with 'low-price, minimum-quality' strategies. These are not direct competitors, and act as further proof for discerning buyers of the necessity to pay the premium price.

Indeed, one of the hallmarks of success is the thorough integration of the product with all aspects of its presentation to the customer. The premium price acts as part of the evidence for the superiority of the product, which would tend to be undermined by price promotion.

By contrast, an established premium brand has to be continually vigilant to maintain its reputation. If the supplier economises on the added values, allows others match the advantage, or even undergoes some external disaster, the premium that buyers will be prepared to pay can disappear almost overnight, and may be very expensive to re-establish.

ADDING VALUE IN BUSINESS-TO-BUSINESS MARKETS

Those who sell to businesses have even more scope for charging premium prices than do those who sell to domestic households. Firstly, sales are usually made directly with the user without a distributor acting as a cut-out.

Secondly, the number of significant customers is small. Thirdly, demand is relatively heterogeneous, and the needs of most customers differ from each other.

In other words, it is often practicable to treat each major sale as a separate case, and the scope for tailoring the offer to individual needs is much greater than in mass-marketing. Extra value for money compared with the competition can be created not by cutting price but by making individual improvements in specification or terms of trade, and offering guarantees and services free (or even at modest additional charge).

Orders can often be customised in formula or packaging in exchange for a minimum quantity. Deliveries can be tailored by time, place and quantity to whatever the customer can use most efficiently. Extra services can be offered such as on-site surveys, installation, staff training, trouble-shooting, insurance, help-lines and up-dates. These might be supplied free if the competition charges for them, or at nominal charge if they do not. For example, suppliers of computer hardware now expect to include free software which will be familiar to the users and compatible with their existing equipment.

The terms of trade themselves can be negotiated in ways that avoid direct discounts. The needs of both supplier and customer might be better satisfied or values added to the deal by payment in instalments, by a lump sum in advance, in a different currency, by a contra-deal in kind and so on. For example, airlines and newspapers have been known to make no-cash exchanges of tickets for advertising space. This is highly profitable because the marginal costs of supply are nearly zero in each case.

CONCLUSION: THE BENIGN AND VICIOUS SPIRALS

The results of the strategic choice between cutting prices and adding values are most easily summarised by Figure 12.4, which shows that the rewards of success for a premium brand are substantial and progressive. Once it has been established in a niche above the main part of the market, yet more values can often be added and premiums increased to the point where it will be difficult for any other brand to match them convincingly. This simultaneously provides greater satisfaction for the customers and higher security and profit of the supplier.

The penalties for those who rely solely on price-cutting are also progressive, leading to the treadmill of commodity marketing and in terminal cases to bankruptcy. The great guru Theodore Levitt said: 'There is no such

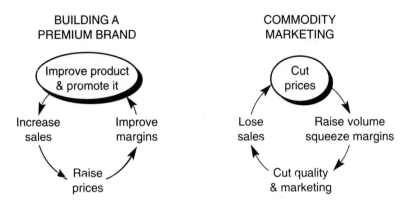

Fig. 12.4 The benign and vicious spirals

thing as a commodity – or, at least from a competitive point of view, there need not be.' (*Harvard Business Review* January–February 1980).

To recapitulate: 'pile it high, sell it cheap' has its place as a business strategy but will generate profits in only specialised circumstances. While most business markets still contain a segment of customers who insist on the lowest-priced 'commodity', a more profit-orientated strategy is 'charge high and give more', leading to a positioning of giving value for money to the more discriminating buyers.

(A version of this chapter appeared in *Marketing Intelligence and Planning*, Volume 10, Number 11, 1992.)

13 COMMUNICATING WITH THE CUSTOMER: SELLING AND PROMOTION

FROM STRATEGY TO TACTICS

It would make life (let alone writing a book) much easier if everything could be put in watertight compartments. But the distinction between strategy and tactics is inevitably blurred. Businesses vary greatly in the time-scale within which changes can be implemented, so that a few light-footed companies can modify almost anything at any time; while others, because of their technology or organisation, have very long lead-times for changes in most activities.

This is one of the reasons why a small company can act entrepreneurially and recoup strategic errors by making huge tactical changes in direction like a fairground dodgem car. A large market leader, such as a multi-national (even if 'regionaliscd'), moves more like a supertanker and therefore has to get its strategy right, because if its course has not been plotted a long way ahead, it will not be able to initiate any change in direction soon enough even when approaching obvious danger. Big companies often appear unable to react to trouble until it is too late, especially if the difficulty is a gradual change in the market environment.

A good example is General Motors who lost a major part of their market share in USA to Japanese imports before taking the steps to restructure their product range and its methods of production which a smaller company would have initiated years before. IBM failed to diversify away from the mainframe computers where it had dominated the market until long after a number of small entrepreneurs had established themselves in personal computers and work stations.

It is tempting to define tactics as activities where a major change can be implemented within a financial year; thereby, for example, classifying a new advertising campaign as a tactical decision, and diversifying into a new product field as a strategic one. However, most strategic decisions have profound effects on the range of tactics that are available for implementation. If the strategy requires advertising to build a specific corporate image in the long run, then the *campaign strategy* ought not to be changed for tactical reasons, only the choice of individual advertisements chosen to present the image to the customers in a particular year. Local conditions may also exert a strategic influence, for example in order to get good representation in some third-world countries, a supplier has to tie down a local agent with a long-term contract which specifies most of the required selling and promotional activity.

---

1. THE OFFER
   Product specification
   Name, packaging, sizing, design
   Price, terms of business
   Customer services
   Corporate reputation, product image

2. DISTRIBUTION AND SELLING
   Distribution, delivery, availability
   Intermediaries
   Direct personal selling

3. MARKETING COMMUNICATIONS
   Media advertising
   Direct response, database marketing
   Public relations
   Trade fairs
   Print, video
   Sales promotion
   Commercial sponsorship

Figure 13.1 From strategy to tactics: the marketing mix

In theory, all the elements of the marketing mix shown in Figure 13.1 are tactics available for implementing a marketing strategy, but in practice most 'product offers' have to remain unchanged for long periods. Indeed, for a successful product with loyal buyers, changes in such matters as formula, name, terms of business, after-sales service, channels of distribution and image are made at the supplier's peril.

All modifications to an established product, even believed 'improvements', must be assumed to be risky. They should proceed only after detailed customer research and live market testing to make sure the market appreciates the improvement. What may bring in one or two new prospects may put off far more of the most regular buyers through its unfamiliarity. Consumer marketing has many sad case histories of successful 'number-two' brands destroying their business through insisting on matching the characteristics of the market leader, only to discover too late that their customers were the minority who did not like the number one and now had nowhere to go.

While the decisions whether or not to use any of the remaining items in the marketing mix, namely personal selling and all marketing communications techniques, are also largely strategic ones, their applications and approach can be changed relatively quickly in line with tactical needs. This chapter will deal with the way these tactical techniques can and cannot meet objectives and the grounds on which the selling and promotional mix should be decided.

THE FIRST CHOICE: PERSONAL CONTACT

From the beginning, this book has reiterated that marketing is about mutually satisfactory relationships between a supplier of goods and services and its customers, and that in the case of business-to-business marketing the relationships are interactive personal ones between the staffs of the supplier and the customers.

This is possible only because the base of actual and potential customers is usually small, and only a few people are involved in each customer's DMU. The exceptions are markets in which the product can be bought by almost any business – such as stationery, insurance, parcel delivery – where suppliers may have to rely on 'consumer' mass-marketing techniques for all but their biggest customers, particularly the use of intermediaries for distribution and mass-media advertising for direct communication with customers.

The spearhead marketing technique is therefore personal contact, or 'selling' in traditional jargon. In the great majority of business markets negotiating a deal and closing the sale can only be done face-to-face, and such activity is often initiated by the buyer's representative calling in person for proposals or tenders from a short-list of potential suppliers.

Traditional sales-forces therefore pioneered sales by 'cold-canvassing', and once successful called regularly on the buying departments of existing customers to build up good relations as a preliminary to repeat sales. As knowledge of the structure and needs of individual customers grew, such activities were often reinforced by technical sales forces who liaised with known specifiers and provided after-sales service for the users should any technical problems arise; or in the case of the largest buyers by 'key account managers' whose task was to get behind the buying department and to pin down the authorisers at senior management level.

The results of this fully-personalised approach can be very good: the problems lie in the ever-increasing costs per personal call and in the large number of calls made in between sales which do not appear to be income-generating, and which keep the sales staff away from pioneering more new business. Some much-quoted figures from McGraw-Hill suggest an average of six calls per sale, at a total cost of $4,000 or 3,300 ECU at 1986 prices, which by the mid-1990s will be at least half as much again. This burns up a high percentage of gross margin on small orders.

Country	Cost per call $	Average number of calls per sale	Cost per sale $
Denmark	1,440	5.0	7,200
Switzerland	920	6.3	5,800
Italy	809	6.8	5,500
Sweden	710	6.5	4,620
France	772	5.4	4,170
Belgium	687	6.0	4,120
Germany	678	5.9	4,050
Netherlands	639	5.9	3,770
U.K.	303	6.4	1,940
Ireland	128	5.5	700
AVERAGE	640	6.0	3,840

Figure 13.2 Cost of a business-to-business sales call
Source: McGraw Hill, 1986

There seems no question that inter-personal contact must remain the central technique of business-to-business marketing. In particular, any supplier who values customer loyalty must reassure regular buyers that they can at all times expect a quick response from someone both qualified and authorised to deal with their question or problem, and who will usually be someone they already know. (Sales management should also reassure themselves regularly that this promise is fulfilled!) It is possible that maintaining a good 're-active' customer service when the customer needs it is more important for growth of turnover and profit than unwelcome 'pro-active' visits to encourage new sales. Certainly, as pointed out earlier, keeping existing customers happy is a more cost-effective use of resources than pioneering new business, even if it is less well regarded in many companies.

Whatever their purpose, human resources are costly and their time is by definition limited. If a substantial proportion of the time of a 'customer-contact-and-service' force has to be set aside to service key customers and stand by to deal with incoming enquiries how can the pro-active selling needs be covered?

IMPROVING THE EFFICIENCY OF SALES CALLS

The solution obviously lies in eliminating the calls which have the least effect on actual sales, and maximising the effectiveness of the rest. Concentrating the calls where they most matter is a task for sales management, firstly, by identifying from analysis which are the most worthwhile customers (as opposed to the easiest to contact or the most pleasant to visit!) and by anticipating the times when their decisions are being taken and suppliers' input is likely to have the greatest effect.

Secondly, by encouraging field staff to use faster and cheaper means, such as fax, telephone and mail, for minor or routine contact.

Thirdly, by providing from head office adequate back-up facilities to minimise clerical work, so that the field staff can concentrate as much of their time as possible on the customers, for example, by employing a team specifically building schedules of calls, setting up appointments and making travel arrangements. Fourthly, by setting up a telesales operation to handle routine repeat orders and preliminary canvassing for new business.

Fifthly, by the supply of portable terminals to field staff for use on-line from home or hotel to deliver the latest information about customers interactively from the sales database ahead of a call; and also in the customer's office to check such facts as product availability, delivery times, special terms and credit limits. When the customer is willing to close the sale, the order can be put in directly to the system and printed confirmation of terms and delivery issued to the buyer in real time. Faxes and electronic mail can keep a field worker in constant touch with head office even when in a non-compatible time zone. The paperwork on which the old-time salesman spent his evenings should have been totally eliminated by information technology.

Sixthly, by the use of techniques whereby the sales-force can build goodwill and make new contacts efficiently away from the customers' offices through the planned use of trade fairs, conferences, in-house visits, technical seminars and pure entertainment opportunities provided by well-chosen sponsorships of sports and arts. The sales-force can in this way be given overt backing by their senior management, which may or may not impress the customers, but usually adds greatly to staff morale!

Even though not much hard business can (or should) be done on these sponsored occasions, one large-scale and high-profile event can substitute for a great deal of later individual entertainment; and the resulting contact with other and more loyal customers can help reassure the doubtful. For example, Trafalgar House, a British group, found it economical to sponsor a horse race meeting and invite all its key customers in one go for an all-expenses-paid day out. It has been a great success from the outset, but has also created a problem because the event now has to be repeated every year, and any customer not invited is mortally offended!

Business entertainment has to be seen as a necessity, and must be pitched at the right level. Being over-lavish wastes profit, and the appearance of bribery must be avoided at all costs, yet doing too little or appearing mean can adversely affect reputation and eventually sales income.

LOW-COST NON-PERSONAL CONTACT THROUGH MARCOMS

Reducing the number of occasions on which a supplier's field force make sales calls on each customer, even if the calls still continue on key people at key times, creates a risk of lost goodwill through 'out of sight out of mind'. At a minimum there will be loss of interaction and a better chance for the competition to get a foot in the door. This can be countered by substituting cheaper but more flexible, and if possible, more appropriate forms of communication, namely by harnessing the techniques of *marketing communications* (marcoms) which can reach the buyer's whole DMU, cost far less per contact and are well suited to take over certain parts of the task of the traditional sales-force.

Two such sub-tasks are the supply of hard factual information, and the generation of favourable attitudes to the company. Both of these can be done effectively by the use of marcoms, with the added benefit that they can be targeted at those members of the customer DMUs which the field sales-force find most difficult or inconvenient to contact and also at potential new customers which are not yet called upon at all.

Marcoms should be looked on less as a substitute for personal contact than as a back-up system which maximises the cost-effectiveness of each call by pre-selling and following up.

As common and obvious examples, a sales visit can be preceded by a letter reminding the customer of the date and purpose of the call, and suggesting tactfully that mutual time will be saved if certain facts such as current rate of usage are on hand. Hard information on product specification or performance can be included for prior evaluation by the contact's experts. The visit can be followed up by a telephone call of thanks and written confirmation of what was agreed. If a sale was made, this creates the opportunity of follow-up offers that might increase it; and, even if not, another approach can be tried. A background campaign of corporate advertising will help to smooth the sales negotiation, particularly if (as was suggested in Chapter 10) an order to a well-known and respected supplier obtains authorisation more easily from the contact's top management.

THE CHOICE OF MARCOM TECHNIQUE

The final choice of technique should depend on who the target customers are and what the communications task is. Too often the decision is taken on quite different grounds (to give real life examples): 'we are using public relations because the agency quoted us a very low retainer' (but perhaps has in consequence to provide a low-level or inappropriate service?); 'we must have a stand at all the trade fairs because our competitor will be there' (who possibly has a different marketing objective or might even have got it wrong?); 'we are sponsoring kayak racing because the CEO's son knows a lot about it and can make sure we get a good deal' (certainly it is inadvisable to put money into a minority sport without inside knowledge, but is this one relevant to the target audience and the marketing objectives?).

Choosing the communications mix starts at the marketing audit stage (see Chapter 10). Within that there should be carried out a *communications audit* of all external channels which have been used in the past to contact target groups and which records materials, content, styles, frequency and cost.

Regular tracking research (see Chapter 14) will provide awareness and image data among target customers. As far as is possible, competitive activity should be monitored on the same basis.

Such an audit will show where the set communications objectives have and have not been achieved, strengths and weaknesses compared with main competitors, which of the techniques used have been effective or a waste of money, where the intended messages have been received and accepted and where there has been confusion and misunderstanding. From this a short-list of relevant (and perhaps even proven) techniques can be drawn up. A useful planning aid is a grid listing the messages to be communicated and the targets to which they should be addressed.

Figure 13.3 is such a grid, but should be read as an example, not as a general recommendation of possible target audiences, communications tasks or the most suitable marcoms techniques!

Target market	Communications task	Technique
Customers		
– existing	create loyalty cross-sell	direct mail, telesales
– potential	attract leads new business	advertising, PR, direct mail, telesales
Agents, distributors	maintain customer contact	advertising, PR, sponsorship
Influencers	put company case corporate image	advertising, PR
Suppliers	tie-in	direct mail, sponsorship
Employees	brief on company objectives, reinforce loyalty	newsletters, meetings, sponsorship

Figure 13.3   Markets, tasks and marcoms techniques

Unlike consumer marketing where a company may well spend a very high proportion of its communications budget on a single technique, such as television advertising, most business-to-business marketing problems need a *combination* of techniques to solve them cost effectively and a trade-off between alternative choices will usually be necessary. Criteria for judging include the budget available (see Chapter 15), the expected market environment and competitive climate, the apparent effects of past activity, the likely overlap between techniques and their relative suitability for the creative approach to be used. For example, if the best selling points of a machine are its effectiveness or ease of use, then relatively expensive film, video, personal demonstrations and trade fairs will have higher priority over more economical print. If the advantages relate to good maintenance service or low installation cost the case may be put effectively and cheaply through direct mail and media advertising.

Such decisions are specialised tasks, and most companies will need input from professionals on such matters as the cost and availability of different media, and advice on creative approaches. If possible this should be gathered from an agency which does not have a vested interest in any one technique (see Chapter 16).

PROBLEMS ABOUT CHOOSING TECHNIQUES

Each market, and each supplier in it, presents a different problem, and there can be no general recommendations. However, there are a few common misunderstandings. For example, funds are always limited, and a common mistake is to try to do too much and fragment the effort among too many techniques. It is far better to limit the tasks to the most important or a few which can be tackled properly: a visibly effective activity aimed directly against one objective will often have a 'halo effect' over some of the others. Often more than one technique or medium might be used to achieve an objective, but, rather than splitting the budget, it will always be better value to put all the money behind the one which is believed to be most cost-effective.

Another common error is to plan each activity in isolation. Intentionally or not, customers are likely to be exposed to more than one activity and can be confused and even put off if they receive conflicting messages. The minimum common element in all marcoms is the corporate image of the originator, and all supplying agencies must be properly briefed and supervised to make sure they adhere to corporate guidelines.

Suppose you choose your usual airline because its advertising has convinced you that it is very efficient with superior maintenance schedules and a high safety record, and then you find in your destination country that instead of being a 'high tech' airline it is positioned as a 'high touch' one, stressing the attentiveness of the cabin crew and the luxury of its pre-flight service. How will you then view its image and the credibility of its future communications?

A further common problem is to choose a communications technique because it has a low minimum cost irrespective of whether it delivers what you want. This is a bit like buying a cheap rail ticket from your office in Brussels to Amsterdam because you cannot afford the airfare to Rome. You will have spent time and your travel budget, yet ended up further from your real destination than ever. It is surely better to postpone the journey until you have the fare, or to look for a cheaper means to do at least part of your business in Rome, such as sending a letter?

For example, some companies put all their communications money into sports sponsorship to achieve 'cheap media exposure'. Certainly the name is seen on television and in press photographs, there may even be image spin-off by association with something rugged, fashionable, high-tech, traditional or whatever. But at any international sports event a viewer will see, among a few familiar brands, rows of unknown names round the edge of the stands. Are they banks, beers, computers? To have any commercial value, high awareness of the name and a desirable image should have been established earlier, usually by media advertising. And even then the audience to the sponsored medium has to contain a sensible proportion of potential customers or the exposure will be wasted.

This is not to denigrate sponsorship in any way. There are many case histories of its intelligent use giving sponsors large and cost-effective benefits. For example, the pioneers of sponsored sport such as Gillette and the oil and motor car manufacturers who have long used carefully selected sponsorships as a *supporting* technique to their media advertising. If Ford win a rally sponsored by Shell, both will exploit the news value for all it is worth in advertising, public relations and point-of-sale activity.

I live in a rural area with narrow roads and am frequently forced to follow commercial vehicles displaying a message such as 'XYZ for quality and service. Telephone 012 345 6789'. Clearly XYZ optimistically believe all who see their vans know who they are. I might well be a potential customer for XYZ, but since I have no idea what they do, I never write down the number or remember the name.

Every marcom technique has a different audience, works in a different way and will be more appropriate for some purposes and less so for others. When properly used, the more expensive usually deliver more effect than the cheaper ones (if not, nobody would buy into them!). Some such as media advertising and direct mail are highly controllable, so that the advertiser knows in advance exactly what will appear and when, to whom it will be exposed and how much it will cost. By contrast, many of the techniques of sales promotion and public relations cannot be guaranteed so precisely (even though they may on occasion deliver more for less money). A combination of more controlled and more flexible but risky techniques usually delivers a better end result than a single activity on its own.

INTERACTIVE DATABASE MARKETING

As a pointer to new opportunities, the increasing awareness of the need for 'relationship marketing' in the business community is being matched by the development of computerised 'database marketing'. In future, the use of marcoms will become more precise in keeping track of customers and prospects and in building a dialogue with them. Computer-created direct mail and controlled-circulation specialist media will enable commercial messages to be tailored to the individual characteristics of the recipient and be delivered with less and less wastage. Naturally the cost per message is likely to be high, but it will be delivered at a much higher cost-efficiency than the relatively broad-scale techniques of the past.

Yet further ahead, the development of specialised data-networks and the growth of user-friendly videotex terminals in business (as discussed in Chapter 8) will permit the customers to request the specific information they need: in effect each designing his or her own personalised catalogue or specification sheet on-line from the supplier of their choice. The technology for this has been available since the early 1980s, and is already in extensive use within limited markets such as the travel trade and international finance where the instant availability of accurate information in real-time has a large cash value.

If each customer had a personal computer including a modem and a compact disc reader, a supplier could provide a complete catalogue on CD, which included not only the usual technical data but also audio-visual demonstrations, user testimonials and interactive questionnaires which answer most buyers' queries. Members of the customer's DMU could in their own time and in private browse through the information, and if necessary check on-line with the supplier about prices, delivery and deals, and then either actually place an order on line or book an appointment for a personal visit. For large and regular customers, it may be worth the supplier providing this equipment.

To recapitulate: the essence of business marketing is to form mutually satisfactory interactive relationships between the staffs of suppliers and customers. As a tactic for achieving this, there is nothing better than regular personal contact with all members of each customer's DMU. But profitability demands that the costs are limited by concentrating increasingly expensive personal calls where they can have most effect.

This means first developing good in-house sales-force back-up and customer support services and using marcoms to pre-sell and follow up each customer call. Secondly, marcoms can be used as a background to generate a favourable corporate image which will improve the effectiveness of all marketing activity and also in a more tightly targeted way to deliver specific information to those who specifically need it.

Choice of marcom techniques is a specialised task whereby the marketer and specialist advisers review the alternative techniques against the specified target customers, the marketing objectives and the communications budget. In almost every case a mix of several techniques will be appropriate, provided this can be done without fragmenting the effort over too many different tasks.

14 EVALUATION: MARKETING IS JUST AN EXPENSE UNLESS IT SELLS

THE MARKETING BUDGET: AN INVESTMENT OR AN EXPENSE?

In earlier chapters we have noted that the rules of the accounting profession have resulted in classifying advertising and much other marketing expenditure among the 'expenses', the items which have to be written off within the financial year in which they are incurred. Yet one of the most common objectives of such activity is the long-term building and reinforcement of the reputation of companies and the 'brand images' of their products. It is only recently that such benefits have been treated as assets in balance sheets, after it had been found that corporate raiders were able to take over companies owning household-name brands at prices which reflected only the value of their physical assets, thereby obtaining the value of years of marketing expenditure almost free of charge. More recent practice admits that intangible assets (which were traditionally labelled 'goodwill' and written off as fast as possible) ought to be capitalised in order to value correctly a company and its profitability.

It is part of the thesis of this book that any marketing activity is indeed an expense and a luxury unless it generates a profit, and should therefore be planned and assessed in exactly the same way as any other business expenditure. To the extent that the effects of such activity extend into the long term, the cost should be judged as an investment in the same way as capital expenditure on other assets such as vehicles or raw materials which depreciate but are in use beyond the financial year in which they are bought. This chapter discusses ways in which such assessments can be made.

One of the well-known maxims of marketing was first coined in the 1930s: 'I know that at least half of my advertising money is being wasted, but I do not know which half'. While it has long been accepted that advertising 'works' (or it would have died out!), the lack of reliable methods of assessing its sales effectiveness has been used as an excuse for taking its value on trust, leading to a great deal of imprecise planning by advertisers and wishful thinking by their agencies.

This is no longer permissible because of the development of market research techniques to assess advertisements and of cheap multivariate analysis to relate sales to marketing variables. There is now a great deal of information available about how advertising (and to a lesser extent other marketing activity) works in practice. As mentioned in other chapters, many case histories, at least from consumer fields, have been published in the admirable *Advertising Works* series, and the most recent volumes include examples from business-to-business. While such information cannot be transferred wholesale out of consumer markets, there is no reason why the business community should insist on inventing the wheel.

One such finding is that much advertising appears to spread its effects over quite considerable periods of time. The analogy is made of a bath containing water which is fed in by a tap and leaks out through a drain. The pressure exerted by the water at any moment relates to its depth (or the volume of water in the bath) rather than the amount then flowing in from the tap. When more water enters through the tap than leaves through the drain the water level and hence the pressure will gradually rise. If the tap is turned off the pressure will gradually fall. By setting the tap to match the drain, a given pressure of water can be constantly maintained.

Similarly the current effects of an advertising campaign are believed to relate not so much to current expenditure but to an accumulated and discounted sum of past advertising. This has led to a concept called 'adstock', rather like 'goodwill', which has helped to disentangle the effects of advertising from other marketing variables. It explains why it is that when a product is first launched the full effects of its advertising take time to build up, yet when the advertising ceases these effects may linger on. It is expensive to build up a high-pressure adstock quickly, but maintaining it from year to year is cheaper.

This is why most advertising agencies recommend their clients spend smaller amounts of money regularly every year rather than a large sum in one year and then waiting until sales increases justify a further large burst. The evidence is at present patchy, but it is likely that other forms of marketing communications such as public relations and sponsorship work over the long term in the same way.

It should not be controversial to say that the visible effect of any marketing campaign (advertising, below-the-line or combination) is the product of three factors:

1. How much money is spent (i.e. the size of the *budget*)
2. How efficiently the expenditure is targeted (i.e., choice of *technique* and *media* which provide the most impact on the target with the minimum of wastage)
3. How motivating is the message which is delivered (i.e., the *creativity* of the material used).

While general evaluation systems may permit the measurement of the overall effects of a campaign, they will not be able to evaluate the separate contribution of these three (largely) independent factors. To make improvements, each must be evaluated individually and different means used to diagnose their weaknesses. This does not mean that they should also be *planned* in isolation, and indeed, as discussed in Chapter 13, both the size of budget and the creative task can have a great deal of influence on the technique and media chosen.

For example, if an advertising campaign shows no apparent effect it may be because its creative content delivered the wrong message to the target audience, or because it was delivered to the wrong people, or because the right message was received by the right people but not often enough to persuade them to take action. An effective evaluation system must be capable of distinguishing between these three cases.

THE IMPORTANCE OF ACTION STANDARDS

The starting point for all evaluation is a clear understanding from the outset of what is needed to be achieved. If *any* positive effect is deemed to be satisfactory, then almost any activity can be shown to be effective. To be capable of proper evaluation, objectives have to be specific to the activity and preferably unique (as discussed in Chapter 13, there is rarely sufficient money to justify using two methods of achieving the same result). And for quantified evaluation, objectives have also to be quantified.

Each type of marketing activity therefore has to be set *quantified action standards* for success: what it should achieve, by how much, where and when. It is not usually realistic to expect optimum effects as the goal posts move too frequently in real life, and a more useful and widely applicable benchmark is 'last year'. Any company which continuously beats its own norms will eventually lead the field, even if it started a long way behind its competition.

Each activity will have different objectives, and therefore will need different evaluation systems. The action standards will indicate what has to be monitored. For example:

'We need x new sales leads per month (or y per cent more than last year)'

'We want buyers of our main competitor to be made aware that our specification is better than theirs on these three points.'

'We want to raise the order-to-call ratio on telephone canvassing by 10 per cent'

'We want 60 per cent of known specifiers of widgets to attend one of our technical seminars by end-December'

'We want our new product launch to be the lead story in these trade magazines with at least one follow-up per month between them'.

MONITORING

Some of the necessary measurements will be internal to the company, such as the logs of the telephone sales team, and back data may be available for past years. If so there will be the added benefit of identifying trends so that the effects of any changes in marketing activity will show up more quickly. It may be necessary to check the recording systems so that the information is fully and correctly input in a form which facilitates analysis (see Chapter 8).

Other measurements will relate to the outside world, such as customers' knowledge, attitudes and behaviour. To monitor changes here will almost invariably demand market research, particularly interviews with valid samples of members of the DMU in target companies. Baselines for comparison have to be established before the beginning of each year's activity, but tracking studies can then be repeated annually (or more frequently) to build up trends, thereby increasing each year the significance and value of the data collected.

Since the required response is quantitative, this must be done by quantitative research, and through professional market researchers as the biases caused by company staff in effect checking on themselves will be unacceptable. This may be expensive but can be justified if as a result the cost-effectiveness of the marketing budget is increased year by year.

PITFALLS AND MAGIC TECHNIQUES

There is one major pitfall in evaluation. Every marketing campaign will have different objectives and therefore need different evaluation techniques. Worse, because some objectives are expensive or difficult to monitor, there is a temptation to be switch-sold to something cheaper particularly if it is of general application. Indeed every so often some research guru appears with a 'magic technique' whereby good advertising can be distinguished from bad by a single measure, irrespective of its purpose, medium or approach.

One such popular measure of so-called 'advertising research' back in the 1950s and '60s was 'memorability'. Researchers found it easy to ask people such questions as 'Have you seen any advertising for beer recently? What brand was it and what did it say?' Companies who should have known better spent hours poring over their own and competitors, recall scores. Their agencies did not mind much because they knew it was easy to get high recall by using simple slogans and images with wide appeal such as children or animals. It was certainly easier than the communication of complex messages! After conducting and analysing dozens of such studies I was able to show my clients that much of the total recall of their advertising came from a minority of people who had good memories, while most people could play back only one or two brands or frequently none at all. While the advertising for most leading brands had higher recall than for minor brands, changes in recall scores bore no consistent relation to changes in brand usage or any other measure of sales effectiveness.

Researchers later showed from other more complicated measures of effectiveness, such as brand images, that most people attributed to their usual brand the same characteristics which had been stressed in the advertising they professed never to have seen. (As the old lady said in the London pub: 'I have never seen any advertising for Guinness, I drink it because it is good for me' – thereby repeating the slogan from 40 years of Guinness advertising in Britain!).

Consumer advertisers have now largely abandoned memorability of the content of advertising as a measure of effectiveness, although it is surprising that some business-to-business advertisers, their researchers and agencies appear not to be aware of this. Certainly where it is thought necessary to implant a name or slogan into buyers' minds a test of memorability will be appropriate for evaluation: but it must be recognised to have no necessary connection with sales.

ASSESSMENT OF RESULTS

Once reliable data have been collected, the main problem of interpretation will lie in the fact that sales and profits depend on the combined effects of all the activities of the company, and it is not easy to disentangle the contribution made by marketing from that of the product specification and its services, price and distribution, from competitive activity and from the many outside influences such as economic trends which were discussed in Chapter 5.

The monitors for specific activities will be helpful in determining which appeared to do a good job and which did not, with some diagnostic information on what went wrong. But any objectives set for advertising, PR, sales-force and so on have to be intermediary steps along the path to profits (such as building awareness of particular aspects of the product and favourable attitudes to the brand, or identifying and making direct contacts with prospects), all necessary but not sufficient conditions for sales. If everything hit its targets and the expected sales did not result, then at least the company will have learned that it has not been concentrating resources on the most important issues, and can plan a more profitable reallocation for next year.

At the minimum, as one of the first moves in the planning cycle, there should be a post-mortem to review objectively the results of all activities. It is important that these reviews are seen as attempts to improve understanding not to allocate blame for failures.

One of the companies for which I worked had a very efficient internal monitoring system so that comparisons of actual costs with estimates were available by department and by project on a weekly basis. Top management used these not for strategic planning but as a tactical method for controlling staff. Anyone whose costs overran even temporarily or looked as if they might do in future was hauled up and bullied by the managing director. As a result we all became experts in window-dressing our figures, and reallocated costs from the least profitable projects to the most, and the less scrupulous of us from our own responsibility to other peoples.' As a result the excellent monitoring system did nothing to increase overall cost-efficiency nor even to improve the company's collective skills in cost-estimating. We just got better at spotting errors ahead of management and spreading their effects thinly. Consequently the whole company appeared uniformly unprofitable and top management were never able to improve this by reallocating resources to the people who were doing the best job or by rejecting business which was inevitably going to be unprofitable.

A manager who never makes mistakes will almost certainly be one who has neither courage nor creativity and whose work will be safe but of low profitability. The whole point about risk management is that some of the chances will come up favourably and some unfavourably. By proper monitoring, the failures can be spotted early and their costs minimised, thereby releasing more money to exploit the successes. Managers should be encouraged to learn from their mistakes for the future rather than being forced to cover them up through fear of punishment. Certainly the accident-prone should be moved to a less risky role and must inevitably end up less well rewarded. The entrepreneurs must be allowed to make mistakes without penalty provided they are able to compensate for them by the rest of their activity.

The purpose of a monitoring system is not to *eliminate* errors but to contain them and then improve overall performance year by year. The dangers to profitability which eventually do have to be removed are those managers at all levels who learn nothing by experience (such as the apocryphal hereditary Captain of Industry with 'one year's experience repeated 20 times').

EXPERIMENTAL MARKETING AND MARKET MODELS

Monitoring individual activities as described above will give only a partial view of how sales and profits can be controlled. At present modelling is the only technique available for linking changes in the multiple inputs to a business with changes in final results. Very simple financial models can be run using spreadsheets on a manager's own PC.

Unfortunately, most of the pre-set computer modelling programs which come in financial packages (despite their apparent sophistication) take a simplistic view of how markets work, and can be dangerous if used for strategic planning. It is better to study how the market actually responds in real life. Chapter 9 described the methods, value and limitations of econometric modelling which is well-tried and probably the best generally applicable approach for doing this.

Given a suitable database, econometric modelling can indicate which variables appear to have and have not affected market sizes and market shares, and to quantify such effects. It can even indicate whether and by how much a sudden change such as a new competitive product launch or distribution strike has changed the structure. It can add a great deal more precision to the evaluation of the effects on sales of the types of marketing activity on which significant sums are spent. The financial modelling systems mentioned above then come in useful to determine what this does to profitability.

A further benefit available to companies who have built market models is to use them as a basis for designing market experiments. They can deliberately extend the natural degree of variability in marketing activity by means of small-scale 'pressure tests' of mix or weight of various techniques. This can give early warning of the activities to which the market is most and least elastic. Competitors who notice the experiments going on may attempt to cloud the issue with counter-activity, but a good model can take such spoiling tactics into account. I believe that experimental marketing will become much more widely used during the 1990s by pragmatic businesses, which will rarely be without one or more experimental test of new strategies or tactics designed to 'beat the norms' of past activity.

To recapitulate: all marketing expenditure should be treated as a luxury unless it can be demonstrated to have contributed to sales and profits. However, it is usually possible to make marketing at least as accountable as other major business expenditure (such as capital equipment, pricing or staffing).

To do this, it is necessary to set specific and quantified objectives for each type of marketing activity, and to set up relevant monitoring systems. Whether any set of results counts as success or failure can never be decided after the event except against its pre-determined goals and in comparison with previous baseline 'norms'.

The results of such monitoring must be analysed objectively, not as a basis for identifying scapegoats for failures, but rather to increase understanding of the market so that the organisation and its management may learn by experience how to improve performance consistently. 'Beating the norms' can be further encouraged by conducting small-scale market experiments evaluated by econometric models.

Most of the problems of evaluation stem from the lack of past data from the monitoring systems so that it is difficult to disentangle the many factors that affect sales. Once the systems are in, however, they will justify the trouble and expense many times over in regular improvements in the cost-effectiveness of the marketing budget.

This has been a short chapter, because it deals with one of the central themes of the whole book. Many other chapters deal with aspects of it, particularly accountability and the need for action standards against which all expenditure – marketing or otherwise – should be evaluated. The ultimate goal of an evaluation system is to change marketing expenditure from an 'expense' to an accountable asset whose long-term effects can actually be capitalised in the balance sheet.

15 MANAGING RESOURCES: MONEY AND PEOPLE

WHO IS IN CHARGE?

A Chief Executive who has read this far may wonder if this book is trying to suggest that 'marketing' is just another name for his or her job. In a small company, the answer is 'yes'; whoever runs the company is responsible for everything including generating sales income, and is therefore Director of Marketing.

But marketing is about customers, and although they are of central importance for survival and growth, a business has also to concern itself with a great number of other things. In larger businesses, where one person cannot cope with the complexities alone, the management of marketing and of other functions such as accounting and production have to be delegated. Certainly whoever runs the business must have ultimate control over the actions and funding of the marketing department and should therefore be prepared to recognise its essential role in the generation of profitable sales income. But, putting it the other way round, running the business is certainly not the responsibility of marketing management whose role (however fundamental) is subordinate to corporate policy like any other function. A company which is run by its marketing department will eventually end up in different but equally bad trouble as a company which does not have one at all.

The ultimate responsibilities of a Chief Executive (different companies use different titles) can be distilled down to two: the company's internal resources and its relations with the outside world. The most important part of the activity concerned with the outside world is dealing with customers and gaining sales income from them: in other words marketing. The internal resources are of two kinds: people and money.

It could be argued that all the resources are financial because capital and labour both end up on the balance sheet as costs, and certainly all physical assets such as plant and intangibles such as goodwill can be measured in money terms, and each employee has an accountable cost in wages, benefits expenses and overheads. But companies who look on their staff as a 'wage bill' rather than an asset tend to create industrial relations and even sales problems for themselves. A certain multinational company used to refer to its very large sales-force as 'stencils' presumably because under the technology of the time, sales management normally communicated with them by feeding their name and address templates into a machine which sent out standard stencilled letters. ('Sales are down in the North East, how many stencils do we have up there?') Surveys showed that not many of them ever worked very hard, despite knowing that those that did earned very large commissions.

So, in effect, corporate management has three tasks: Finance, Staffing and Marketing (since it is no longer politically correct to use the alliterative '3Ms of Management' – men, money and marketing). This chapter is about the relationship of these three, or how marketing should interact internally.

MONEY: THE BATTLE BETWEEN FINANCE AND SALES

Marketing management have to negotiate with top management for the funding of their operation. Hence, a perennial question at budget time is 'how much should be spent on marketing?' to be followed immediately by 'how much of that should be spent on advertising/public relations/extra sales-people?' Companies have different approaches to the problem.

The two extremes are described as 'top down' and 'bottom up'. Most companies use a mixed method, but with one or the other predominating according to their management style. In 'bottom up' budgeting, executive departments submit to top management estimates of what they believe they will need, who add them together and (as is usually necessary) scale them down, either proportionately across the board or according to some view of priority. This contrasts with 'top down' methods where top management first indicates the total sum which the budget makes available, and then the various departments compete for shares of it. Under either method the result is one political battle between departments and another between corporate financial management who wish to minimise expenses and safeguard profit and line management as a body who wish to invest to expand the business. There is no guarantee that the winner will be the department that is going to make the largest contribution to profit.

In particular, marketing tends to lose out because much of its material (such as advertising and public relations) is ephemeral and its results often long-term and difficult to check: such as improving customer attitudes, making sales calls more effective or containing a competitor's inroads. Chapter 14 recommended methods of evaluation whereby marketing expenditure can be made more accountable, thereby helping to restore the political balance.

Allocation of money to specific activities can be done in a number of ways. Figure 15.1 lists the commonest in the context of advertising, and similar lists can be made up for other marketing activities.

A. Pragmatic methods

- a pre-determined advertising-to-sales ratio (per cent of sales at ex-factory price or a fixed sum per unit or tonne)
- a 'residual' after required net profit, fixed overheads and higher priority costs have been subtracted from gross margins
- dominating, matching or otherwise relating to competitors' expected expenditures
- maintaining previous years' levels, taking into account inflation of media costs

B. Task-orientated methods

Estimating the costs of achieving tasks which advertising could be expected to carry out:

- pre-determined investment or numbers of impacts per customer
- calculated marginal revenue needed to justify a marginal increase in expenditure
- matching share of advertising expenditure to desired share of market
- matching changes in advertising to desired changes in sales volume or market share

C. Analytic or experimental methods

- simple models of the advertising process which relate advertising levels to absolute or relative changes in volume or share
- dynamic models such as econometrics which relate past changes in sales to advertising and other key variables in the market
- marketing experiments such as 'weight testing' so as to increase variations artificially and measure the effects of alternative advertising strategies

---

Figure 15.1 Methods of setting advertising budgets

Of the three approaches, *pragmatic* is the least recommendable, because it begs too many questions. Traditional norms can give a ball park figure at the beginning of planning, or could give a rough cross-check at the end to see if the results are reasonable, but they are no substitute for proper planning. How were the 'rules of thumb' derived in the first place, and have the conditions prevailing at the time changed? Why match competition if they are over-spending, and do they have the same objectives as us anyway? Last year's figure will always be either too much or too little for next year if we expect any changes at all in the market situation.

Task-orientation is always to be preferred because it permits 'zero-based' budgeting. First of all, specific tasks have to be set for marketing and given priorities. This permits management to short-list and cost alternative methods for carrying out each task; and to set goals for each method which would make the final choice cost-effective. The selected goals then become the 'action standards' for evaluation as discussed in Chapter 14.

A company which regularly uses task-orientated budgeting is able to move on to *analytic* budgeting methods which are the most effective of all. Instead of having to guess which alternative activity would best achieve the goal and find out afterwards if it was right or wrong, hard evidence from the past can be used to reduce the risks in the choice. Experiments can be built in to the plan to generate better evidence more quickly, and to reduce the number of surprises.

THE BUDGETING CYCLE

Marketing management have the best chance of getting their fair share of corporate funds if they can persuade management to adopt the sequence of Figure 15.2.

This method is an interactive one which allows both corporate and executive needs to be considered together. The starting point is for top management to set the objectives for marketing within the corporate plan. Finance then works out (on whatever methods) how much money can be allocated to achieving the objectives. Marketing then drafts a plan to spend that sum on achieving that objective (it may be necessary to call in outside specialists such as the advertising and PR agencies to recommend and cost alternative techniques).

Marketing management should then discuss the draft plan with top management (and ideally also the agencies) to decide whether it can be expected to achieve its objective. If the consensus is 'yes', then the budget is satisfactory to all and the plan can be finalised.

If not, this is usually because the objective is unrealistic or the budget too

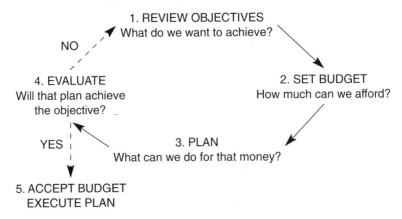

Figure 15.2   The budgeting cycle

low or both. Management negotiate amendments and repeat the cycle until a realistic objective is agreed which justifies a budget that can be expected to achieve it. Under this approach, neither objectives nor budgets can be considered final until agreed as viable by both line and staff management.

The most difficult step is the fourth: will it work? This has to be taken on the best judgment available. However, once the cycle has been used, each year provides more hard evidence on what can and cannot be achieved. This enables the company to move on to analytic and indeed experimental methods for evaluation of marketing activity which will progressively increase confidence in the whole budgeting process.

MANAGING BUDGETS

Finance Directors understandably prefer to authorise expenditure whose effects can be overseen directly (such as additional administrative or production staff) or better still for tangible assets which can be shown in the balance sheet or even sold off in emergency. For example, a fleet of new delivery vans, which can be costed in detail before purchase, and its performance subsequently logged so that it can be evaluated as 'cost-effective' if costs-per-delivery are sufficiently below last year's.

Marketing managers who learn the principles and jargon of business finance do better at budget time, because they are able to put forward their propositions in a form that looks justified in accounting terms, in particular to state clearly why the money is needed, what it will be spent on, and the return that is expected from it. Financial departments inherently prefer the visible purchase to the invisible and give priority to those which appear to save costs elsewhere or contribute to income. They are not implacably against spending money, only open-ended commitments, which marketing projects sometimes turn out to be. For example, sales promotion schemes such as games and incentives if not designed by experts.

Once any item is approved, it is usually easier to get 'last year plus' into subsequent budgets than it was to get authorisation for it in the first place. If large new schemes are sub-categorised as much as possible, each item looks more reasonable, and a concession on one can be traded against retaining another. The experienced executive always makes sure that a budget is spent or at least committed in its year because under-spent budgets tend to be cut in the year following. The unscrupulous even spend their full allocations as early in the year as possible to protect them from any mid-year axing spree as discussed in Chapter 2.

CAPITAL AND RETURN ON INVESTMENT

Chapter 1 argued among other points that 'profit' was a movable feast, that gross margins on products were less important than the speed at which they were earned, and that the two keys to financial success are Return On Investment (the terms on which the company borrowed its capital) and cash-flow, the daily lifeblood without which companies go bankrupt.

In general, a going business (even the most dubious) seems to have little difficulty in raising extra capital from one source or another, the problem being the rate of interest at which it is provided. Interest is the price of money, and as money is the most widely used raw material, it has to be considered as part of the ingredient costs for every product.

When interest rates are high during a good year, businesses are able to maintain margins by passing them on in higher prices to customers. This is inflationary, but inflation makes high interest rates tolerable at least for business because the real value of their debts is continually devalued. In the long term, governments which keep interest rates high create high inflation, as is easily demonstrated from international financial statistics.

In bad times, high interest on borrowings forces businesses to pay a higher proportion of their earnings to the providers of capital, thereby creating the same effect on company finances as the 'sales under budget syndrome' of Chapter 2. Such businesses have to retrench and if already in an insecure position may well go bankrupt.

It is therefore not only highly desirable for a business to choose to borrow its capital during years and from providers which offer historically low rates, but it should be prepared to pay a slightly higher than market rate in return for having it fixed for the length of a medium-term plan. Better still is to finance as much as possible of new capital needs out of gross income. This will reduce the amount of net profit available for dividends, but a business with a consistent growth record (which does not mean high growth in bad years, only above average!) is not expected to provide yields as high as a torpid or risky enterprise.

Marketing management should therefore try to anticipate any long-term needs for capital far enough ahead to give the company financiers plenty of notice to negotiate a good deal with the backers (a further argument for medium-term planning).

MAKING GOOD YEARS PAY FOR THE BAD

Marketing management should plan to match net profit margins to the total business environment. Even those who do not believe in the existence of a regular world business cycle will agree that some years are better than others, and that in many cases they can anticipate which are going to be which. Good years are ones where sales are easy to get at good prices. It is then important not to declare more net profit than was promised in the budget. The reward for doing so will be little more than a handshake and a round of applause at the Annual General Meeting. The penalty is higher profits tax in the current year, followed by the corporate financiers requesting an increased contribution to profits next year and raising the floor of the brand manager's profit-share scheme.

Far better is to squirrel the surplus money away for the future. For example, by increasing stocks of raw materials and work in progress but running down stocks of finished goods. Regular suppliers will be only too happy to accept and invoice for advance orders for all kinds of goods and services. Proposed capital expenditure can be undertaken early and written off more quickly. Since customers are willing to buy, this is a good time to negotiate long-term contracts with customers, and to do so on terms and prices to which they will be pleased to commit themselves. When a bad year comes they will have to cut back on their purchases from your competitors not from you.

In a bad year, by contrast, stocks of raw materials should be run down, and any advance contracts called in and converted into finished goods so that the wheels can be kept turning, the overheads spread and all orders can be supplied and invoiced immediately. Now is a good time to negotiate long-term contracts with *suppliers* who will be very conciliatory in exchange for advance guarantees, which will be very helpful when the next boom again creates shortages of raw materials.

Back in the 1960s, the Thomson Organisation ran a large fleet of delivery vans for its newspapers. These vehicles had hard wear and one third had to be replaced each year. In less profitable years the replacement vehicles were hired on a three-year contract, in good years they were bought outright, but maintained by the contractors. This had the completely legitimate effect of moving the achieved sale price of the written-off vehicles from good years to bad ones with the cash dropping straight to net profit. An imaginative accounting department should be capable of discovering other stones under which money, which is not needed immediately, can legally be held until a day of crisis.

In other words, in years that look favourable, an organisation should develop an *offensive* marketing strategy which adds volume and should not object to narrowing its margins by so doing. If it succeeds it will still make more money than the previous year anyway. In unfavourable years it should expect to consolidate its position by a *defensive* marketing strategy which holds market share at the same sales volume, or even a little lower, but at a wider margin. Net profit may be down, but if the competition are in the same situation, they will fare even worse. This will protect the company's capital because the backers will have no better haven!

CASH – EVEN BETTER THAN PROFIT!

Companies go bankrupt when they run out of cash, which should be some time after they run out of profit. This means that care of the cash-flow is as important as the development of margins, and marketing has a role here too. When it is certain that profit will be down, the priority must switch to protecting the cash-flow.

This does not mean suddenly deciding not to pay the suppliers for 90 days and sending the man with the pit-bull dogs round to the customers on day 31. This just betrays the trust and mutual relationships which marketing has expensively built up. What a company (and its suppliers and customers) wants is predictability (or less risk, as this book keeps repeating).

How about persuading suppliers, instead of the usual minimal discount for cash (which the unscrupulous take anyway, however late they pay), to give a larger credit note against the next order for early payment of this one? What about offering good customers the chance to pay in regular monthly instalments based on 90 per cent of average consumption, with adjustments only at long notice? (The cash comes in when expected and the outstanding debt is a relatively small and good one.) This should take the heat off the price negotiations, and encourage the customers to give you a higher share of their total purchases when the competition are pressing hard, and which you can probably consolidate later by offering volume overriders. As Chapter 12 suggested, terms of trade negotiated to fit the mutual needs of buyer and seller give better margins for both than low prices (particularly in those cases where the invoice is never paid!). Hard times should provide many opportunities for buyer and seller to develop loyal commercial relationships which should become even more beneficial when conditions improve.

MANAGEMENT STRUCTURES

Besides money, marketing has to negotiate with top management for staff: how many, what qualifications and experience, what pay and benefits? And when they arrive: what should they do, what structure and working conditions will get the best out of them, how to motivate the best and should the rest be trained, moved, demoted or fired?

It is an unfortunate hang-over from the days of product-orientation that many companies still give more attention to the care of the physical assets such as the plant than they do to the staff. Experience of the market, knowledge of the company and its funny ways, good relations with the customers and loyalty are valuable assets not quickly replaceable in the way that machines can be. Managers are rarely given professional training in interpersonal skills or the techniques of managing. Even 'personnel departments' are sometimes staffed by people filling in time before retirement and in extreme cases quite large companies have no one on the staff with any professional qualifications in staff management, despite the growth of protectionist employment laws.

There is a great deal to be said for the view that departmental managers should be picked for their managerial not technical skills. There is an old saying that if you promote the salesman with the best figures you gain a bad sales manager and lose a lot of business on the ground. This illustrates the 'Peter Principle': in any hierarchy, every employee tends to rise to his level of incompetence, so that in time every post tends to be occupied by an employee who is incompetent to carry out its duties. This can be defeated by building managerial training into the programme of everyone believed capable of senior status, and by rewarding the most brilliant specialists for staying in place. The top technician should sometimes earn more than his or her manager, and both should be happy about that.

MANAGEMENT STYLES

A great deal depends on the management style of the organisation. Although a case can be made out that 'marketing is different', people who think and behave (and get paid) differently are not happy in or useful to an organisation with a strong ethos. In *Mind Your Manners* (Mole, J., Nicholas Brealey, 1992), there is a useful classification of management styles on two dimensions, *systematic/organic organisation* and *individual/group leadership*, which can be summarised as follows:

a. Organisation

Systematic companies (otherwise task-orientated, formal, mechanistic) treat an organisation as a machine, designed and built to achieve a precise objective. Success depends on whether well-defined, logical job functions relate well to each other and are efficiently carried out. They require loyalty to the company above loyalty to individuals. What a manager *does* is more important than who he or she *is*.

By contrast, *Organic companies* (people-orientated, informal, social) believe they are more like living organisms, growing out of the needs and abilities of their members. Success depends on how well managers work together as people. Their functions and relationships will change depending on their views of common goals. They make no distinction between loyalty to the company and loyalty to individuals.

b. Leadership

Individual leadership systems (or autocratic, top-down, authoritarian, directive), assume that employees are intrinsically unequal. Hence decisions will be most effective if the most knowledgeable or competent are given the right to exercise power over the rest.

Group leadership systems (democratic, bottom-up, egalitarian, participative) accept inequality of ability and performance, but believe that success comes from *everyone* contributing to decisions that affect them. Leaders are designated to elicit and represent the consensus.

These dimensions are both continual, and individual companies of all types (both successful and unsuccessful) are to be found in all countries. Few will show the extreme of either dimension. But it is extremely useful to know whereabouts a company lies before attempting to sell anything to it, or indeed accepting a job there. The Mole survey even claims that just as there are meaningful national stereotypes of individuals so there are of companies, as summarised in Figure 15.3, a useful concept for companies selling internationally.

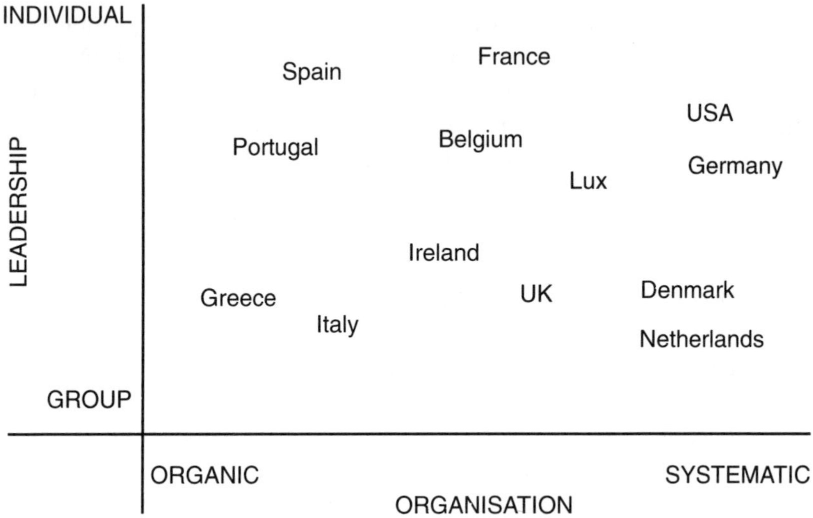

INDIVIDUAL

LEADERSHIP

Spain   France

                                        USA
Portugal   Belgium
                          Lux   Germany

              Ireland

Greece   UK   Denmark
        Italy   Netherlands

GROUP

ORGANIC   SYSTEMATIC
              ORGANISATION

Figure 15.3 Euro-management styles

Source: Mole, J., *Mind your Manners*, Managing Culture Clash in the Single European Market, Nicholas Brealey Publishing, 1992

It is in the nature of many marketing people to be 'group-organic'. They like decisions to be taken by whoever is best qualified, irrespective of job title, usually after considerable personal contact and discussion, and then implemented informally.

When the writer's staff were all in a trades union 'closed shop', I was told that my market research team had been barred from attending union meetings. This was not because they were politically suspect, indeed they were further to the Left than most of their colleagues, but the union was strongly 'individual-systematic', and the meetings were called by the leadership to tell the rank-and-file what to do. The researchers, who had degrees in social and political science, analytical minds and an anarchic instinct to argue the toss with everyone, would interrupt emotive harangues with unanswerable questions. They were permitted to pay their union dues, but expected to stay at their desks while the union spoke to the rest of the staff.

THE IDEAL MARKETING EXECUTIVE

If a group of heads of marketing were asked to list the most desirable qualities for a marketing executive, they would probably all include: experienced, hard-working, numerate, creative, analytic, realistic, 'good with people', a generalist, high technical skill, an intelligent enquiring mind, a good communicator, and (more recently) computer literacy and speaking several languages.

Naturally no paragon has all these virtues, and if one turned up no marketing director would dare hire him or her! In fact a team has to be picked which will cover the departmental needs collectively. The one with flair and creative ideas will need a numerate analyst to comprehend and summarise the problem, who will work on data supplied by the enquiring mind, and the solution will have to be implemented by someone with an eye for detail and sold to top management by the communicator!

MANAGING THE MARKETING DEPARTMENT

Complex organisation charts do not work with this varied gang, and although pay rates will vary, and everyone knows who is really their boss, it is better for day-to-day purposes to treat everyone on the same level.

What helps control are good *job descriptions*, whereby everyone has in writing to whom they are responsible, for what they are responsible, and the specific functions they must carry out. These should be taken seriously and discussed and updated regularly (perhaps at an annual review with the boss's boss). It is a good discipline if each executive drafts his or her own job description in the first instance, discusses it with the superior and both together submit the final version to the marketing director for approval.

Motivation is multi-dimensional. Money is important to the kind of people who are likely to be successful in the profit-making sector: 'the labourer is worthy of his hire'. Good, self-confident staff who feel underpaid find it easy to do better elsewhere; the rest may stay, but transfer their emotional involvement to their hobbies, and really disaffected staff try to get even: they steal the stationery, lose documents, scramble the computer files and even drop organisational banana skins on the boss's path. (When a student, I had a friend who worked during vacations as a slave-labourer in a cannery. 'We let the mice go through in the cans,' she said, 'it cost us too much in piece-rates to stop the line.')

There is a problem with matching pay to effort. During a downturn, the factory will be able to contain its wage bill by going on short-time. Marketing will be working extra hard to diagnose the problem and find a new approach. Yet (as discussed in Chapter 2) the salary bill at the end of it is likely to be frozen. If, as a result of the new marketing strategy, the following year is a good one, marketing may be able to take it relatively easy and be given a good pay rise at the end of it, as the result of work credited to other departments. This is a demotivating set of signals for a management to give any part of its work-force.

By the same token, in years of high inflation, a salary increase less than the rate of inflation is the award of a pay cut. In the 1930s when inflation was not an issue, a pay cut was the last sanction a firm imposed before firing an unsatisfactory employee. Do management or employees realise this parallel? We all of us pick up signals almost unconsciously from those in authority (parents, teachers, bosses), and act accordingly. Marketing people are trained to be quicker on the uptake than most. So inequity of treatment between management and staff for whatever reason is likely to cause demotivation, and it may well start in the marketing department. Similarly, profit-sharing schemes are good for senior staff, but for those whose work can have little direct effect on profit there is no incentive in a bonus which just fluctuates arbitrarily. The further away from policy, the more pay and benefits should relate to personal effort and less to corporate results.

Career structures are important in building loyalty with executive staff. One by-product of job descriptions is that senior staff should have designated deputies. Good marketing people feel the need to 'go walkabout' regularly, to see the product in use, the customers in person, the sales-force in action, the competition at first-hand. This should be encouraged, as an ivory-tower team who never talk to anyone except each other can never understand the customers and their needs. However, everyone must provide cover for their absences, and this gives juniors the chance to gain experience, to show their worth in decision-taking and to enhance their chances of promotion.

If vacancies are always filled from outside, then the best staff will look elsewhere when they feel ready for promotion, leaving gaps which may be hard to fill. I once knew the Chairman of a small shipping line who in his early 60s acquired a young second wife and a villa on the Algarve, and decided to retire to devote his time to them. Unfortunately, he had never given any thought to a succession and suddenly realised that his Board were all his age and the next layer down were the clerical staff. There had been no designated successors, or training for management, or even delegation of authority. All the management potentials had become bored with waiting and gone elsewhere.

When young, I left a job in a good company for a much bigger job in what turned out to be a bad company. I was too inexperienced to spot this ahead of time and had three unhappy years before escaping. It was only years afterwards that I learned that the first company had me on their 'will-go-far' list and regretted my decision: they never told *me* that and made no serious attempt to stop me leaving. Obviously it is not possible to have exactly the right person available internally when someone leaves unexpectedly, but those with a future should at least be told about it, and given the pay and conditions to encourage them to take the statement seriously.

Training needs to be planned and budgeted. Good marketing people are eager to learn more, and should be given a programme of opportunities to get better at their job. For example, the chance to meet experts and their opposite numbers in other companies in an environment where their boss is not present. Management training courses are expensive, but carefully matching course to executive can well repay the investment. Yet, as shown in Chapter 2, training is usually an early victim of cash-saving programmes. Similarly, attendance at trade fairs, conferences and seminars should not be a reward but a regular exercise in business intelligence. Only one person should go (or one and the boss if it is that kind of event) but all major events should be covered. As a regular discipline the attender should be expected to debrief to the whole department and to provide copies of relevant material.

Delegation can a problem if management are not good at it. Delegation means asking (with a smile) someone else to do a job you know you would do better and faster, and thanking them for it afterwards. Good delegators tell their subordinates what needs to be done *and why*, but do not tell them how unless they ask. All the writer's best and most respected bosses informed their staff of what was going on, and trusted us with what were often highly confidential matters. We responded accordingly, thought managerially and acted more responsibly in consequence.

On the other hand, I once worked for a company where everyone was told as little as possible on a 'need-to-know' basis. As a result, nobody dared to delegate anything in case they were blamed if it was done wrong. The MD did the directors' jobs and was worked to death, the directors did the senior executives' and were bored, the seniors did juniors' jobs and went home early or found better employers, the juniors made coffee and filed but were never ready for promotion. Consequently, the costs per hour were uncompetitive, every vacancy had to be filled by someone from outside who was more expensive and less qualified than the person who left, and the key task of planning, resourcing and guiding the company was not done by anyone. It was an unhappy and unprofitable operation which drifted from one unforeseen crisis to another.

A manager should take care that each job should be appropriate and satisfactory to the employee as well as useful to the employer. Robert Townsend, in *Up the Organisation*, reminds us that Hercules slew Augeus after he finished the labour of cleaning his stables! The job should also be permanent. As discussed in Chapter 2 companies with the reputation of firing their middle and junior management every time there is a cash-flow problem find trouble in recruiting or keeping good staff. This means that creating a new job should never be undertaken lightly. I was once hired in a boom year and fired in the subsequent recession on a 'last-in-first-out' principle, despite this possibility being raised and assurances given during my recruitment discussions. Management must have the right to hire and fire, but this implies they should overtly discuss a career structure or its lack when hiring, and have a responsibility to look after anyone who leaves the company through no fault of their own. This is prudent policy, because draconian behaviour by management is noted well and the survivors all start looking for safer employment.

It implies that a marketing department should be lean but of top quality. Numbers should be kept too low to require regular pruning, and the staff should be too good for anyone to be willing to lose any. Chapter 16 will discuss the value and use of outside marketing resources. Unless an executive task is constant and vital it is usually more efficient to sub-contract it to an outside specialist. An internal expert should be able to match tasks as they arise to suppliers with the right mix of skill, experience, quality, and price. By means of a stable of permanent agencies and a card index of specialist contractors and consultants, a small in-house team can cope with large variations in demand for a wide range of marketing services.

As discussed in Chapter 16, the key internal skill is in briefing and implementation, which demands staff with a high level of technical knowledge and wide experience. Such people come expensive, and so to keep hourly costs down each has to be supplied with less experienced back-up staff who can work under their direction, thereby becoming trained and experienced in their turn.

To recapitulate: almost any fool can make a profit in a boom year. The wise operator will not be too grasping in the short-term in order to build up goodwill and financial cushions so that in the inevitable bad years later on there will be better options than to 'eat the seed corn'. Capital is not usually as serious a problem as cash, and a medium-term marketing strategy should include methods of keeping the cash-flow from customers regular and predictable from year to year even if margin has to be conceded in return. Those who correctly anticipate the good and bad years will need to make smaller concessions than those who have to rebuild their strategy from scratch in each crisis and they will also be in a better position to exploit the subsequent upturn.

Staffing a marketing department requires the usual skills of personnel management (in which every manager should have the opportunity to get professional training) plus a few more, because of the special nature of the work and of the kind of people best qualified to do it. A typical department is a multi-disciplinary and experienced team of extroverts who, when given proper briefing and considerable freedom of action, work hard and effectively. They are liable to become demoralised, if not subversive, if subjected to the office discipline and hierarchical structures common to many organisations. In order to gain the undoubted benefits which marketing can provide, businesses have to find a *modus vivendi* with those who can best implement it.

16 USING OUTSIDE RESOURCES

BUYING MARKETING SERVICES: DOES IT HAVE TO BE LIKE MARRIAGE AND DIVORCE?

As recommmended in Chapter 15, many companies choose to delegate part of their marketing activity such as advertising and public relations to full-time outside agencies and to contract out by the project other parts such as market research and print. Others set up internal departments to carry out all such work, or employ internal specialists who sub-contract part and do part in-house. Many marketing managers are unsure which is the best thing to do, and whether the right solution should be the same for all types and sizes of business, or for every type of activity. Further, those with little direct experience of the marketing services world may not know how to set about selecting a suitable supplier, or how to get the right work from one at the right price.

The marketing business abounds with rumours of traps for the unwary, and stories of tricks played by the unscrupulous. Any discussion about hiring a new agency quickly drops into the terminology of marriage and divorce. Does it really have to be as potentially fraught and expensive? After all, few companies agonise so much about appointing or changing their supplier of raw materials, stationery or coffee for the canteen. This chapter discusses the criteria on which such decisions should be taken; and in cases where outside suppliers are appropriate, how to select and then get value for money from them.

The initiative for this book came from Primary Contact Ltd, an advertising agency, part of one of the largest worldwide marketing communications networks. They will readily admit to a vested interest in mutually successful and profitable relationships with an increasing portfolio of clients and naturally intend to use this book to serve that interest. However, it is not the purpose of this chapter (or any other) to make a sales pitch, not even a disguised one. Anyone who has gained that impression ought not to have read this far.

Through working on both sides of this fence, I became aware that of the many problems of agency–client relations, many stem from a misunderstanding of the other party's role or a lack of willingness to believe that the best route to long-term satisfaction is mutual benefit (to drop into the terminology of marriage guidance as threatened!). This chapter looks at these issues from the buyer's point of view, and any readers from the supply side will have to go elsewhere for therapy!

THE KEY QUESTIONS AND THE ALTERNATIVE SOLUTIONS

Before considering the selection of a supplier of marketing or management services, it is vital to decide whether outside or inside resources or some mix are most appropriate. There are four questions to be answered:

1. How often do we need the service: infrequently (e.g., management consultancy, market modelling, legal advice); frequently but irregularly (e.g., sales promotion, market research, trade fairs); almost constantly (e.g., print, advertising, public relations)?
2. How much money do we spend on this service each year or per occasion? Is that an important sum to our company? Would it make us important to an outside supplier?
3. How much is a good job really worth to us and what are the consequences of getting it wrong – just a nuisance? Wasted time? Lost profits? A total disaster?
4. How much knowledge and experience does our company have on this subject and could we easily increase this expertise: we are already expert; we do not know much, but could easily hire someone who does; this is way over our heads and we do not even know where to start?

Depending on the answers, one of five solutions can be adopted:

1. A complete service in-house – 'do it yourself'
2. A co-ordinating internal department or group of experts which do in-house jobs within their own capacity and capability, and select, brief, supervise, co-ordinate and interpret outside specialist suppliers where needed – 'à la carte'
3. A specialist full-time buyer/interpreter liaising with outside 'full-service' suppliers for almost everything
4. An outside consultant on retainer to act as technical adviser and inter-

preter but only when needed – 'at arm's length'
5. Buying 'ad hoc' in the open market as necessary.

Clearly, there can be no universal 'right' solution, and a company will probably need to vary its approach from one service to another. The savings and control over an in-house department have to be weighed against the flexibility of a 'black-book' of specialists to be used ad hoc and the value of a permanently-briefed but independent 'second-opinion' from an agency in partnership.

THE BENEFITS AND PERILS OF THE IN-HOUSE MARKETING OPERATION

'Do-it-yourself' is a sensible solution only for services in constant, uniform and predictable use. An in-house facility which is not kept working close to capacity is expensive to run and can even 'go rusty'. For example, most companies face patent problems only rarely, and will then consult a specialist patent agent, 'ad hoc' or perhaps via the company lawyers. A giant conglomerate carrying out large-scale R&D and frequently launching new products may well be able to justify a full-time patent expert in-house. With the development of cheap high-quality desk-top publishing facilities, an increasing number of companies are taking on board a proportion of their traditionally sub-contracted print where this lowers costs, increases flexibility or shortens lead-times.

On the other hand, even when financially justifiable, in-house service departments can have serious drawbacks. I was for a while in charge of the marketing services division of the Thomson Organisation, a large newspaper publishing group which had become widely diversified. Thomson Group Marketing Services was a combination of in-house advertising agency and generalised management and marketing consultancy employing about 100 people. It offered to all the operating divisions a wide range of advisory and executive skills, both the general and regularly used ones of advertising and economic forecasting, and the more rare and intermittently used ones such as operational research and new product planning. My senior staff were highly qualified, concerned about the opportunities and problems of the group and able to push back the frontiers of marketing expertise (at least as far as the newspaper industry was concerned). The work done was of recognisably high quality; for example, the creative group had as large a cabinet-full of international awards as any comparably-sized advertising agency, and the market research done in support of the media sales-forces was unquestioned at a time when most research published by media owners was dismissed by media planners as hopelessly biased. Where work had to be sub-contracted, our specialists knew the relevant suppliers well, and negotiated for excellent prices and quality because they were large, regular and sometimes feared buyers. Advice and internal work was free of charge and any external costs were passed on without loading.

Yet this apparent marketing paragon was widely disliked by its users and was eventually (and quite rightly) disbanded. Why? Firstly, because the Thomson Organisation headquarters defrayed its costs by a compulsory levy on its operating divisions in proportion to their turnover: as a result of which some, particularly the largest, believed they were subsidising smaller divisions who might be over-using the service as free marketing consultancy. Secondly, headquarters made it mandatory for the operating divisions to use the central service unless it could be shown that they were unable to fulfil a particular task. Thirdly, the marketing service executives had inevitably a great deal of knowledge of the whole Thomson business (sometimes more than the operating divisions did) and by reporting directly to headquarters had considerable political power. Some would on occasion use this to pressurise an operating division to undertake marketing activity which perhaps they needed but did not want, or to refuse briefs for work the service executive thought unnecessary. So the users resented the loss of choice, of full control over expenditure, and indeed of the respect (to say nothing of the entertainment) they would expect from the use of outside suppliers.

There were internal problems too. The range of 'clients' was limited, and the consequent boredom or clashes of personality could not for long be solved by reallocating the teams as an independent supplier would. Long-serving staff had solved their clients' most recurrent problems (to their own satisfaction at least) and tended to offer standardised solutions. If rejected too often, the most highly creative would take themselves and their bright new ideas away to other employment. Every attempt to provide a more flexible structure and more responsive service were foiled by having to operate under the rigid constraints of 'closed-shop' newspaper trades unionism. The end came when one division was granted special permission to hire an outside advertising agency, and the others leveraged the precedent for all it was worth. The inevitable disbandment degenerated into a preliminary skirmish of the war of attrition between British newspaper proprietors and their trades unions about the introduction of computerised publishing (which they were still quaintly calling 'new technology' some 20 years after its invention!), which ended a full decade later in bitterness and indeed violence.

To complete this history, the most far-sighted staff found other jobs early and took voluntary redundancy. The operating companies agreed to absorb some of the key staff (thereby depriving the rest of the group of their services), while the remainder were disposed of in bulk with the high-handedness for which British newspaper managements used to be famous. One of my staff who remained, thoughtfully sent me a copy of a memorandum circulated round her operating division explaining the new methods of working, which ended '. . . and in this company the term "marketing" will not in future be used.'!

In-house operations can be highly successful and profitable, but appear to work best where they are able to sub-contract wherever this is better, cheaper or more flexible. I earlier ran a small in-house market research team for Rowntree. It specialised in product testing, and provided a continuous flow of small-scale, high-quality, low-cost surveys, to standards and techniques which were comparable from year to year. This was particularly important for such problems as maintaining consumer acceptance of chocolate when the quality and flavour of cocoa beans varied by source country and by annual crop. In-house was also felt to be appropriate for highly-confidential new product work. Occasional spare capacity was used for pilot studies, non-urgent general research and technical development projects. However, all large-scale research work such as retail auditing and usage and attitude studies or occasional specialist tasks such as qualitative research were sub-contracted to a short-list of outside research agencies with appropriate skills and capacity.

As the range of specialist suppliers and their degree of competitiveness has grown, so more companies have taken the opportunity to divest themselves of the overheads and responsibility of running in-house operations. For example, Unilever, ICI, Mars-Pedigree Petfoods and Nestlé all used to have large, high-quality and well-respected all-purpose field market research operations in Britain but eventually sold them off or turned them into independent profit-makers serving other clients as well. Many companies who once ran large delivery fleets now have sub-contracted their distribution.

USING AN EXTERNAL SUPPLIER

Buying a service such as an advertising campaign or a place on a management training course is more difficult than buying a good such as lubricating oil because there is no 'sample' to try or agreed specification with which the delivered product can be compared, and even obviously defective work cannot afterwards be returned to supplier for replacement. At the extreme, return of the agency fee or even of the whole media spend would not compensate the buyer after the event for an advertising campaign which actually put customers off! This makes good briefing and supervision of all suppliers essential.

Outstandingly good work will obviously be rare, cannot be guaranteed by any supplier and should not be assumed by the buyer. But most professional suppliers of marketing services can produce at least a competent and effective piece of work if they understand what is wanted. Most of the many failures with which the writer has been associated (on both sides of the fence) were traced afterwards to deficiencies at the briefing stage. Either there was no proper written brief; or it did not describe what was really wanted by the buyer; or it was misunderstood or even ignored by the supplier (who knew better!); or was changed significantly at the eleventh hour (known as 'moving the goal-posts', one of the worst handicaps a buyer can inflict on a good supplier); or was later set aside through over-enthusiasm about an irrelevance ('this idea is absolutely brilliant and will set the market alight. I know it is not *exactly* on brief, but perhaps you could see your way to modify in just this case . . .?').

Briefing for a new campaign or major project where the effectiveness of the results is vital to the buyer should be put in writing and then discussed face to face by all concerned on both sides. This is often a good opportunity for top management of agency and client to meet (and assess) each other's team.

Almost all businesses are both buyers and sellers, yet often behave towards their suppliers in the very way they complain about among their own customers. A good relationship can happen only if both parties find it profitable: buyers must allow their suppliers to make a fair profit from them. Every supplier knows that if it allows one client to subsidise another, it will eventually be found out and lose both; which happens most frequently during a period of cut-back when it can least afford to lose anyone. Therefore a buyer who over-uses buying power is likely either to lose the supplier and have to substitute a cheaper and probably lower quality one; or to have the 'small print' of the Terms of Business invoked in time of trouble; or to be given second-team service except for window-dressing occasions. By eon-trast, a supplier will go to great lengths – such as throwing in extra support in times of temporary crisis – to keep happy a client which is profitable and easy to get on with, and the best staff will actually compete to work on this account.

When a junior advertising agency executive, I had a client (a very shrewd multinational giant) which occasionally asked all its advertising agencies to give their views on some trendy topic and would even volunteer an extra fee. Agency management knew this was a chance to do well (or badly) against the opposition, the team knew that while we worked on 'project x' our time and expenses were covered and would not be subject to normal scrutiny. We therefore gave of our best and ended up not only with good answers to the 'exam questions' as we used to call them (which we suspected the client knew already and was only cross-checking), but better briefed on the client's general business and how these new problems or opportunities could be tackled when they arrived for real. Of course the agency would eventually have done something about each topic of its own accord; but looking back, I believe this client knew they would get exceedingly good value for money for those modest extra fees!

An advertising agency or any other normal supplier of a marketing service earns income only from its clients. There is therefore no such thing as 'free' service (or as has been said elsewhere, lunch). It is a reality of the life of a service business that each client or project must be made to pay its way by charging the client one way or another or by cutting the costs. The client therefore must expect to pay for everything done on his or her behalf, and so should find ways to control how the money is spent. Competent client-service executives are sensitive to client needs and will tailor the service to provide more or less contact, thinking, execution, presentation or entertainment as appears to receive the most approval and create least hassle.

Buyers who pay regular negotiated fees (as is usual in business-to-business) have best control and can encourage concentration of future expenditure on what analysis of the past shows to be most needed or most productive. Work paid by project can best be controlled by rewarding good work through offering more afterwards; and by discussing alternative specifications for each project at the proposal stage.

THE VALUE OF THE IN-HOUSE SPECIALIST

Wherever there is an on-going relationship with a supplier, money can best be saved and crises minimised by employing a liaison person who is an expert on the topic (advertising, PR, transport, etc.) *and has worked on both the buyer and the supplier sides.* He or she will be able to 'short-hand' with supplier staff, build trust (so that any supplier crisis is confessed not fudged), can modify or reject tactfully quotations or proposals which are unrealistic, unnecessary or poor value and ensure that completed work is within budget and on brief. Internally this person can help the product marketing team to develop actionable briefs for outside suppliers, and help to interpret, implement or reinforce their output afterwards.

For example, an in-house lawyer can minimise that part of the costs of law suits which is created by barristers having to explain the legal position at great and expensive length and to translate legal terminology into laypersons' language. Such an expert may even be able to confine chargeable external advice to those areas where court action may be in prospect.

The habit of some financial institutions (and others) of putting in charge of their advertising a senior accounting clerk who is filling in time to retirement burns up unproductively a great deal of the agency's remuneration in basic tuition in the elements of advertising practice and also inhibits the agency from offering anything remotely 'creative' in case it frightens off the client by its unfamiliarity.

A marketing consultant specialising in advising lawyers told this story at a seminar. When the rules were changed in 1987 to allow legal firms in UK to advertise competitively, several of the largest commercial lawyers all went through the same highly unproductive sequence of events through lack of internal skills. The first act (quickly, to get in first) was to distribute large quantities of promotional material in the form of the glossy self-congratulatory brochures traditionally loved by lawyers. They then found these looked somewhat old-fashioned, and commissioned a trendy designer to give them a new house styling, letterheads and so on. To capitalise on this they then hired a Public Relations consultant to promote their new up-to-date image. The consultant, as professionals will, demanded to be briefed with the firm's business and marketing objectives. These concepts were so foreign to their way of thinking that they finally had to recruit their own marketing expert; who turned round and told them that brochures were not the most cost-effective medium to achieve their objectives!

Those firms who took the same steps but exactly the other way round lost nothing by the delay of planning ahead, saved themselves a great deal of money and launched themselves effectively with properly planned and targeted *multi-media* campaigns.

SELECTING A NEW AGENCY

Returning to the marriage–divorce metaphor, no agency–buyer relationship is perfect, and the prospect of a change and especially the process of courtship is always exciting. Some companies change their advertising agencies every three years, and are in consequence on the blacklists of the new business directors of all the best agencies. A standing belief of the marketing services business is that most new marketing directors on appointment automatically change their agencies to demonstrate quickly and in a macho fashion to their colleagues that 'things are going to be different around here'. Yet if the working relationships have been productive, these will be hard and time-consuming to re-establish with new agencies, and the process itself very demoralising to the in-house liaison staff who had put much time and skill into getting the old agencies into line.

If, on the other hand, an agency is no longer giving satisfaction, it is a better bet to have it out with them frankly and give them one chance to adapt to your new needs before asking for a re-pitch. Any agency knows it is safer and cheaper to keep an established and profitable client happy than to find and bring in a new one, and will jump through hoops given such an ultimatum.

Yet, every so often, a change has to be made or a supplier in a new area has to be found from scratch. This process is at its most difficult when looking for a full-time partner such as an advertising agency, data processing bureau or legal adviser where there will be a time contract and a lengthy period of briefing and learning to work together. The objective of a search should not be to find the heaven-made match of the romantic novels but rather a relationship which will be workable and profitable for the medium term.

It is important to choose an agency of a size who will be able to respond at your level of expenditure as equal partners: a client which dominates its agency tends to suffer the 'what time would you like it to be?' syndrome, particularly on the occasions where the agency ought to be arguing its hardest for some counter point of view. And when the inevitable happens of changing to a bigger agency, you have to live with the responsibility of putting out of a job the nice people who have worked so hard for so long on your behalf.

At the other extreme, a small advertiser may enjoy the idea of having an international giant on the end of the telephone; but should be aware that while as a matter of policy every agency tries to do its best for every client, there is a tendency in times of crisis to concentrate the best resources on the 'top 20' clients which the agency can least afford to lose.

Further, such organisations usually have high minimum charges which include services which the small spender may have trouble in accepting or making use of. For example, they will certainly offer strategic advice and total campaign planning, and probably have departments for TV production, research and print. It is a waste of money to appoint such a 'full-service' agency and then to use them as if they were just an art studio, and the agency staff will have trouble in giving of their best to a client who appears uninterested in their full range of skills.

A problem which is often raised is whether or not to look for an agency with previous knowledge of the client's industry. This has obvious advantages; but as was pointed out in Chapter 7 in the context of market research, it is far more important to choose someone with expertise in *their* business (where you cannot teach them). Good agency people are by nature 'quick studies' and will pick up the essentials of your business as fast as you are willing to brief them.

Indeed an agency with long experience of one of your competitors may have difficulty in learning to do things your way; and if part of their pitch to you is a willingness to reveal knowledge gained in confidence from a former client, it might be unwise to appoint them. One of the bases of a good agency–client relationship is mutual trust, and life becomes impossible for both parties if the client feels unable to share confidential information. A permanent agency should be a *partner*, who can be expected to supply a great deal more than advertising and other marketing material, however good. As an outsider, and one with experience of a wide range of markets and business situations, an agency should be able to offer objective advice and an informed second opinion on strategic marketing issues.

As was pointed out in Chapter 13, marketing communications in business-to-business require a range of techniques. There are many advantages in having them planned and coordinated through a single agency, even if some are executed elsewhere. At the selection stage it is worthwhile investigating the range of services on offer, and to give preference to those with the internal resources and outside contacts to take over and coordinate a number of the marketing activities which are a nuisance to commission directly with specialists.

COMPETITIVE SHORT-LISTS: SWAINS OR GLADIATORS?

Another benefit of having in-house experts is that they will know the structure of the supplier industry, and have first-hand experience of (or at least know by repute) most of the competing firms and can act as marriage-broker. It should usually be possible for them to produce a medium-to-short-list of likely candidates from examination of their current work, size and client list, reputation in the trade and 'business intelligence' about their resources, staff and methods of working.

This list of possible agencies can be visited informally (you always learn more by holding such meetings at their offices) to get 'credentials present-ations' at no obligation. This weeds out those which are visibly inappropriate or which are not interested in the business for some reason. The remainder become candidates for competitive presentations or 'beauty contests'.

The writer has taken part in enough of these, on both sides of the fence and for several different types of marketing service, to believe that the competitive pitch in its traditional form is a modern equivalent of the Roman gladiator circus and a totally inappropriate way of identifying a good agency–client match. The structure and atmosphere of the presentation is untypical of normal working conditions, often with both sides fielding people who will not be in the actual team and omitting people who will. The suppliers do what they think will win the business in preference to discussing what they believe will be in the prospect's best marketing interest but fear will be dull or conventional to present. It is not even usual for the winner's material to be used: too frequently at the first meeting after the competition the new agency asks 'when can we start running it for real?' and is told 'Ah, wonderful stuff! But we cannot actually *use* it for a number of good reasons we have not yet told you.' And the frequently significant costs of the failed presentations have to be paid for. The new client will be unwittingly con-tributing to the agency's future pitches, perhaps at ever-increasing cost: 'We usually lose if we don't show plenty of roughs, and look how well the telephone research went down at the XYZ pitch, and why don't we use those stunning laser-light people again!'

Some years ago the creative director of the advertising agency for which I was then working sent a full production unit to Italy to shoot a very expensive speculative TV commercial on the assumption that the prospect would not be able to understand the power of 'atmosphere' from a storyboard (no animatics in those days) but would be unable to resist real creativity on screen. Unfortunately the prospect was the hard-headed type who commented 'you haven't left room for the price and specification' or words to that effect and took his business elsewhere. We all suffered the effects of that episode in our Christmas bonus, but I at least was mollified because a lesson was learned and in future new business pitches we listened more carefully to what the prospects said they wanted, and were never again seen to be so unprofessional as to produce finished creative work without being asked (and paid) to do it.

It is unlikely that buyers will give up the excitement of being competed for, and indeed certain types of contract have to be seen to be 'open to tender'; but perhaps the less bloodthirsty could be persuaded to replace gladiatorial combat by mutual courtship. Indeed, business-to-business is more civilised than consumer (more business, less show business); but this may be a temporary phenomenon related only to the relatively smaller budgets during the 1980s and may change as marketing activity moves to a European scale in the 1990s.

What a buyer really needs from a marketing services agency (like any other supplier) is evidence that they have the resources to handle the business, to the appropriate level of quality and service, at an affordable price, using compatible staff and methods of working. This is much better done by asking for meetings (plural) with the team that will actually do the work in order to hear them give case histories from their own clientele and to discuss their preliminary reactions to the prospect's situation. This will inevitably still be superficial and may call forth only unusable solutions. But this will give a much better idea of the calibre of the people and ideas on offer and how they are likely to respond to your company in real life. If it is announced ahead that the losers will be offered a token sum in consolation, all may spend significant time on deeper thought and research.

The number of contenders in a beauty contest of any kind should be strictly limited. A team of selectors that spends two days seeing a new potential supplier every hour on the hour ends up only confused ('Was it no. 5 or no. 8 who gave that excellent case history of XYZ Widgets; I can't find it in this pile of leave-behinds?'). The most business-like of the contestants (perhaps the one the buyer is looking for?) will relate the quality of their pitch to the size of the business on offer and to their perceived chance of getting it. If facing six competitors, a contestant can calculate they have a 75 per cent likelihood or worse of losing even if they believe they have twice the chance of any other. For a small slice of business they may decline to pitch or send in the trainees, for a big one they may be encouraged to try a shock approach rather than a safe and mainstream one. Is this what the selectors really want?

When working for a research company I frequently had to respond to mailed requests for proposals from unknown prospects. A proper reply would involve thinking out the problem, costing a solution and setting it down on paper after consultation with several of our specialists (sampling, field, data processing), probably a minimum of a day's work. I would of course first telephone the enquirer for clarification of what was really wanted and to gauge how serious the request was. But sometimes not only the briefing document but also the covering letter was an impersonal photocopy, which had manifestly been sent to everyone on some list. I knew some of my less scrupulous competitors would reply to such a request by themselves photocopying an absolutely standardised proposal, which might by luck hit the jackpot. For an average-sized (say 6,000 ECU) job on which the agency would be relieved to make a 10 per cent profit, if I had only a 10 per cent chance of getting it, could I even justify the cost of making the phone call?

MANAGING SUPPLIERS FOR 'AD HOC' CONTRACTS

Where business is given on a project basis, such as 'ad hoc' research, trade fairs, much of print or some types of sales promotion, the task is less fraught. It is usual to parcel such work out among a small stable of proven suppliers giving the highest share to the most satisfactory performer. This encourages competition and provides insurance against capacity problems in the favoured supplier. Regular work leads to good mutual relations.

In this way the buyer builds a picture of the specialist skills and weaknesses of each supplier, fully detailed briefing is not necessary each time and the buyer will have a shrewd idea of what is the 'right' price for normal projects so that only the biggest jobs need be put out to tender. It is becoming quite usual (particularly in the Sales Promotion and Direct Mail businesses) to put the most favoured supplier on retainer, thereby getting access to regular expert advice to help planning as well as execution, and a higher level of guarantee of receiving real help in time of crisis.

Candidate new suppliers can be tried out cheaply on small or low-risk jobs without complicated competitions or tenders. The choice can be based on reputation in the trade or personal recommendation. In most businesses there is a good grapevine for regular users based on the trade press, professional associations and the trade fairs. Indeed the user's on-going agencies will often be a useful source of information about companies with which they do not compete.

LOCATING A SPECIALIST SUPPLIER

But supposing a 'first-time buyer' does not have the necessary specialist experience in-house, and no one to give advice, how can they locate a suitable supplier for a technical marketing service, and how will they know the price and quality offered is right for them?

It has to be realised that, unlike legally-protected lawyers, doctors and accountants, anybody can put up a brass plate saying they are market researchers, advertising agencies, premium-merchandise specialists or econometricians. In times of boom when business is plentiful (and established practitioners have capacity problems) cottage industries spring up in many areas of marketing service. The redundant, the retired and mothers on extended maternity leave offer their services from home. Senior practitioners feeling their progress blocked or reading the gross margin figures in their employer's balance sheets form breakaways without much in the way of financial backing or expertise in running a business beyond their own undoubted speciality. Cowboys with no skills or resources other than good letterheads lay ground bait for the innocent.

Experienced buyers can find their way through this jungle and will have their own tests to distinguish the competent unknown from the cowboy. Indeed they may deliberately give business to a new breakaway knowing that at least until a second client comes along they will have 100 per cent of the attention of the proprietor!

But the buyer should play for safety in any area where the company has no backlog of experience, and the first rule should be to give business only to members of a recognised professional body. To counter the lost business and bad reputation created by the incompetent and the unscrupulous, practitioners in most European countries have formed professional bodies (some of them now international) to facilitate the relations between buyers and sellers of the major marketing services. Most require their members to fulfil certain basic criteria in financial backing, technical qualifications and length of experience. They raise technical standards through training schemes, Diploma examinations and annual Award competitions. They publish and police Codes of Conduct for members' behaviour towards their clients and the community generally. Aggrieved clients can apply to a Professional Standards Committee for impartial advice, and if there has been incompetence the professional body will put pressure on the delinquent member to make restitution, because it is in the interests of all parties to keep such cases out of the law courts.

The buyer without background experience is seriously advised to go first to the appropriate professional body, scrutinise its conditions and codes with care and ask for advice in drawing up a short-list from the list of registered members. Choice should not be at random, it is usually better to start with large, well-established, generalists in the area: they are likely to have the resources to carry out any type of work, have no vested interest in any single technique which may be inappropriate for a particular problem and will not be so hungry for new business as to over-sell.

Discussion with candidates should concentrate first on what resources they have, what types of work they do and for whom. It is reasonable to ask for and to take up client references. Where the replies are satisfactory, raise the marketing problem, and the objective to be achieved and let the specialist recommend a technique (i.e., say, 'I need some sales leads among specifiers of air-conditioning systems', rather than 'I want to do a mailing to architects'). It is better to specify up front the budget or scale of operation required. It wastes both parties' time if the supplier recommends a scheme costing 10,000 or 1 million when you have 100,000 ECUs available. If what you say you have is too much, true professionals will tell you so (and maybe offer a second project to help you spend the rest!). If it is too little they will tell you what is really needed and discuss how a project with a reduced objective might fit the budget. An illustrative example of the nature of a brief to and response from a supplier is given in the context of market research in Chapter 7. Certainly a first-time buyer in a new area should never take the cheapest offer, but concentrate on getting the right technique and quality and then if necessary tailor the scale of the project to the available budget.

To recapitulate: buying marketing services is not really very different from buying other inputs to your business. Too much counter-productive mystique and emotion has become attached to making appointments by high-profile competitive pitching. To be fair, a long-term relationship with an advertising agency (or corporate lawyer) requires more care than choosing a printer for a short-run catalogue. But what is needed in both cases is someone with the resources and skills to do the required job at an acceptable combination of quality and price, plus in the case of the agency the staff and methods of working which will make the relationship harmonious. There may well be more than one suitable partner available and it will be easier to identify one of them in extended face-to-face discussion than at an emotionally charged, high-tech, competitive 'agency presentation'.

Depending on circumstances, the chosen solution could be a full-time agency, a regularly used consultant on retainer, or just one of a well-known short-list used occasionally on a project basis. In each case it is usually safer for buyers to stick to established professionals, and to insist on the standards and codes of the relevant professional body which provide some reassurance of technical competence, financial stability and commercial probity. This also gives the buyer an external source of redress in case of disappointment, before going to law.

In every case, good service comes from maintaining good relations with full time agencies and 'ad hoc' suppliers. These depend first on both parties finding their association profitable, and secondly on the staff in regular contact building up mutual respect and trust. The cost of an experienced expert in-house can almost always be justified through improved cost control, agency relations, quality and effectiveness of work. Failures usually stem from the briefing stage if either the objectives or the proposed action are inadequate, misinterpreted or not agreed in writing. Failures along the line through unforeseen circumstances cannot be obviated, but businesses in good partnership will usually find a way of dealing with them.

To use the marital analogy for the last time, most of the most admired agency–client partnerships are successful because (as in good marriages) both parties have put a great deal of effort over a great deal of time to make them so.

17 THE LAW AND THE PROFITS: HONESTY AS THE BEST POLICY

BUSINESS: PIRATE'S PARADISE OR REGULATOR'S PLAYGROUND?

There is one piece of advice which all marketers must take; get a good lawyer. Throughout Europe and North America business is more regulated in the 1990s than at any time in history, and new regulations are added year by year, not only by local and national governments but originating increasingly from supra-national bodies such as the United Nations and the European Commission. This chapter discusses the reasons behind this legislative burden and the actions which the business community should take in response.

This is not a plea for a return to 19th-century *laissez-faire*. The weak private individual needs state protection from the strong, selfish, rich and ruthless. Instead of burglary and robbery with violence, some criminals go in for commercial fraud and extortion, sometimes on a very large scale. It should be the duty of the state to deter and prosecute all such people, and to compensate their victims.

But some newer commercial laws set out to protect people from activities in which the evil is by no means self-evident (such as the laws against 'free gift' promotions in Germany), and others protect people not from other people but from themselves (such as bans on smoking). Yet others provide benefits (such as the ban on non-returnable packaging for soft drinks in Denmark) which seem somewhat trivial in relation to the amount of money that has to be spent and eventually recouped from everybody in compliance. Yet others cause more problems to the honest than to the immoral who easily find loopholes. A law in Britain aimed at preventing spurious price cutting actually prohibited a number of honest practices related to specifying the 'worth' of products, yet permitted the truly dishonest to get away with numerous deceptive wordings.

All businesses except the intentionally criminal do their best to obey the law, if only to avoid the penalties and the bad publicity following prosecution. But the position of even a totally lawful business could still be under threat. In addition to the law, many industries now self-regulate themselves by voluntary Codes of Conduct and their business activities through professional bodies (such as accountancy, advertising and market research). And even for those who act legally and ethically, there are many self-appointed watchdogs such as the consumer and environmental lobbies and investigative journalists ready to publicise and pressurise any business which they suspect is acting in what they consider to be an immoral or anti-social way. It is the nature of trial by media or by professional body that the burden of proof is reversed and (once accused) the suspects are deemed guilty unless they can prove themselves innocent.

There are genuine moral dilemmas; for example, insider trading, cartel agreements, industrial espionage are illegal, but all are the opposite side of fair and legal coins. How do we draw the borderlines between the legitimate, the unethical and the criminal? I devoutly hope that contact with deliberate and serious crime in business is as rare for my readers as it has been for me. The only course of action is to lay any such evidence before the top boss and the police as soon as possible.

But ethical dilemmas are another matter. Suppose, for example, my marketing database needs a copy of each competitor's specifications sheet and price list. They give them to customers, so why not just pick up my telephone and ask? But supposing I used my home address, or asked one of my customers who also buys from them to pass the literature on, or got my personal assistant to pose as a potential customer, or paid a private detective to get it, or accepted an offer from one of their employees to supply me with it and other documents on retainer? Two useful tests to distinguish where legitimate business intelligence crosses over into industrial espionage are: 'does anyone have to make a false statement?' and 'how would I feel if they did the same thing to me or my company?', and if these leave any doubt, not to do it.

When I was a very young market researcher, a client of mine was ordered (by a top boss in another country) to arrange some figures in a way that he and I considered highly misleading. If he refused, he might be fired. If he complied, he might one day be accused of unprofessional conduct. So we took our dilemma to my department head, a man of long experience, high integrity and indeed a founder of the UK Market Research Society. 'Well, old lad,' he said, 'you can't win 'em all!'. So we swallowed hard and did it.

Part of the responsibility of authority is never to order staff to do something you would not be willing to do yourself. If the boss gives an apparently dubious order, query it with reasons, if necessary go to the boss's boss for confirmation. It is unrealistic to resign every time a borderline case comes up, but if the matter seems substantial and serious, protection for oneself and perhaps for the company would be to put the objections in writing, circulate them upwards and take a copy home.

High moral dilemmas of this kind should be extremely rare in the marketing field. If not much money or reputation is at stake, it seems reasonable to err on the side of the customer, be generous to anyone with a legitimate complaint and leave it at that. But some issues are important and difficult, and advice should then be sought from a specialist lawyer or the professional standards adviser of the relevant organisation. The complexities are now such that regular and skilled advice is necessary for the certain compliance with all the law and all the codes. As a minimum, it is essential to cross-check in advance all new business activity against existing and impending law, not only in the home market but in every country from which sales are expected.

This is even true within Europe. It was one of the principles of the Single Europe Act of 1987 that EC member states would 'approximate' their laws so as to eliminate barriers to trade between them by the end of 1992. However, this has happened only to a limited extent, as ratification of the central harmonising Directives has been slow, individual countries have found many loopholes for special treatment (such as economic and environmental protection), the problem of technical standards has been too large for the time scale allowed, certain key areas such as electrical voltages and road driving regulations have not even been put on the agenda, while the more recently enshrined principle of 'subsidiarity' has ensured that in some areas of business legal positions that were once common will actually diverge.

It is therefore highly likely that the final arrival of a Single Market with no internal physical, technological or fiscal barriers will have to wait at least into the 21st century. Some, but not all, of the EC's legislative package will be ratified by some but not all other European countries. Non-European countries already have and may further increase tariff and non-tariff barriers against any increases in discrimination by 'Fortress Europe'. Redress against any inequity through the international courts will be a lengthy process beyond the means of all but the largest businesses. Since the offenders will mainly be national governments a victory will be counter-productive to those wishing to continue to trade under their jurisdiction. World trade has always been a legal jungle, and all the evidence is that it is getting worse not better. Caveat vendor!

THE RISE OF BUREAUCRATIC POWER

Governments of almost all parties in all countries support the principles of economic growth, higher living standards and increasing world trade. So why is it that they place an ever-increasing pile of restrictions in the way of those whose business it is to create the additional wealth, employment and base for taxes necessary for the economic miracle?

There are two causes: one is the inevitable growth of governmental bureaucracy, whose members surely believe in the value of governing and must therefore be continually on the look-out for new areas on which to extend its blessings. In 1957 C. Northcote Parkinson first published his eponymous Law that 'work expands to fill the time available for its completion'. He proved that, as an inevitable consequence, the number of people employed in public administration will rise irrespective of the amount of actual administration done or needed. He demonstrated by reference to the British Civil Service that the average annual rate of growth of numbers was five per cent. His most entertaining illustration was that between 1914 and 1928 the number of warships in the Royal Navy declined by 68 per cent while the number of Admiralty officials rose by 78 per cent.

His conclusions appear still to stand, since most of Europe has pursued a policy of divesting itself of state-managed enterprises, yet the number of government servants in most countries has not declined, and indeed large new bureaucracies have grown up through the European Commission and various other international bodies such as GATT, NATO, UNESCO, WHO and so on. As we now have more people to govern us, we must therefore expect more government, and this will inevitably include business.

Secondly, the majority of those in positions of greatest administrative power, career politicians and senior civil servants, have never worked in business, and certainly few of them in managerial roles. They therefore have little comprehension of how wealth is created, the nature of commercial profit, the mechanics of supply-and-demand or even how a business operates. Some also appear deeply suspicious of the motives and even of the integrity of people who work in commerce. This appears particularly true in the European Commission where until recently more consultation has taken place with consumerists than real consumers and business schools than businesses. As a result the stance of much Euro-legislation, at least as originally drafted, is interventionist, consumerist, environmentalist, with a protectionist view of industrial relations.

Most recent and known forthcoming legislation affecting European business originates in Brussels, where there is a view that the actions of business (especially large and multi-national businesses) and of the forces of the market-place generally, are not for the good of the community. Many draft Directives not only have an anti-business tone but also would be difficult and expensive to work in practice.

Nowhere has this been more true than in laws that affect marketing. It appears that marketing is the unacceptable face of business, and 'advertising' (which until 1992 has been Euro-speak for all marketing communications) is the unacceptable face of marketing from which the public is believed to need a great deal of protection.

Business has now formed an EC lobby, which to be fair has been listened to with some sympathy. The final version of the Directive on Misleading Advertising (signed off in Brussels in 1985) gives an acceptable degree of consumer protection and is workable, whereas its first draft of 1975 would have brought all advertising to a halt while test cases were fought out. Nevertheless 'freedom of commercial speech' (which the European Court of Justice has ruled is a category of 'freedom of speech' guaranteed by the 1957 Treaty of Rome) is still under threat at least in the programme of Directives under discussion in 1993. It is important that all businesses support the lobbying bodies such as the International Chamber of Commerce and the European Advertising Tripartite. Everyone should keep a close watch on policy issues as they arise, and give the lobbyists early warning of the unfair, the unworkable, the extravagant and the unnecessary, so that they can raise objections at the stage when draft legislation is still plastic.

SELF-REGULATION OR LAW?

This is not to suggest that honest business-people never get anything wrong, nor commit anti-social or immoral actions through error or carelessness. In the end, all human actions need and ought to be limited by law. But business law is slow and expensive to enforce, and should concentrate on protecting society from major ills such as fraud or dangerous products.

Many of the sins of commerce are relatively trivial such as exaggerated claims in advertisements, or sales calls purporting to be market research interviews. Business has had considerable success in dealing with these by self-regulation through Codes of Conduct formulated by professional bodies, funded by joint action, policed and enforced by mutual consent. The first International Code of Advertising Practice was produced in the 1930s by the International Chamber of Commerce and has become the model for similar national codes. Other disciplines such as Sales Promotion and

Market Research now have national and international Codes, and industries such as building and the travel trade are self regulated in some countries.

The value of self-regulation is that it can act quickly and cheaply, its sanctions are highly specific (such as enforcing the amendment or withdrawal of a misleading advertisement or the removal of an offending company from a list of approved suppliers), and the Codes can be up-dated regularly to take account of changes in public opinion, new business techniques and the issues of the day.

As a result of lobbying, the EC has been persuaded that self-regulation is capable of providing an economical and efficient protection for the public; so that where an effective system is in place the law is necessary only as a 'safety net' against a minority of renegades who refuse to co-operate with the system. This is good news for business, which in return must encourage the Eurocrats, other legislators and indeed any groups which are suspicious of the motives of business, by making codes wherever possible, and enforcing them to a high standard.

BUSINESS POLICY: DOING WELL BY DOING GOOD

As pointed out in Chapter 11, doing the right thing is never enough; in all forms of corporate activity a business has to be clearly seen to be virtuous. There is much corporate goodwill to be gained by being not just law-abiding, but conforming to every relevant Code and then publicising the fact.

For example, it is very attractive and reassuring to buyers to know that a particular supplier offers not just their minimum legal obligations but will do its best when there is trouble to see customers right even if the fault is not the supplier's. The costs of 'or your money back' is often less than the difference between inspecting to (say) 98 per cent and 100 per cent perfection, yet is a much more believable claim than 'zero defects'.

Those who work in advertising know that advertisements are much more strongly regulated than the editorial or television programmes in which they are embedded. It has been said that if politicians had to conform to the 'legal, decent, honest and truthful' principle of the Code of Advertising Practice which now applies over much of Europe, elections of governments would be conducted in silence!

Any established business knows that telling lies in advertising has always been counter-productive. Most suppliers would go out of business if their customers were not regular buyers, but few people ever become repeat buyers of a product which does not come up to the claims it makes. David

Ogilvy wrote his best-known aphorism in *Confessions of an Advertising Man* (Longmans, 1963): 'The consumer isn't a moron; she is your wife.' Few know the rest of his paragraph: 'You insult her intelligence if you assume that a mere slogan and a few vapid adjectives will persuade her to buy anything. She wants all the information you can give her.' That was true of consumer advertising in 1963, so how much more so for business-to-business marcoms in the 1990s where a duped buyer has not just wasted a dollar from the housekeeping money but has laid him or herself open to criticism from the entire Decision Making Unit. Indeed, the published reports of the regulating bodies suggest that flagrant and deliberately misleading advertising has almost been stamped out. Most offences against the codes are either technical matters where even the experts are not all in agreement, or hyperbole attributable to over-enthusiasm, or just sheer ignorance of the code from very small or new operators.

Yet significant minorities of the general public still criticise advertising, watchdog bodies keep it high on their hit-lists, and bureaucrats still draft yet more legislation to curb it. Why? Perhaps because some types of advertising are intrusive. People see it not because they choose to, but because it is there, even if they are not in the market for the product. (Analysis shows that most critics mostly condemn advertising for products they do not buy; those in the target market are much less likely to complain.)

Perhaps the problem is simply that all advertising is advocacy and people assume that it must therefore be partially untrue. After all, when we sell our own home, we draw attention to the new paint inside and the view of the park from the front rather than the leaking drainpipes and the view of the railway from the back. Commercial advertising (and the rest of the marcoms) puts the case for suppliers who genuinely believe in their products and who cannot reasonably be expected to feature possible disadvantages. The product will have to be safe and 'of merchantable quality' as English Law puts it, and any misrepresentation of fact about it will be liable to prosecution in law. Plenty of official watchers (and the supplier's competitors) will be eager to take action if they can. Is this not enough to protect society? Some critics appear to expect every advertisement to be a judge's summing-up with the strengths and weaknesses tabulated for each competing brand! But we do not all want the same thing, and the aspects of a brand which make it most attractive to me may be the ones that repel somebody else. Which is the plus, which the disadvantage?

THE 'BAD APPLE' SYNDROME

I believe from personal experience that the vast majority of businesses are run honestly by people of integrity. The few that are not cause disproportionate damage to the reputation of the rest. It is therefore vital that the business community should police itself. When a major scandal is uncovered, it too often appears that many people who were not part of the conspiracy, sometimes including those in official places, knew what was happening but did not speak out, for fear of the consequences or (less acceptably) unwillingness to get involved. This is unfortunate, and the business community for the sake of its collective reputation should find ways to protect all who help to uncover those who commit fraud on businesses or the public and so create problems for their honest competitors.

It is a fact that there are no barriers to entry into many sectors of business, and in times when profits look easy to come by, some become infested by the unqualified and the unscrupulous. I know of several services in the UK which suffered at different times from the invasion of such 'cowboys'.

Some years ago, there were many unqualified and under-financed travel agents. Some went bankrupt, leaving travellers stranded at their destinations and creating very bad publicity for the whole travel trade. The Association of British Travel Agents responded by requiring that its members demonstrate minimum standards of financial backing, including paying to indemnify their customers against being stranded by any financial failure by the agent or carrier. Yet more members' money was demanded to promote this scheme, so that while unscrupulous travel agents could not be closed down, travellers were aware they undertook risks by not going to a registered ABTA member and this discouraged the further entry of those unwilling to operate responsibly.

The Market Research Society (and its business-to-business counterpart the Industrial Marketing Research Association) had always demanded and published minimum standards of skill and experience from their members, who also had to agree to uphold a detailed Code of Conduct which specified practitioners' responsibilities to buyers of research, to respondents to surveys and to the general public. They then set up training schemes including an examined Diploma, to raise standards of good practice, and funded public relations activity to spread knowledge about the differences between professional and amateur research among users in business, the media and government. Almost all professional researchers have been persuaded to support the Society for their own good and to subscribe large amounts of time and money to its efforts. While this has not eliminated 'cowboy' research, the activities of the least competent have been greatly restricted, general standards of research have improved and not least of all, the professionals have gained additional business by being able to compete on quality rather than simply price.

Gresham's Law from the 17th century that 'bad money drives out good' still applies, and unless the honest band together and fight, dishonesty can take over a whole business sector to the permanent detriment of all. The magnet to the 'cowboy' operator is a level of profit disproportionate to the quantity and quality of work done, and the best deterrents are transparent pricing policies and a widely publicised and properly policed code of conduct which defines good practice and offers redress to those who do not get it. Such codes and the self-regulatory bodies to run them may seem expensive nuisances, but in the end will protect the business and profits of those who support and obey them, from both unscrupulous competitors and unsympathetic legislation. Chapter 16 advised buyers of marketing services in their own interests to patronise agencies and other suppliers who put themselves under the jurisdiction of the relevant professional bodies, and act according to their Codes of Conduct.

HONESTY AS A CORPORATE OBJECTIVE

It is a statement of faith that dishonesty never pays in the long run, but it is certainly true that once they know they have been deceived by a supplier even in a trivial detail, customers will take their business elsewhere, and no amount of later promise of improvement will bring them back. Further, even an inaccurate rumour of such trouble can do almost as much harm as the trouble itself.

Therefore, any business which wishes to keep trading and to serve a clientele of loyal satisfied customers must build and maintain a reputation for scrupulous dealing in all aspects. This implies that all aspects of the business should be well run to the highest standards, that errors when they arise should be put right and any aggrieved customers compensated. It should be a matter of policy to obey not only letter of the law and any other regulations but also their spirit. 'Sailing close to the wind' for a temporary competitive advantage is a dangerous temptation. And the policy of fair dealing should be promoted as part of the 'corporate image' through media, public relations and any other appropriate means.

The benefit of this is that customers who are convinced (because they have hard evidence) of the integrity of their supplier give a fair hearing when trouble strikes. As argued in Chapter 12, no company, however well run, can be totally free from risks such as defective ingredients, dishonest employees, natural disasters or just human error. If problems are admittedand put right as soon as possible, good customers will support good suppliers.

Further, public opinion is now an important factor in the business environment. Gaining and keeping the goodwill of the business community and the general public should be on the corporate agenda of all businesses if for no other reason than keeping down demand for expensive, inconvenient and possibly unworkable official intervention. This demands fair dealing with customers and suppliers, and (as discussed in Chapter 15) with staff. In any deal, one party will be in a stronger position than another (for example in buyers' and sellers' markets). It is up to the party with the most power to use it responsibly and not extort the last ECU of profit or insist on every clause in the small print. A business needs regular buyers and suppliers and loyal employees, and today's power structure may be reversed later. If customers cannot reciprocate loyalty and kindness, it may be better to do without their business anyway!

To recapitulate: honesty is the best policy for a business, not just for the warm moral glow it provides, but for the sound marketing reason that mutual loyalty between supplier and customer is an asset which is worth investing hard cash to build and will provide profit in hard times if maintained.

Honesty in this sense means a great deal more than obeying the law of the land; it implies maintaining the highest standards of conduct and professional behaviour at all levels, and contributing time and money to the organisations who define and police the self-regulatory codes. It also means watching for unprofessional conduct and law-breaking in the market: and bringing evidence to the proper authority however inconvenient or even 'disloyal' that may be.

The benefits are numerous: honest businesses seek out and deal with each other to their mutual profit, and a whole industry with integrity gains the support of governments and a good press. The less scrupulous may make extra short-term gains in good times, but will eventually lose customers, suffer constant publicity crises and if not otherwise brought to book, will bring down unnecessary and unhelpful legislation on their whole industry.

18 EPILOGUE: THE MARKETING BRIEF

Robert Townsend prefaced *Up the Organisation* (Michael Joseph, 1970) with: 'If you're not in business for fun or profit what the hell are you doing here?' This book does not presume to tell the reader how to get fun out of business, and inevitably there are periods where it is no fun for anyone. Managing a business inevitably uses up a great deal of your time and money, if there is *never* any fun in it for you, my advice is to move on to a more congenial occupation.

If, on the other hand, you are not making money, someone will eventually take your business (and all its fun) away from you. This book is intended to illustrate how marketing can help prevent that happening. A reader who would like a summary of its content is respectfully requested to re-read the recapitulation paragraphs at the end of each chapter. This final section will instead restate the book's approach to marketing as a means to running a business at a profit.

Ray Willsmer's *Directing the Marketing Effort* gives a succinct encapsulation: 'Marketing is selling goods (or services) that won't come back to customers who will!' A marketing strategy could be generated most simply by answering his six 'questions for marketing self-analysis':

- What are we selling?
- To whom are we selling?
- Why are we selling?
- How are we selling?
- When are we selling?
- Where are we selling?

If everyone in a business gives the same answer to these questions, that business is likely to be customer-orientated, and its decision-taking staff will be co-ordinating their work with each other so that the resources available are used to satisfy the customers' needs at a profit. If the answers differ, or some are missing, then that business needs more research, more discussion or more communication, and it will be taking higher risks with its resources than are necessary or desirable.

An admired entrepreneur who was once invited to address the UK Marketing Society told them: 'I know nothing about marketing, I just give my customers what they want at a price they can afford!' and the assembled elite of British Marketing applauded him enthusiastically. But within three years this star of the business world was bankrupt because the price he was charging for his service was not one *his company* could afford. Reduced price (or best of all free sampling) is an excellent sales promotion technique for gaining rapid trial and consequent repeat purchasing if the product is a good one; but it is no substitute for a proper pricing strategy which offers both value for money for the customer and a profit for the supplier.

Marketing is a philosophy of doing business, not a set of techniques (such as 'advertising and selling') nor the mindless application of rules of thumb. There is always a section of the business community who hurry to respond to the latest fashion, and there are always new gurus to provide them with slogans: 'small is beautiful', 'excellence', 'globalisation', 'Just-In-Time delivery', 'Total Quality Management', 'flexibility' and 'mass-customisation' are recent examples. There is nothing wrong with any of these concepts in the right situation, only that they are not panaceas, they are not substitutes for analysis and thought, and if all competitors end up offering the same thing they are not even selling points.

This is because the listed concepts do not inevitably offer benefits to the customers: adding quality above the level that the customers require for their particular need only adds to costs and prices, offering JIT will create problems for the buyers if they are not geared up to ordering accurately with the necessary lead time. Even the originator of 'excellence' as a management philosophy later recanted some of his views when he found that several of his 'excellent' firms had run into trouble shortly after his book about them was published.

There are no 'universal magic solutions' to business problems: if research into a market suggests that customers are concerned about the number of faults they find in the products and services from all competitive suppliers, then the first to offer 'zero defects' will capture more business. But if the problem is too narrow a range of specifications or slow response to orders or lack of reliable technical advice, then it probably will not.

A useful reference source for business research is the PIMS (Profit Impact of Marketing Strategy) database at the Strategic Planning Institute, Cambridge, Massachusetts, USA. This contains the financial, sales, marketing and profit records of a large number of American and European companies. One of the earliest analyses of PIMS which was published in Harvard Business Review unfortunately concentrated on the strong correlation between ROI (Return On Investment) and share of market. As a result a number of companies (presumably without greater depth of thought than 'it says in HBR we must go for market share!') then devoted all their resources to increasing their share of market at any cost and even in recession years, and consequently became extremely unprofitable.

The correlation is genuine, but its implication is no conceptual break-through. It does not mean that companies with high market shares will automatically have high ROI, but rather the other way round. Successful companies (almost by definition) have a high ROI, and not surprisingly, they tend to have higher shares of their markets than the less successful.

Later analysts have shown what most of these successful companies really have in common. For example, Alexander Biel of the Ogilvy Center for Research and Development, drew five conclusions from a recent study of the 1,500 business-to-business enterprises in the PIMS database:

1. Products that are perceived as being of relatively higher quality than their competitors earn higher prices and profits
2. Advertising affects perception of quality: provided product quality is genuinely high, advertising can amplify and reinforce this perception
3. Relative advertising pressure and market share are related: businesses with low advertising-to-sales ratios operate at substantially lower levels of market share than businesses with higher ratios
4. Market share is related to return on investment, because both are related to quality, price and sales volume
5. Businesses which invest in advertising obtain higher ROIs; and advertising-to-sales ratios are directly related to ROIs. In the sample analysed, the average ROI was 24 per cent. For companies with a/s ratios much higher than their competitors the average ROI was 32 per cent, for companies with much lower advertising-to-sales ratios the average ROI was 20 per cent.

I believe that these companies are successful not just because they advertise, but rather because advertising is a visible indicator of their total marketing effort. The PIMS database does not contain the information to prove this, but it is highly likely that the companies with the highest advertising also spend significantly more money on market research, new product development, good customer contact and a wide range of other marcom activities.

Marketing is certainly about satisfying customer needs, but it is also about the responsible and efficient use of the resources of people and money, and it is above all about the management of risks.

To provide itself with the necessary resources, a business must offer an attractive reward (or 'profit') to those who supply them, namely the backers and the staff. But there is no profit in the business world without taking risks. These cannot be eliminated, only estimated and minimised. The essential of good business management is to make sure the degree of exposure to risk is understood, that the reward for success is at least commensurate with the degree of risk and that the penalty for failure (which must happen sometimes even to the best of management) is not so high as to destroy the company.

The contribution of marketing to developing a sound business strategy is to provide a good understanding of customers and their needs, of the competitive market situation and of the business environment which must be faced by the company in the immediate future. The method for doing this is the proper use of market research and business forecasting, whose costs should be looked on as an insurance premium which reduces the risks of serious failure. Although marketing is a vital input to the business strategy, it is only one of several: finance, production technology, and the corporate philosophy 'what kind of a company do we want to be?', are among the others.

Once the strategy is agreed marketing has a major role in its implementation, which can be summed up as developing and maintaining good interactive relationships with the customers. Much of what has been written so far in this chapter is general to all markets, but this is the point where business-to-business marketing diverges from consumer.

These relationships are between members of the supplier's staff and the DMUs of the customers. The numbers of people involved are usually sufficiently small to make it possible for the supplier to know the names, job functions and a great deal of other information about everyone. This permits a much greater degree of personalisation than could ever be possible in mass-consumer markets.

The key technique is and will remain personal contact. But as the costs of doing this go up and the alternatives become more sophisticated and capable of being personalised, an increasing proportion of the marketing budget will have to be devoted to backing up the customer liaison managers (once called 'the sales team') quickly, flexibly and cheaply, through a variety of marketing communications techniques, for instance mail, telephone, fax and electronic messaging, print and video, media advertising of the product and the company's corporate image, public relations, sales promotion, trade fairs, sponsorship of events and so on. By the turn of the century we should expect most routine clerical work, factual enquiries and even routine orders to be handled by interactive links between the supplier's and customers' databases. Humans can be freed from drudgery to concentrate on what humans are best qualified to do: helping each other, through fair and honest trading.

Because all this work is concerned with the customers, it rightly falls under the responsibility of marketing management. Proper control will depend on each part of the marketing mix having (and accepting) its own brief which specifies its unique contribution to the common task, the money and other resources available, any constraints such as time and the method by which success will be evaluated.

The essential to effective management is the *brief*. As has been said in several places earlier, most business failures can be traced to inadequacies at the briefing stage. Unless the brief is based on a sound view of the reality of the market-place, unless the tasks and budgets are clearly specified and understood by all who have to implement them, the risks will be high of misunderstanding, confusion of effort and waste of resources. There are enough external risks facing any business operating in a competitive market without adding to them internally!

Figure 18.1 gives a sample check list for a general marketing brief. Each separate activity (selling, advertising, PR, etc, whether handled by internal departments or outside agencies) should also have the general version in addition to its own brief to ensure proper co-ordination and reinforcement between one activity and another.

Marketing management must regularly monitor all activities and evaluate them with the staff or agency concerned against their objectives to identify causes of failure and under-exploited opportunities. If the rewards of success are properly shared, all will be able and willing to work towards progressive improvements in the effectiveness and cost-effectiveness of their task. In this way, sound marketing will ensure the survival in bad years and growth in prosperity in good years for both company, management and staff.

A few months before being asked to write this book I was sent to Africa to advise the largest manufacturer in a small country which was facing great marketing difficulties. I was unfamiliar with both the country and the industry, and while I found many issues which I recognised, some of the economic, financial and managerial problems facing the company and the country as a whole were totally unlike anything in Europe or North America. All I could do was apply the principles set out in this book and ask for the answers to Ray Willsmer's six questions.

They led me to believe that the company should make drastic revisions to its whole marketing strategy. To give just one example, instead of using

1. Business Objectives

Where the company is headed, the requirements for turnover and profit, the resources of capital, labour and intangible assets available to achieve them.

2. Market Appreciation and Forecasts

The essential elements in the market and the business environment that will influence the achievement of the Objectives. What changes are expected in customer demand and the competition?

3. The Product Offer

Specification of core product and associated services, pricing and terms of business. What customer need does it satisfy, what are the (unique) competitive advantages, what is the required image?

4. The Target Customer

How many, what kind of company, industry, locations, structure of Decision Making Unit, names, job titles and addresses. How do they differ from non-targets?

5. Marketing Objectives

The (specific and unique) role of marketing in achieving the Business Objectives. How does this relate to the role of other activities (e.g., production, finance, distribution)?

6. Marketing Budget

Expressed in money, as percentage of sales, investment per target customer, as percentage of total budget, comparisons with previous years and competition.

7. Constraints

Timing, legal, corporate, other.

8. Evaluation

On what criteria will marketing activities be judged? What are the 'action standards'?

Figure 18.1 The Marketing Brief

exports as a sink for dumping surplus capacity in bad years, the company ought to reduce its risks by developing regular contracts in relatively stable rich countries and using the desperately poor and much more volatile home market to take up any surplus at very low (marginal) prices. This would also earn more foreign exchange and act as a bargaining counter with the government over various administrative problems. I was very diffident about offering such radical solutions after such a short acquaintance with such horrendous problems. I put them forward in small doses, starting with the least controversial, and I ran discussion groups among the managers to test whether I had missed anything fundamental. Finally, and still in trepidation, I put the whole revised strategy together. The Executive Manager in charge of Sales and Marketing read it through and said: 'I suppose it is just common sense when you think about it.' If a marketing strategy is sound it should be common sense; if it does not make sense it is probably nonsense.

In his Preface to *Foundations of Corporate Success*, Professor John Kay points out how much data we have about successful and unsuccessful companies, and that the problem is to develop a framework which makes sense of it. He says that one will be successful if the thoughtful senior executive, instead of reacting 'That is something new,' thinks 'That makes sense of my experience'.

I have tried to put down the sense I have made of a very varied personal experience. For example: that added-values are a better indicator of success than profits; that risks have to be quantified; that good customer relations, branding, pricing and advertising are vital to generating regular sales; and that the marketing audit is a key step to developing a profitable business strategy.

This book will have succeeded if it helps any of my readers to make better sense of their own experience.

APPENDIX 1
Further reading

Barnard, N. and G. Smith (1989). *Advertising and Modelling – an introductory guide*, Institute of Practitioners in Advertising, London. The principles and practice of econometric modelling for the lay user.

Biel, A. (1988). *The impact of business-to-business advertising on profits*, Ogilvy Center for Research & Development. Copies of this analysis of the PIMS database are available from Primary Contact Ltd. 33 St.John St., London EC1M 4AA, UK.

Broadbent, S. (ed., 1981). *Advertising Works: Papers from the IPA Advertising Effectiveness Awards 1980*, Holt Reinhart Winston. This is the first of a two-yearly series of winning case-histories using many quantified methods of evaluating marketing campaigns (including econometrics). Most are consumer products, but there is a business-to-business category.

Clifton, C., et al. (1992). *Market Research: Using Forecasting in Business*, Butterworth Heinemann. A student's textbook, but written by a team working in-house at ITT. It covers a lot of 'nitty-gritty' in research and forecasting.

Davidson, H. (2nd ed., 1987). *Offensive Marketing*, Penguin. Still totally up-to-date, positive and practical.

Ehrenberg, A. (1983). *A Primer in Data Reduction*, Wiley. An introductory text in statistics for non-specialists.

Huff, D. (1973). *How to Lie with Statistics*, Penguin. Funny, but very helpful to the non-numerate before reading Ehrenberg.

Kay, J. (1993). *Foundations of Corporate Success: how business strategies add value*, Oxford University Press. A scholarly discussion of several of the issues in this book.

McKenna, R. (1991). *Relationship marketing*, Random House. Mainly about high-tech markets in USA, but the only book on the subject and very good on 'positioning'.

Mole, J. (1990). *Mind Your Manners*, Nicholas Brealey. The differing management cultures of 12 European countries, USA and Japan. A most useful guide to those selling in the European Community.

Piercy, N. and M. Evans (1983). *Managing Marketing Information*, Croom Helm. A specialist text.

Sutherland, K. (ed., 1991). *Researching Business Markets*, Kogan Page. A collection of papers by business market researchers, sponsored by the Industrial Market Research Association.

Turnbull, P. and J.-P. Valla (eds., 1986). *Strategies for International Industrial Marketing*, Routledge. Academic, but fact-based.

Thurow, L. (1992). *Head to Head: the coming economic battle among Japan, Europe, and America*, Nicholas Brealey. A stimulating review of world business strategies.

Walton, S. (1992). *Made in America: the Story of Wal-Mart Stores*, Doubleday. The memoirs of a highly successful entrepreneur.

Willsmer, R. L. (1971). *Directing the Marketing Effort*, Staples Press (reprinted by Penguin). Old, consumer-based, but still authoritative.

Wilson, A. (1991). *New Directions in Marketing*, Kogan Page. One of the few texts dealing exclusively with business-to-business.

APPENDIX 2
Glossary of key marketing terms

Ad hoc (project): a self-contained piece of marketing work such as a customer survey or print job which is placed with an outside supplier with whom the buyer has no on-going contract. This contrasts with continuous or 'agency' relationships.

Advertising: a controllable channel of communication between those who supply goods and services and their customers and users. In marketing terminology it is confined specifically to measured media such as newspapers, magazines, television, radio, posters, direct mail. In governmental and legal terminology it may be taken to include any form of marketing communication such as leaflets, catalogues and packaging.

Below-the-line/Above-the-line: the term originates from accountancy in the 1930s to distinguish in a company's marketing budget activity under tight cost control (meaning at that time media advertising) from sales promotions and public relations whose costs and outcome were at best imprecise and at worst open-ended. The terms have survived a half-century despite the fact that professionals in 'below-the-line' can now cost and deliver their work with almost as much precision as advertising. Further, there are newer techniques such as database marketing and telemarketing which are hard to classify and sometimes referred to as 'through-the-line'.

Benchmarking: the process of seeking improvement in efficiency and profitability by making comparisons of the company's own performance last year on a variety of indicators against successful competitors. Where there is a deficiency the company attempts to match and then improve on the 'benchmark'. Many Japanese companies are believed to use benchmarking.

Boston Matrix: a general classification of products made by the Boston Consulting Group during the 1970s. It divides them according to whether their market share and total market growth are high or low, as 'stars', 'cash cows', 'problem children' and 'dogs'.

Branding: the active and consistent projection of the qualities which differentiate a product or the organisation which supplies it from its competition. See also *Image*.

Break-even point: the level of sales where the income gained by a product exactly equals its costs. In theory all sales above this point will be profitable. Not a precise term in most business operations because prices are subject to negotiation and there are many ways of allocating general fixed costs between different products.

Budget: a plan to allocate resources (on plant, raw materials, staff, transport, advertising, etc) in order to earn money through later sales.

Business intelligence: the informal collection, appraisal and internal dissemination of facts and rumours of interest to a firm. Employees at all levels should be aware of their duty to pass to the company database any relevant information they acquire. See also *Market Research and Industrial Espionage*.

Corporate image: see *Image*.

Customer-orientation: the approach to business which starts with the nature and needs of potential customers and develops a means of satisfying them which simultaneously provides value for money to the buyer and profit for the supplier. As opposed to **production-orientation**, whereby the proprietor of a given product (or production process) seeks buyers willing to pay profitable prices. The philosophy of marketing is to reduce commercial risks through customer-orientation. See also *Marketing*.

Database marketing: the use of computer technology to hold on file and update regularly data about customers and prospects in such a way as to be able to build a dialogue with them, for example, to be able to identify prospects with common business characteristics or product needs (known as 'profiling').

Desk/field research: Field or primary research is new research to find out (for example, by sample survey) information not otherwise available. Desk or secondary research is the reanalysis of information collected for other purposes but held in-house or published. Despite the names, secondary research is normally carried out before more expensive primary field research.

DMU (Decision Making Unit): the group of people in a company most concerned with making a specific buying decision. Their roles will comprise Authorisers, Specifiers, Purchasers and Users, sometimes augmented by internal or outside Corporate Specialists. Members of a DMU can be at several levels in different departments and while few can authorise expenditure many more have an effective power of veto over a supplier.

Econometric model: an analysis of a time-series of data (e.g., sales) against trends in independent variables such as seasonality, economic, social, technological and market factors to quantify consistent correlations. Econometric model (Murphy's definition): a set of mathematical equations which explain a high percentage of past variation in the market and a very low percentage of future variation.

Elasticity: the quantitative response of a market to changes in stimuli. For example, if a price cut of one per cent increases sales volume by one per cent the price elasticity is defined to be 1. If sales increase by two per cent, elasticity is 2 and the market is said to be 'elastic to price'. By extension, elasticities can be calculated for other stimuli such as advertising or customer profitability.

Entrepreneurism: a management skill which enables the holder to generate profits from risky situations through tactical flexibility.

Forecast: a quantified and objective estimate of what is most likely to happen in future, based on an analysis of the past, with evaluation of the degree of uncertainty, and with any necessary assumptions identified. See also *Budget, Target*.

Halo effect: a well-recognised, strong, positive characteristic of a good or service is likely to be reflected in a good rating by customers for number of other elements in the image of the product. If a machine is believed to be 'well-engineered', its users are likely also to report it as 'efficient', 'safe', 'easy to maintain' and so on, even if it does not have any particular competitive advantages on these other points.

Image: the perceptions and beliefs about a product or its supplier in the mind of those in its market. It is usually multi-dimensional and can include both objective and subjective criteria. A 'brand' is a product with a strong and distinctive image, a 'commodity' has little or none. Companies have 'corporate images' which tend to reflect on all their products and activities. See *branding*.

Industrial espionage: information about competitors, customers, suppliers and government acquired by means which are illegal such as computer 'hacking' or unethical such as misrepresentation. Adherence to professional Codes of Conduct such as that of the Industrial Marketing Research Association can help to indicate what is within the ethical borderline. See also *Business Intelligence, Market Research*.

Marketing: the management process responsible for identifying, anticipating and satisfying customer requirements profitably. (Chartered Institute of Marketing). See also *Customer-orientation*.

Marketing audit: a comprehensive, objective and precise evaluation of a company's assets and resources to determine competitive strengths and weaknesses. See also *SWOT analysis*.

Marketing communications (marcoms): any controlled channel of communication between suppliers of goods and services and their customers. Principal techniques are media advertising, public relations, sales promotion, direct mail and telephone, trade fairs, sponsorship, print and video. The general public and institutions such as the European Commission usually refer to these collectively as 'advertising'.

Marketing Information System (MIS): the regular collection and storage of in-house and external data in a form which facilitates access for the purposes of marketing planning and evaluation, for example, analysing trends in the market and tracking the progress of the company's products.

Market Research: the systematic collection, collation, storage, retrieval, analysis and reporting on data about customers, competitors, markets and the total business environment. MR should be combined with other external and internal sources of data to help improve the quality of marketing decision-taking. MR is a professional task, requiring skills in the social sciences, resources in fieldwork and analysis and understanding and objectivity in communicating with business users. See also *Desk/field research* and *Qualitative/quantitative research*.

Multiple linear regression: see *Regression*.

Positioning: an agreed statement of how a product best suits a defined target customer and need by differentiating itself from its competition. This will ideally be unique and all marketing activity should be designed and 'branded' to reinforce the product's positioning in the market.

Prediction: a subjective view of the outcome of a single future event, implying certainty without alternative possibilities. See also *Forecast, Projection*.

Price elasticity: see *Elasticity*.

Profit: the surplus of all sources of income for a commercial business (or individual products) over all attributable costs. *Pure profit*: profit as defined above but with the return on capital employed included in costs, also known as the *added values* created by the business.

Projection (or extrapolation): a statistician's term meaning the past extended forward assuming no change in trend. See also *Forecast, Prediction*.

Public Relations (PR): activity used in a market-place to create climates of opinion or to influence purchasing by indirect means, for example through opinion leaders or the media. The techniques of public relations are also used in a variety of non-marketing contexts.

Qualitative/Quantitative Research: Field research is called *quantitative* if done on a sample structured to be representative and large enough to provide numerical data which can be subjected to evaluation. It requires structured questionnaires on a limited range of pre-determined topics. *Qualitative* research is carried out on a small number of interviews where respondents are questioned more extensively over a wider range of topics by specially-trained interviewers. No structured questionnaires are used, and the results are used to determine customer language, and to develop ideas and hypotheses about a market which can be quantified later.

Regression: a statistical technique which measures the extent to which series of numbers do and do not move up and down in step with each other. For example, if sales are higher on warm days than on cold days, they are said to 'correlate positively' with temperature. If equal changes in temperature produce approximately equal changes in sales, then the correlation is said to be 'linear' and the relationship can be represented by a straight line on a chart. Most marketing situations are more complex and involve many variables which interact simultaneously and not necessarily linearly. Their relationships need to be measured by 'multiple regression'. See also *Econometrics*.

Sales Promotion: marketing activity at the point of purchase or place of use (usually of a short-term nature) designed to add interest or value to a product.

Sponsorship (commercial): a subsidy paid to an activity not directly concerned with the sponsor's own business (e.g., sport, art, media, environmental rehabilitation), in order to achieve specific objectives relating to the promotion of the company or its products. Subsidies given with no expectation of commercial return are *patronage* or *charity* depending on how good the cause is believed to be.

SWOT analysis: an assessment of the internal competitive Strengths and Weaknesses of a company in the light of the external Opportunities and Threats in the market-place. See also *Marketing audit*.

Target (e.g., for sales): what management would most like to happen, and will strive (and incentivise others) to achieve.

Target market: a tightly-specified group of potential customers for a product on whom all marketing activity will be concentrated.

INDEX